6678

B
SHORTER
Shorter, Frank,
1947-

Olympic gold

15 X 2/0, 9/02

1595

Olympic Gold

Also by Marc Bloom

Cross-Country Running

The Marathon:
What It Takes to Go the Distance

OLYMPIC GOLD

A Runner's Life
and Times

Frank Shorter
with Marc Bloom

HOUGHTON MIFFLIN COMPANY BOSTON 1984

6678

Library of Congress Cataloging in Publication Data

Shorter, Frank, 1947–
    Olympic gold.

    1. Shorter, Frank, 1947–   . 2. Runners (Sports) — United States — Biography. I. Bloom, Marc, 1939– II. Title.
GV1061.15.S48A36 1984   796.4′26 [B]   83–49180
ISBN 0–395–35403–X

Printed in the United States of America

V 10 9 8 7 6 5 4 3 2 1

Chapter One originally appeared in *The Runner*.

Acknowledgments

We would like to thank the following friends, colleagues, and sources for their assistance: Jack Bacheler, Janet Beyer, Dr. Steven Bittner, Amby Burfoot, Bill Clark, David Costill, Tim Cronin, Dr. Kenneth Davis, Dr. Andrew Fischer, Steve Flanagan, Al Franken, Jeff Galloway, Robert Giegengack, Samuel Greene, Dr. Gary Guten, Ted Hayden, Bob Hersh, Dr. Stan James, Don Kardong, Pat Mooney, Kenny Moore, Walt Murphy, Bob Newland, Katherine Shorter, Dr. Samuel Shorter, Mark Young, and the Yale Sports Information Department for filling in memory gaps; Rich Clarkson, Art Klonsky, Jane Sobel, Paul Sutton, Steve Sutton, and *Track & Field News* for photographs; Phil and Renee Benson, John and Susie Cabell, and Ethel Shorter for their hospitality; Kathy Gettings for her clerical help; Tom Hart and Larry Kessenich of Houghton Mifflin for their care and wisdom; and George Hirsch, publisher of *The Runner*, who helped bring us together.

Frank Shorter
Boulder, Colorado

Marc Bloom
Marlboro, New Jersey

Contents

Foreword

Frank Shorter and I worked on this book about his life in much the same way he does everything — it couldn't interfere with his running. Because Frank runs twice most days and travels a good deal — and because he lives in Boulder and I in New Jersey — finding the time to meet or even work by phone became the trickiest part of the project.

We worked in a Chicago hotel room; in an airport and on a plane; while Frank pedaled away on an exercise bike at a Cape Cod Nautilus Center to stay fit while injured; on his grandmother's front porch in Middletown, New York; in Manhattan at the home of George Hirsch, publisher of *The Runner;* at a race director's home on the Jersey shore; in Frank's office in Boulder; at the Orange County (N.Y.) Fairgrounds, where Frank used to hang around as a kid; on the steps of the Los Angeles Coliseum; and elsewhere.

It took fifteen months, from the spring of 1982 to the summer of 1983, when we had to be finished. Frank was about to launch into his training for the Olympics, and I didn't want to be stealing any of his time, even for this. In the course of the year-plus, we taped many hours of conversation, from which Frank's story took shape.

☆

I can't remember the first time I saw Frank Shorter run. It was probably at an indoor meet in New York a year or two after he was out of college. My memory of his marathon victory at the 1972 Olympics also is cloudy. I watched it on TV, and my only vivid recollection is of the imposter and an outraged Erich Segal, commentating for ABC, screaming at him. I really don't have a picture in my mind of Frank running it.

I have sharp memories from 1976. I attended the Games in Montréal, and as I sat in the stadium on the final day of competition, I could only keep up with the marathon through the periodic scoreboard notices of the lead runners. When Frank entered the stadium second and immediately acknowledged his supporters with an I-did-all-I-could gesture bordering on apology, I was struck by it. Years later I would realize the significance of what he had done: He had, in a way, personalized the marathon.

Frank's defeat, and his gesture, was as important a symbol of running as his glorious victory in Munich four years before. Should he get as far as the Olympics in 1984, how fortunate we should feel as a nation of runners. We have no greater example of the runner than Frank Shorter.

Marc Bloom
Marlboro, New Jersey
August 1983

Olympic Gold

Olympic Gold

The Light at the End of the Tunnel

It is the stadium tunnel above all else that distinguishes an Olympic marathon from all others. It is the tunnel, cool, dark, and eerie, that comes to mind first when I think back to the Olympic marathons I've run. It is the tunnel, an unnatural link from the track to the world outside, that is in effect the start and finish. In 1972 in Munich the tunnel was a destination that meant victory; in 1976 in Montréal it was a destination that meant merely that the race was over.

Both times I longed to reach it. The first time the tunnel was alluring — it symbolized triumph, which seemed secure after I'd built a sizable lead and had only a few miles to go. The next time, even in defeat, the tunnel was welcome — then as a symbol of relief from having run the hardest marathon of my life.

Not every Olympic marathon has its start and finish inside the stadium, requiring the runners to leave and return through the tunnel that leads into it. In 1984 the marathoners will finish in the Los Angeles Coliseum but they'll start several miles away, on the track of Santa Monica City College. Before 1972 I don't believe I'd ever run through a tunnel. It's rare to find the site of a major marathon with a stadium big enough to have one. The famous Fukuoka Marathon in Japan uses a stadium, but it is a small facility, and the runners are taken in and out through an open gate.

In Munich, as I left the stadium at the head of the pack after the customary two laps of the track, the tunnel became a goal. The reality of running in the Olympic marathon hadn't hit me until then and, suddenly confronted by it, I said to myself, "Only 25 miles to go." There were closer to 26 miles left, but only about 25 to get back to the tunnel, which I considered the finish.

The Olympic marathon is won outside the stadium. The initial half-mile or so around the track doesn't count for much; you use that time to settle into a comfortable rhythm and avoid falling down. There has rarely been a duel at the end. Except for the weird 1908 race, in which the leader, Dorando Pietri of Italy, was disqualified for being assisted by officials, and the finish of 1948, the first man inside the stadium has always been a decisive winner.

I knew as I ran through the streets and parks of Munich that if I made it to the tunnel in first place, I would win. I had history on my side. Leaving the English Garden with 4½ miles to go, and with a lead of more than a minute, all I could think about was the sight of that tunnel. I had broken away early in the race and run very hard for several miles to gain the lead I wanted. Pressing this way had tired me, and as I tried to preserve the lead and the victory, I waited for the tunnel. Once inside, it was land to a survivor.

After almost 26 miles of running, even with the victory in sight, my spirit ebbed, but the tunnel had a strangely awakening effect on me. Its solitary darkness was startling, and its downward slope into the stadium made my legs buckle. I was whipped through its dark and eerie stillness into the jeweled light of the arena.

Suddenly it was very bright, and that, combined with the noise of the 60,000 people, was at first jarring. That I would pop out from the somewhat mysterious confinement of the tunnel and into the stage that is the Olympic stadium had not occurred to me until I was just about to do it, and there was an exhilarating unreality about it.

In Montréal I felt the startling contrast of the tunnel going out. As we gathered for the start it began to rain, which I find a discomfort in a race. It even caused me to alter my strategy at the last minute. But the stadium was roofed (except for a small hole) and masked the intensity of the rain, which I first felt upon leaving the cover of the tunnel. I knew then that the race would be tougher than I'd expected.

Eventually it was, and though the man ahead of me was running away toward the end as I had in Munich, I could not concede him the victory until I was inside the tunnel. He was a fine runner, strong and determined, but only when I reached the stadium tunnel did I feel that there would be no chance for me to win. The race had gone on long enough, and I remember thinking as I ran through the tunnel that despite the disappointment of defeat, I was satisfied for having run the best race I could.

CHAPTER ONE

Middletown and Mount Hermon

I was well prepared for my first race. It was the spring of 1959 and I was at choir school in New York City, excited about the annual Field Day activities coming up. By then, at age eleven and a half, I had developed a sense of achievement, and though most of the other boys at the strict boarding school considered the event of only moderate significance, I considered it a competition — not in the sense of beating other kids, but of doing my very best. I wasn't particularly aggressive, but I did consciously try to move up in status at the school. They gave an award every year for "best all-around boy," and one of the winners three years before had been a boy from Middletown, New York, up in Orange County, where I was from. His name was Gerald Arnold Ash, and I'll always remember gazing at the plaque in the school corridor with his name on it, thinking how nice it would be to have my name up there too.

The full name of the school was the Choir School of the Cathedral of St. John the Divine, a huge gothic cathedral occupying a full block on the Upper West Side of Manhattan, near Columbia University. I'm Episcopalian, and this was a proper Episcopalian boarding school (though being Episcopalian was not an entrance requirement). I was sent there mainly at the urging of my mother, Katherine, who saw it as an educational opportunity for me. I had been a good student in the public schools of Middletown, always had my homework done before leaving school. That was the problem. Though I did well, my mother felt I was not kept busy enough, was not sufficiently challenged. At the choir school there was a more accelerated academic program that my mother, an artist, felt would better develop my potential, so off I went to St. John's, 70 miles away, in the fall of '58. The school consisted of grades four through eight, with only five boys in each grade, most of them from other states. Some attended for the full five years; others, like me, stayed for only one year — the sixth grade, in my case.

As Field Day approached, I looked forward to it. I had always enjoyed the outdoors and grew up joining in whatever organized sports were available. Playing both outfielder and first baseman, I was home run champion of the Middletown Little League. In swimming I could stay underwater longer and swim farther than most other children. Though not particularly strong, I was coordinated as well as motivated. In the fifth grade, at the Mulberry Street School in Middletown, I broke my right wrist because I tried too hard in the tag relays in gym class. There was some backward running involved, and I went too fast and fell. I'd warned the teacher that the backward running was causing an overzealous type like me to fall, but he insisted I do it anyway.

Field Day consisted of a sprint, a distance race around the field, a long jump (or broad jump, as we called it then), the shot put, and swimming, which we did over at Columbia. The winner was determined by one's overall standing, a small decathlon of sorts. The years have clouded my memory, but I do recall winning the running events and then the overall championship, outscoring even the older eighthgraders. I felt very proud and gratified and was given as a prize a book, *Famous American Athletes of Today*. I vaguely remember an awards ceremony, but that didn't matter to me. I had learned that I could set a goal and, by trying very hard, quite possibly succeed. It was my first real athletic experience.

This attitude was not confined to sports. There was choir practice every day at school. I could tell when we were doing well and enjoyed our successes. I'd gone to church in Middletown and felt comfortable in the ornate cathedral of St. John the Divine. Though some of us would doze off now and then during services, there was real work and discipline involved, because your position in the choir was determined by how well you sang. I moved up in rank, and that meant as much to me as the Field Day victory.

But even with good grades, good singing, and good athletics, I was not good enough to be judged "best all-around boy." Another aspect of my personality came out in choir school — the nonconformist. There was a demerit system based on rules infractions and I was an occasional transgressor — a repeat offender when it came to certain things.

This was not a case of a child rebelling against parental authority. I'd welcomed the news that I'd be going off to school; I thought it would be an adventure. On family trips, I'd gotten a taste of the outside world; to me, Amsterdam Avenue was as exciting as traveling out west.

A demerit system was maintained less to preserve order — how much trouble can twenty-five essentially decent boys get into? — than to preserve authority. My demerits were not the result of premeditated mischief but rather my refusal to conform absolutely to what I saw as a rather inflexible system. I guess I've always been that way. I'll play by the rules as long as I feel they're sensible and fair. But when I feel they're not, I'll look for alternatives.

My biggest problem was returning to school after a weekend of skiing with my father. "Weekends" at school were

Monday and Tuesday, and during the winter my father, Samuel, a physician, would pick me up on a Sunday afternoon for a drive upstate or to Vermont for two days of downhill skiing. I had to be back for classes early Wednesday morning, but we'd frequently get back a few hours late. My father, who has always worked long hours, has had a certain disdain for schedules and never took to rushing back from the slopes just so I might be on time for class. I guess it was his fault, but I never thought of it that way. I viewed it as an inflexible system.

If you received up to two and three-quarters demerits in the course of a week, that was equivalent to a misdemeanor. But three or more — that was a felony and you were punished for it. During the evening's free time, serious offenders would have to stand in silence for a half-hour in the dining hall, facing the wall. There were a number of clocks in the room, and all you heard as you stood there was *tick-tock, tick-tock . . .* it was enough to drive you mad. To make sure you took your lumps like a man, an older boy would be stationed as a proctor. I hung in there, letting my thoughts pass the time and occasionally listening to the *tick-tock, tick-tock . . .*

Returning late after a weekend was worth two demerits, so I was frequently in the hole at the start of the week, at least during the ski season. Demerits also were given for such things as improper attire and being late for dinner. There was also a subtle pressure put on the younger students by the older boys, who could turn you in for any infraction, real or imagined. With five or more demerits, your travel privileges could be taken away. Just before that point, my practical side would override my individuality — I didn't want to lose travel privileges.

After the sixth grade, I went back to public school in Middletown. I had started to feel uncomfortable around the other boys, many of whom were lonely and never saw their

families. My parents understood. There was no fuss about
it. I just told them, "I've had enough, and I don't want to
go back."

☆

The Shorters go back many years in the Middletown area.
My mother and father both grew up on the same block
on Jackson Avenue. After a two-year courtship they married,
in Middletown, on December 27, 1943. In the fall of '46,
my father was called to serve as an army doctor in postwar
Germany, and for most of his tour, he was stationed at an
air base in Wiesbaden. After a series of moves following
that, my parents finally settled in Middletown in 1951 to
raise a family that would grow to eleven children.

Late in '46, with one-year-old Samuel Jr. in her arms, my
mother traveled to Europe on the S.S. *United States* to join
my father. His brief stint in the service was fairly uneventful,
but I think he enjoyed it because he likes practicing volume
medicine. He doesn't much care about hours or schedules;
he loves working to exhaustion treating people. He's a very
good GP — it's been his life. He never spoke much about
the army, except to tell how on Monday morning he'd sometimes have to administer penicillin shots to soldiers back
from a weekend of hell-raising — the same men every time.
My father saved one man from a court-martial. According
to the tale, my father intervened in an argument between
an enlisted man and a general in a bar. When the enlisted
man became abusive, my father told the general a story
about how he was treating the man for a serious emotional
condition that was causing his ill-mannered behavior.

About a year after my mother arrived in Wiesbaden, on
Halloween 1947, I was born in the U.S. military hospital in
Munich. The next year my father was discharged from the
service, but before returning to the States, the four of us
traveled around Europe for a month in a '46 Chevy he'd

purchased for $1,600. (Not many people in Europe had cars at that time, and I have always been impressed that my father was able to obtain one. He's always had a certain ability to get things done, to buck the system a little if necessary, usually to help someone out or occasionally for his own benefit.) My parents visited Bavaria, Austria, and Switzerland, carrying me around in a wicker laundry basket. They sold the car and returned by boat to the States, to Middletown, for a brief period, before moving on to Philadelphia so that my father could complete his residency near Temple University, where he had received his medical degree. At year's end, his residency unfinished, my father became the company doctor for the Valley Camp Coal Company, a mining outfit in Ward, West Virginia, a small town 115 miles southeast of Charleston. He figured it would be good experience for a young GP and, since we had run out of money, it seemed like a pretty good deal. So off we went to the coal country of Appalachia.

We moved into an old wooden house with a backyard that faced the railroad tracks where the coal trains went by. My father had a dispensary and also made house calls because many people had no means of transportation to get to his office. He'd acquired a jeep, and I would frequently accompany him on his rounds into the hills. Once when we were riding along on a rather high ridge, my father stopped the car and said to me very calmly, "I want you to get out and stand over there." I got out. Then he jumped out of the jeep, which moments later slid off the road and rolled down the hill. I guess he felt the earth giving way. Though only two, I was old enough to be struck by his calm reaction, and I was spellbound by the sight of the jeep rolling down the hill. Afterward, we proceeded to walk up the hill to the patient's house. I have no memory of how we got home.

It was a rough life. My father had a gun, a .38, which

he kept underneath his socks in the top drawer of his bureau. Once I asked him why he had it; he said it was to shoot snakes. From then on I looked for snakes everywhere until, eventually, I realized he meant two-legged snakes. Fortunately, there was never a need to use the gun. I suspect he worried that the drugs of a physician's trade could attract thieves. (It was the same .38 he used twenty years later, when we were living in Taos, New Mexico, to protect me from the threatening *pachucos,* who were harassing me when I ran.)

Two more of the Shorter family were born in Ward, Susan in 1949 and Tommy in 1950. Susan was born on my father's twenty-eighth birthday, right in the middle of a birthday party, and my father delivered her. Tommy was retarded at birth and blind, always to be bedridden. He lived at home for a while but was in such constant pain, crying and screaming, that he had to be privately institutionalized. Tommy had been born two and a half months premature and therefore was given oxygen and tetracycline, accepted procedure for premature births at that time. But the large dosages impaired his central nervous system and damaged bone and connective tissue, resulting in his severe condition. Somehow my parents seemed to cope with this fairly well — or at least they camouflaged their grief. In 1966, at the age of sixteen, Tommy died.

We left Ward in the summer of 1951 and moved back to Middletown. Sammy was approaching school age, and my mother held the schools of Ward in little regard. Tommy, too, would be better off in the New York area. And my father would take his skills in volume medicine up north.

My father stayed behind to tie up loose ends while my mother, my father's sister Nancy (who'd come over to help with the move), and Sam, Susan, and I set off by car, a moving van trailing, for the 750-mile trip to Middletown. I was very excited by the prospect. On moving day, Father had given

Sam, Susan, and me small doses of a tranquilizer to help us sleep during the overnight trip, but for some reason it had the opposite effect on Susan, and she bounced all over the back of the car.

We settled into a wonderful, twenty-two-room Victorian house at 46 Highland Avenue, on the fringe of the well-to-do section of Middletown. My parents paid very little for it. Built on the side of a hill, it had a huge front porch with large wooden columns — Doric columns, I later learned in art history. At the foot of an elaborately carved wooden stairway was a great chandelier that fascinated me. I remember getting out of bed several times in the middle of the night when everyone else was asleep and going downstairs, just to look at the dimly lit chandelier. With a large family, it was nice to have such a good-sized home so that the kids wouldn't be on top of one another. (Stopping to see the old place in 1982, when I was in Middletown for a race, I found it converted into a home for troubled youths. The counselor, it turned out, was a man named Fletcher Miller, a Little League playmate of mine twenty years before.)

My room was up in the attic. Other than a pool table, there wasn't much to speak of in my room. I was not much of a saver — I'm still not — and couldn't even manage to hold on to my first trophies for very long. Though I spent most of my spare time outdoors, I also spent a good deal of time in my room — reading, doing homework, just being by myself. I'm basically introverted and cherished the space I had all to myself. When I got older, I'd go into my mother's attic studio and watch her paint.

I enjoyed my friends but did not have to depend on them for a rewarding time. I found I enjoyed reading, particularly magazines, and would spend hours by myself on Saturday afternoons at the library, a few blocks away, reading *Life, Look, National Geographic,* and whatever else was around. *The Babe Ruth Story, The Lou Gehrig Story.* I was a consci-

entious student and, though I don't think I realized it at
the time, probably a teacher's pet. When the teacher called
on me, I usually knew the answer, and I got a tremendous
amount of satisfaction at getting 100 percent on a test, at
looking at a paper and seeing all the answers correct. And
I was proud that, though many of my friends were given
monetary rewards for good grades, I was not.

By age eight, I'd acquired a certain amount of self-reliance.
It probably developed from being part of a large family.
My parents tried their best to give no more attention to
one child than to another — which meant none of us received any lavish attention or praise. I realized this early
on and accepted it. Also, because Sam was having trouble
academically, my mother — who kept up with school matters
much more than did my father — wasn't about to hail my
successes at Sam's expense. I played a lot of baseball and
earned a reputation in Middletown as a slugger. I was one
of the bigger boys and had good hand-eye coordination.
Once in Little League, I played the outfield — or first base,
because I'm left-handed. (Though I throw and bat left, I
eat and write with my right hand; I serve tennis with my
right and volley with my left.) By the time I was graduated
from Little League into the Babe Ruth League, I was no
longer such a "big" kid and, against better pitching, couldn't
hit the ball as far as I used to. I went from very good to
just average and realized, probably for the first time, that
ability in sports should never be taken for granted.

Aside from baseball, I played a little basketball. I often
fished alone at a nearby park, where I would later do my
running. My father's grandfather was an inveterate fisher-
man — he would go ice fishing in the winter — but my
father would never go. He hated it.

I guess I was about nine when I first experienced the
feeling of endurance. A whole bunch of us used to play a
form of tag, and often I was the last kid to be caught. We'd

play this on an open field and I could run all around, away from the outstretched arms of the others, feeling no shortness of breath. It did not occur to me then that this open-field capacity might lead to something special. It was just very satisfying to be good at something and outlast the entire group.

I was fortunate, growing up, to be able to travel. There were family trips about every other year — to Mexico, the South, the Rockies and California, across Canada. We had a big trailer and took it everywhere. I became the navigator because my father was notorious for running out of gas. Eventually, the only time he'd run out of gas was when I would fall asleep. Then I was the one who would hitchhike down the road for gas. I learned how to travel and put that knowledge to good use in later years, first when I was seventeen, with a bike trip I took across Europe with my sister Susan, who was fifteen at the time. Susan is the oldest of the six Shorter girls and, like me, an independent sort.

I even attended dancing school. It was my mother's idea, but I don't recall objecting to it. We learned the fox trot, the waltz, and a little lindy. My third-grade crush was there, but by then other nine-year-olds had caught my attention. The girls wore white gloves and pretty dresses and they smelled nice, and it was during those dancing lessons that I first realized that girls sweat, too. That troubled me a little, because it seemed to me then that this dancing was proper and mannered and that the point of it was to instill a certain social grace in a bunch of typically awkward kids. When, after a lindy, my partner would sweat, I thought that was *wrong*.

Many of my values gained as a youngster have remained largely unchanged. My mother's painting gave her a great deal of personal satisfaction and she worked hard at it. As I was growing up, however, I had the feeling that she never had enough time for her art, that the kids and everything

dominated her time. Of course, *I* was among those competing for her time. The memory of my mother's priorities
and the feeling that she has never been able to pursue her
art has stayed with me. I'm rather defiant about certain
things I decide are best for me, perhaps selfish in a way
my mother never has been. If I roll into town for a race
and have planned a workout for a certain time, I'll allow
nothing to infringe on the workout. I guess that's one reason
I've run in airports. I saw in my father the workaholic, the
all-day, all-night country doctor, the healer. He served the
people — but forgot about his own security. He paid no
attention to it. This, too, has stayed with me, and I've felt
a certain need for security in matters of finance and family.

Though I returned to Middletown from choir school in
New York at age twelve with a "race" under my belt, I
had no idea that I would soon start running. I entered the
seventh grade at Anthony J. Veraldi Junior High School and
— partly to avoid football in gym class, partly to get in shape
for skiing, and partly for the pure fun of it — I ran. I can't
recall which came first, running to and from school or running around the field during gym class. Each started at about
the same time, in the spring of 1960, when I was twelve
and a half years old. I knew all about Jean-Claude Killy,
but nothing about Abebe Bikila.

In gym class we played "flag football," not a contact sport
if you adhered to the rules and "tackled" a man by snatching
the piece of cloth that was slipped into the back of his pants.
Some kids ignored the rules and tried to hurt you, which
seemed silly to me, and I wanted no part of it. I wanted
to run. I went over to the gym teacher, and said to him,
"I might get hurt playing football. I'd just like to run around
the field during gym class. I like to run." And he let me
do it, no questions asked. If he thought I was a sissy, he
didn't say so. I'd get in about a half-hour's worth of running,
probably no more than 3 miles. I didn't do it quite every

day, but when I did, I'd simply run laps while the other guys played football. I never counted the laps. No one bugged me about it and no one asked to join me, either.

Those were also the days when kids wore shoes to school. Wearing sneakers was either forbidden or just not done. I was one of the first kids to wear sneakers to school; I had to after I started running to school instead of riding the bus. I think they were Keds, low-cut white Keds. I'd break them in and put patches on them as the uppers wore out. They had a flexible sole for sneakers of that time. I liked the feeling of the exercise and enjoyed the idea of being a bit unusual. Teachers asked me why I was wearing sneakers, and I told them matter-of-factly that I was running to and from school. I don't think they believed me. I felt good about that, about being the first to do something that was enjoyable and good for me. Besides, I could save my bus fare for junk food.

It was 2 miles to school from home. If I had a book with me I'd tuck it under my arm. Like the gym class running, I did it regularly but not every single day. This continued through junior high, and though I suppose I was pretty fit for a kid about to enter high school in the fall of '62 — what with my baseball, skiing, bike riding, and running be- hind me — I knew nothing about organized running because there was nothing of the sort in Middletown for kids my age. Not that I cared. I kept up with the 1960 winter Olym- pics from Squaw Valley, and when I ran, I thought about being a ski racer.

Though we had family ties to the Middletown school sys- tem — my father's father had been president of the Board of Education when the high school was built in 1940 — I went on to a prep school in New England. My grades from junior high (which included ninth grade) were good and Middletown High had a fine academic rating, but my mother thought it wise for me to attend private school, even though it imposed a financial burden on the family. In her mind, I was underachieving. After this was decided, my father's inevitable tardiness led me to one school in particular. We never got around to visiting Exeter, St. Paul's, or Andover (where I wanted to go because my best friend, Alex Preston, was planning to go there), and by the time we finally began looking, the only school with scholastic standing that would consider me and still satisfy my mother was the Mount Hermon School in Mount Hermon, Massachusetts.

Mount Hermon at the time was a boys' school with an enrollment of about five hundred, situated in northwestern Massachusetts, on the Connecticut River near the Vermont–New Hampshire border. (It is now called Northfield–Mount Hermon, having merged with its sister school in 1971.) Most students lived in dorms, but my first year I had quarters with four other sophomores in a faculty house. It was in the attic of a house supervised by Axel B. Forslund, the longtime athletic director. It took no time at all for us to claim territories and form alliances. Donald Chase was a very good skier who had a brother on the Yale ski team (which I later discovered wasn't much of a ski team). Steve Cook was related to the painter Andrew Wyeth. Mike Hannon, a bright boy, was on scholarship because his father was a truck driver. (Doctors' kids couldn't get a scholarship.) And there was a fourth whom I will never forget, a Japanese fellow named Robert Suzuki. He was stocky and had a chip on his shoulder. Anything you could do he could do better. But after Steve Cook prevailed in a wrestling confrontation with Suzuki, things settled down. Four of us had fun while Suzuki tried his best not to.

I decided to go out for football, and I was the starting halfback on the sophomore team, all hundred and twenty-seven pounds of me. I wasn't very fast but I had good lateral movement, probably from all those games of tag I'd played. But in a pileup during a game when someone's cleat cut into my left leg, I decided to quit football and preserve my good health.

I didn't do any running those first several weeks at Mount Hermon, not that the injured leg would have allowed it. In late November, the Pie Race came around. It was an autumn ritual, going on year after year since 1891, longer even than the Boston Marathon, and people were really talking it up. I knew I had good endurance and I've always been one to try anything once. Axel Forslund, our housemaster (who retired in 1970 after forty-one years as athletic director), had set the present course back in 1929. It's a road and cross-country run, 4.55 miles long, around the campus, and is officially called the Bemis-Forslund Pie Race. "Bemis" was Henry Bemis, class of '91, who endowed the race fund; "pie" refers to the apple pies that are awarded to male finishers under 33 minutes and female finishers under 40 minutes — quite an incentive.

It was held the Monday afternoon before Thanksgiving. This day in 1962 was crisp and sunny and I wore a sweatshirt and baggy issue gym shorts and sneakers. I had never before even *seen* a road race. I went into it with the idea of participating, figuring I could run 4.55 miles if I paced myself. I didn't even think about the pie. I was too afraid.

There were about a hundred runners in the field and, as the race got under way, I found myself somewhere in the middle. I remember thinking that the people in front of me seemed to have started out too fast. A half-mile out, on a mild downhill, I began passing people. I maintained my pace and they came back to me. Eventually I was ahead of people in racing uniforms. Then, with about 600 yards to go, winding down another hill, I saw only a half-dozen runners ahead of me, spaced out evenly, and as I approached the finish, I thought, So, this is what a race is like . . .

I placed seventh. Curiously, I'm told, the results that appeared in the school paper, the *Hermonite*, had me thirty-fourth. But I distinctly remember finishing seventh, right behind a guy named Dave Rikert (who *is* listed sixth in the *Hermonite*), a skier who was the Nordic combined U.S. junior champion. There were some pretty good runners from the cross-country team ahead of me, and I said to myself, "Gee, maybe I have some talent." I took the pie back to my room and shared it with my buddies.

The next day, Suzuki decided he had to race me. Perhaps he was still smarting from the fact that a hundred-and-twenty-seven-pounder like myself made the football team and had played ahead of him, so he challenged me to a 100-yard dash. I couldn't back down and, sure enough, he beat me by 5 yards. As I said, I wasn't very fast.

I thought I might go out for cross-country the following fall and for the rest of my sophomore year continued to try other sports. I joined the ski team that winter and competed in downhill, jumping, and cross-country. I did reasonably well. I learned to be "quiet" on my skis in downhill and had the stamina for cross-country. Although I was undefeated in my junior year in cross-country and elected team captain for the next season, I gave it up because I didn't like the idea that you had so little control over the competitive conditions. Your success depended in part on how you were seeded for your downhill run and whether you waxed your skis properly for the snow conditions in cross-country. If you missed the wax, that could affect the outcome.

At the same time, I was finding I enjoyed running more and began to think I might someday do well at it. I knew that, even if this might come, it would take time, and I was prepared to make the commitment. A brief, unsuccessful trial with the track team in the spring after the pie race did not deter me. I'd gone out for baseball and was playing first base when I decided to switch to track. I showed up for practice one day and learned about interval running. The coach had the runners doing 68-second quarters, and

I couldn't keep up. I realized how far ahead the other runners were and, after two or three days, went back to baseball. I figured I'd start clean with track and cross-country my junior year.

Right away, the next fall, we were put to the test. On the first day of practice, the coach, Samuel Greene, sent us on a run over the 2.55-mile cross-country course, and naturally it turned into a race. I was the fifth one back, hence the fifth man on the first team. The four boys ahead of me were seniors. The team, which was undefeated that season for the second straight year, would run 4 or 5 miles a session, and one of the workouts we'd do was a variation of playground tag, in which the last one caught was the winner. By the third meet I was second man on the team, after George Bowman. He beat me decisively almost every time out and tied for first with a runner from Exeter in the New England Prep School championships, which were held at Mount Hermon that year. It was a great finish, not an intentional tie. I took fifth, the first underclassman in the league to finish.

Running proved to be a social advantage at Mount Hermon. To enable interaction between the sexes, the Mount Hermon boys or the Northfield girls would be bused over to the other place for dances or movies. It was very closely monitored. It was five miles to Northfield, and one time I arranged a rendezvous with a girl I'd been dating named Leslie Buffington. Late one night I ran over there, and we walked around campus for hours, with me disguised to avoid being noticed in a long trenchcoat and a girl's hat. At about three o'clock in the morning I ran the 5 miles back to Mount Hermon. That run was my cold shower.

I got the hang of interval running in the spring of my junior year, though it was an uneventful season. I ran the mile in 4:44 and the 2-mile in 10:02, and George Bowman continued to beat me. I can't remember much else about my first track season, probably because I enjoyed cross-country much more.

In my senior year I did quite well. I was in good shape and from the start of cross-country was first man on the team. I was undefeated and broke the course records at Mount Hermon, Choate, Lenox, Exeter, Deerfield — on every course I ran. It was a great thrill to be successful at something I really enjoyed. The New England championship was at Andover, Massachusetts, and my parents drove over from Middletown to watch me compete for the first time. We won the team title for the third straight year, completing another unbeaten season. I won that race and the Pie Race, and was having so much fun, I started to train on my own in addition to the team practices.

But there was an emotional hurdle: I had to inform the coach of the ski team that had elected me captain that I would not be skiing that winter; I'd decided I'd be better off jogging through winter track to maintain my condition for the spring. Richard Kellom was an excellent coach, a fine skier who had taught me well. This was my first real face-to-face experience with someone on an issue of this sort. But he was great. I had expected a rough time; instead, he said he understood and wished me well. It was one of the best experiences of my young life.

My success continued into the spring of my senior year. I was unbeaten in the 2-mile and set a school record of 9:39.6 in the New Englands at Andover. I lowered this a bit two weeks later to 9:39.3 at Mount Hermon. I also ran the mile, but usually on the second half of a double and never below 4:30.

Mount Hermon has continued to produce promising runners, though my record of 13:40 for the school's cross-country course stood longer than I would have expected. I read with interest in the fall of 1982 that, after eighteen years, the mark was broken by David Alden of Brookline, Massachusetts, who ran 13:29. His picture appeared as "a face in the crowd" in *Sports Illustrated*.

I'd made up my mind early in my senior year that I wanted to attend Yale. George Bowman, whom I looked up to in my junior year, had convinced me that the best Ivy League school for a runner was Yale. Bob Giegengack, its coach, had served as the Olympic coach in Tokyo in 1964, and I thought it would be fun to train under a really good coach. I applied and was accepted. I remember watching the Tokyo Olympics on TV during the cross-country season, inspired by the distance victories of Bob Schul and Billy Mills. I thought about those races and about how nice it was to do something like that. But I didn't think it would happen to me.

CHAPTER TWO

Yale

The first time I ever saw Yale was a week before classes began my freshman year. I'd gotten the letter Coach Giegengack had sent, urging the runners to report early for cross-country practice. That late summer's day in 1965, I drove from Middletown to New Haven with my mother and her mother, Ida Chappell, who was sixty-nine and almost an invalid because of a bus accident in which she'd broken her hip. She was a very bright woman with a great respect for education, a sensibility that had evidently been acquired by my mother as well. Ida had been Phi Beta Kappa at St. Lawrence University (class of '17), in upstate New York, and was a voracious reader all her life. That she insisted on accompanying us to Yale impressed me more than anything that first day. She had a reverence for academia, and she made the 200-mile round trip, despite her physical condition, out of that reverence.

As a young boy and then as a young adult, I saw in Ida a remarkable woman who was independent and purposeful in her thinking and able to convey to the people around her a sense of priority and will. She'd always read books to her grandchildren. She'd bring us toys that were constructive. She created an atmosphere of learning. When Ida died, just before my graduation from Yale, I felt a great loss. I still miss her.

I found my way to the Lapham Field House locker room out near the Yale Bowl, and there I met Giegengack. The field house was dilapidated inside, filled with tradition, some said. I thought it was filled with squalor. Giegengack had no complaints. He'd been magna cum laude in classics and philosophy at Holy Cross, head coach of the Olympic track and field team in Tokyo — and this was Yale; but Gieg was no dilettante. You were there to run, he was there to coach, and that's all there was to it. He was balding with a big round face, somewhat portly, and he shuffled when he walked. Physically, he was a strong man but retained nothing of the svelte grace he must have shown as a quarter-miler in college in the late twenties. And when he spoke, from between his big lips came a language readily identifiable as that of his native Brooklyn. And when Gieg wasn't speaking, he usually was chain-smoking. Taking all of this in, I said to myself, "So this is the guy."

Different? Yes. Incapable? No — I never thought that, not for a moment. I'm familiar with eccentricity. I've seen it in the very British side of my mother's family (which is from Liverpool), and I'm probably eccentric myself. Perhaps one has to be to get anywhere, to disarm others into allowing you to take chances.

The bunch of us who reported promptly for duty that day were given lockers and uniforms and a brief introductory talk by Giegengack. He didn't lecture, but he got his points across. He told us that if we were earnest, and honest with ourselves, we could enjoy a satisfying athletic career at Yale. He said he could teach us to train ourselves, to coach ourselves. That was best for the athlete, in Gieg's view, because — for one reason — after college a runner is out on his own to fend for himself (assuming he continues at all) amid the terribly inadequate postcollegiate club system that exists in the U.S. Giegengack, unlike many of his peers, took the long view of a runner's potential. He did not overtrain an athlete because he needed to produce winners. He felt athletics were part of the educational process and treated them as such, which is why he could coach at Yale for twenty-nine years. At the same time, he could develop talent, which is why his teams won fifteen Heptagonal Championships, four IC4A titles, and produced many Olympians.

This was Giegengack's genius — his desire, and ability, to teach you how to coach yourself. Though I think I understood what he was doing at the time, I really began to appreciate it years later. For me, at least, the system was ideal. Since college I've never had a formal coach. I've never wanted one. I've never felt I needed one. I like coaching myself. Giegengack gave me that privilege and know-how by being that rare type of coach who did not need to have his athletes dependent on him. Perhaps I'm an extreme example of the success of Giegengack's system, not because of my victories, but because of my personality. Give me a task to do, leave me to my own devices, and somehow I'll get it done. What existed at Yale for me, though I didn't know it at first, was a compatible coach-athlete relationship that formed the philosophical foundation of my training as a runner.

I might have learned too well. By my senior year I was determining many of my workouts on my own, moving about somewhat independent of the team. Sometimes I'd stroll out to a practice session after things were already under way, inspiring, I understand, the biting Giegengack sarcasm. Apparently, prior to my arrival, as Gieg was setting up the workouts, he'd wonder aloud as to whether "we could start without Frank." In jest, of course. Gieg wasn't about to wait for me or anyone. But even if I wasn't Regular Army, I was on Gieg's system. I'd learned it. That must have given Gieg great satisfaction.

Perhaps "system" is misleading. It was more of an approach. Most of our training was done on the Yale golf course or on a large field near the Yale Bowl. The distance men rarely trained on the track. Though common practice today, this was unorthodox in the late sixties, when punishing speed sessions on the track were a staple in most advanced running programs. Gieg turned us loose on the golf course, and for strength work we did long intervals, repeated runs of a half-mile, a mile, and more with short rests in between. Gieg's method of shortening the rest periods between repetitions as we got stronger was an innovative concept. We took a long run once a week and the rest of the time alternated "hard" days with "easy" days, a method advocated by Bill Bowerman, a Giegengack contemporary, at the University of Oregon. On hard days we did our intervals; on easy days we jogged. That was it. I don't think I ever ran more than 50 miles a week until late in my senior year, when I was running twice a day.

But remember the learning process: Gieg watched us closely when we ran. In the winter he may have been in his car, smoking away with the engine running and the windows fogged up, but he watched us, studied us. He designed his training loops so he could drive to various points and see how we were doing. Before and after the running he'd discuss it with you. You'd report back to him following a workout, and the great thing was that you'd get immediate feedback. How did you feel? Great? Maybe try some more. Uncomfortable? Gieg would alter the workout so it would suit you better the next time. He didn't keep charts, but he got to know each athlete very well. He had it all in his head: your mileage, your split times, the specific training you'd been doing. He could recall it all, and he'd ask you to. Nothing was assumed; you were not running blindly. If you were willing to listen and make a commitment, you could really learn to gauge your running.

Gieg was wise enough to know you just couldn't tell a Yale athlete to do something without explaining why to a certain degree. There aren't many sheep there. He'd explain theory to you and was more willing to discuss it after a workout than before one. However, certain runners were so inquisitive that Gieg established a policy of allowing no more than two questions a day about training theory. This was in keeping with his philosophy. You couldn't very well learn to coach yourself if you always had someone explaining every last detail to you.

Well educated, well read, and analytical, Gieg knew his subject. Like a physician who kept up with the latest medical literature, Giegengack knew the current training theories so he could incorporate into his program new ideas that worked. So knowledgeable was the man that he became a member of the Technical Committee of the International Amateur Athletic Federation, the worldwide governing body for track and field.

Two of the runners on the team, Steve Bittner and Rob Yahn, became close friends of mine. We were probably the best three distance runners to enter Yale in a long time. We'd take the first three places in a cross-country meet, and Yale would win.

Bittner was a top quarter-miler from Flossmoor, Illinois, outside Chicago, whom Gieg converted to a half-miler and miler. He was very compulsive and reflected the kind of academic pressure that existed at Yale. In class he took notes excessively, and he studied more than he had to. It was relaxing for me to be around him; I guess it made me feel less anxious, by comparison. Yahn was a miler and 2-miler from Springfield, Massachusetts. Unlike Bittner, he was not that ambitious about his studies, more the kind who would let his work go and then stay up all night when an assignment was due. It was an interesting contrast: Bittner, intense and consumed; Yahn, rather easygoing and unaffected; and me somewhere in the middle.

Bittner's athletic initiation at Yale was a rather inauspicious one. Instead of running cross-country in his freshman

year, he played freshman football as a running back behind
Calvin Hill, who went on to an NFL career with the Dallas
Cowboys. Hill was also a teammate of ours on the Yale track
team and set school records in the long jump and triple
jump. Bittner, after that first semester, never returned to
football, which I'm sure he'd agree was a wise decision. He
would set a Yale indoor record in the 880 (1:53.6) and run
an outdoor best of 1:49.2. He would share with me the Yale
indoor mile record, the 4:06.4 we'd run together in the Har-
vard-Yale-Princeton meet in our senior year. The record
still stood in the eighties.

Bittner went on to the University of Chicago Medical
School, and now he's a pediatrician in Weston, Connecticut.
In the fall of 1970, when Bittner was in medical school and
I was planning to run in the National AAU Cross-Country
Championship in Chicago, we'd arranged for me to stay at
his university apartment. I was living in Gainesville by then
and Bittner sent me a key, since he was not going to be
in town the weekend of the meet. When I got to his apartment the night before the race with John Parker, a friend
of mine from Gainesville, we discovered there were two
locks — one for the foyer and one for the door — and we
had only one key. Trying not to panic, with an important
race the next morning, I called the University of Chicago
Track Club coach, Ted Hayden, who phoned the building's
security people and convinced them it was okay for him
to let us into the apartment. When I later spoke to Bittner
about it, I told him, "Next time send us both keys."

Yahn was an economics major who, after graduation, went
into the Navy Supply Corps and then on to Harvard Business
School. In the service he was stationed at Pearl Harbor, and
when I traveled to Japan in the early seventies for the Fukuoka Marathon, I'd stop in Hawaii and spend time with
Rob and his wife, Patty. We got along very well, and when
I started my clothing business I invited Rob to become a

partner, which he did. He'd been working as an accountant in Massachusetts, without much enthusiasm, and joined me in Boulder, Colorado, in 1977, and stayed for one year. In this original clothing venture I had two other partners, John Kubiak and Jim Lillstrom, and when a dispute arose regarding the controlling interest in the company, Rob feared that we'd go bankrupt and left. He went back to Boston and struck a clothing deal with Bill Rodgers.

I haven't really spoken to Rob since. It was a very emotional, very disappointing, turn of events. In a way, I felt abandoned. Maybe I'm naive in this regard, but to me friendship is more important than business.

☆

In my first three years at Yale I was a fairly steady distance runner, good for dual meet points, good for the anchor mile on a distance medley relay, improving my times from Mount Hermon, and on occasion scoring well in a conference meet, but I didn't really win anything big. And I accepted that. Despite my success in prep school, I did not go off to New Haven with great expectations. I realized that the selective prep school world was thin in running talent, and coming out of it with the stamp of victory did not entitle me to set my goals, at first, very high. Academic achievement was more important to me, and for a pre-med student in a place like Yale, competition was intense and the career consequences were great.

I need to know how well I can perform in something that I consider important, and in the academic sphere, my pride was at stake. It was a matter of self-respect. When I studied hard and did well, it alleviated the uncertainty of what kind of student I could be at Yale. It also added balance to my college life because I seemed to know where I stood with running.

I truly enjoyed running. It provided a late afternoon release from the rigors of academia, and since I had some talent for it, I could experience the thrill of doing something well, and seeing positive results.

At the outset I established myself as the best distance runner on the team, not just among the freshmen but the varsity too. Our first competition during the fall cross-country season was a practice meet at home, where we raced as well as trained on the golf course. The distance was 4.45 miles and I was the first Yale man to finish, taking third. The winner, as I recall, was Amby Burfoot of Wesleyan, who always impressed me with his shuffling running style, a style that would be adopted by millions of high-mileage joggers in later years. Burfoot distinguished himself as a fine collegiate distance runner and in 1968 he won the Boston Marathon. But he's probably known more for being the role model for his college roommate, a runner who credits Burfoot with helping him to appreciate the virtues of long-distance running, a runner whom I've gotten quite a good look at since then: Bill Rodgers.

In those days freshmen were prohibited from competing on the varsity, and though we all trained together, freshman competition was separate. The highlight of that first season for me was a tenth-place showing in the freshman race at the IC4A Cross-Country Championships in New York. The meet was held at Van Cortlandt Park, a sprawling site in the North Bronx, and the racing distance for freshmen was 3 miles, as opposed to 5 miles for the varsity. In the home-stretch, with about 200 yards to go, I was passed by a Villanova runner from upstate New York named Dick Buerkle, whom I would meet many times again in competition, in college and afterward. That day he finished seventh, in 15:13, beating me by 4 seconds. I got to return the favor in our senior year in the NCAA 2-mile in Detroit when I passed Buerkle, who was leading, on the last turn (only to be passed myself by Ole Oleson of USC, who nipped me at the wire

with both of us hitting 8:45.2). Buerkle developed into an
excellent 5,000-meter runner (and also held the world indoor
record for the mile briefly) and was a teammate of mine
in the 1976 Olympics.

The Van Cortlandt course is a home away from home
for Eastern collegians in the fall. The IC4A and Heptagonal
(the Ivy League plus Army and Navy) meets have been held
there and a number of New York–area colleges, such as Columbia, use it as a home course. We'd run there at least
three times a season, and while I'd seen more demanding
courses, this one was the most dangerous. The wooded trails
are strewn with rocks and debris and punctuated by sharp
turns and downhills. It takes a certain daredevil mentality
to fly through the course without fear of the bumpy footing
and perilous pitches. I recall seeing a Harvard runner splat-
tered on the ground after missing a turn and slamming into
a tree.

I didn't run well on the track against Harvard until my
senior year, and running well against Harvard was important
at Yale. Gieg would stress the importance of the Harvard
meet. To him, as Bittner would say, it was "the championship
of the universe." But I managed not to score in the Harvard-
Yale outdoor dual meet as a freshman, sophomore, and junior. Each time I ran the 2-mile, and each time I didn't
score a point.

☆

At the end of my sophomore year, my father took a position
as a missionary doctor at Embudo Presbyterian Mission Hospital in Taos, where most of his patients were the Spanish
Americans and Indians of the Sangre de Cristo Mountains
of north-central New Mexico. The entire family, twelve of
us, moved from Middletown into a small house in Taos, and
that summer of 1967, while working odd jobs at a resort
ranch for pennies an hour plus room and board, I ran in

the 7,000-foot altitude of the surrounding hills. I was the crazy guy at the place who ran in the heat of the afternoon. While I did not realize until later how much the altitude helped me — that running in oxygen-thin air provides a conditioning effect that can be advantageous in competition at sea level — I knew I was well trained when cross-country resumed that fall and I placed second to Doug Hardin of Harvard in the Heptagonal championship.

But the medical college admissions test was coming up and so was organic chemistry. I worked hard, and while I ran every day, I didn't train hard. I wouldn't always show up at team practice, preferring to run alone. Gieg took me aside one day and said, "You know, you could be better if you came out and trained all the time." He was not angry but disapproving. I knew he was right, but I needed to make sure I got the grades that would earn me a place in medical school. In a funny way, I think my adherence to the study ethic helped my running because I learned how much I had to put in to get what I wanted and at what point diminishing returns set in. This sensitivity is important in running, especially if you coach yourself. I think one of the reasons I've lasted so long in running, even though I've had my share of injuries, is that I have a good sense of how much I need to train and when I have to back off.

There were social diversions that year as well. Skiing that Christmas of '67 at Taos Ski Valley, I was riding the chairlift when I saw a young woman lying immobile in the snow below. I called down and asked her if she was all right, and her matter-of-fact answer was: "No, not really." At midstation I skied down to her and found she'd broken her right hand in a fall. I took my scarf and wrapped her swollen hand and helped her ski off the mountain. Her name was Louise Gilliland, and she was a University of Colorado student from Hutchinson, Kansas. After the doctor determined she had broken a bone, I took Louise over to my father's office to have him cast her hand. We established a courtship by mail, interspersed with vacation visits, and three years later we were married.

☆

My most conspicuous failure in "Old Blue" Yale terms came in the Harvard-Yale dual meet in my junior year, when I was not in very good shape. Five of us ran the 2-mile that day — Doug Hardin, James Baker, and Tim McLoone of Harvard, and Yahn and me. The Harvard men set out at what was a hard pace for me, though through the first mile we were still bunched up. The split was 4:28 — an 8:56 pace for the full distance. I had yet to break 9 minutes for 2 miles. I was straining, and I knew I was headed for worse trouble. Hardin pulled away and I desperately hung on to second, but with little more than one lap to go I just stopped and stepped off the track. I sat down, took off my spikes, and walked away.

I was tired, extremely tired. I'd been running in severe oxygen debt from a pace that had me in over my head. It was more of a vague exhaustion than any sort of real pain, and I simply lost the will to go on. A mile and three-quarters at that speed was all I had to give.

I was disappointed but hardly traumatized. I was not among those who considered the Harvard meet anything special and didn't worry about possible criticism for dropping out in general or for screwing up against Harvard. There was no great crowd reaction because there was no crowd to speak of. Gieg said nothing, though I could imagine what he must have been thinking. The only one whom I recall questioning me on the spot was quarter-miler Mark Young, the team captain.

He came over to see how I was, perhaps out of obligation more than anything else; feeling confused, weak, and a little defensive, I was never sure whether he meant to console me, check my condition, or make me feel that I'd bombed out. The 2-mile was the last individual running event of the meet, and had I carried my second-place position to the end, it would have meant a net gain of six points for Yale. Harvard took first, second, and third in the 2-mile, Hardin winning in 9:12.9, and went on to win the meet, 80–74. The score evened the outdoor dual meet series between Harvard and Yale to thirty-five victories apiece with one tie since 1891.

Earlier in the program the mile had been similarly contested, in Yale's favor. James Baker, second in the 2-mile (9:35.2), set out on a remarkable pace for Yale's heavy cinder track, hitting the 880 in 1:59 and the three-quarters in 3:02, intent on trying for a four-minute mile. That same year, in the Heptagonal Championships at Harvard, Baker would record an exceptional double — winning the mile (4:07.1) and 2-mile (8:54.2) — but in the Harvard-Yale meet he, like me, was in over his head. With 220 yards left, Baker appeared to have the mile sewn up. But suddenly, in the worst case of "rigging up" I think I've ever seen, he receded to a jog, totally spent. I was watching from the backstretch and urged on Steve Bittner, who'd been trying to hang on to *second* until given this gift. Bittner caught Baker, so stricken he was nearly walking, and won with a time of 4:14.9. Baker finished third in 4:19.6.

Young, a two-time IC4A champion who once ran a 45.3-mile relay leg, was a team player at Yale who took his captain's role very seriously. That day against Harvard he won the 220, 440, and anchored the winning mile relay team and was named the meet's outstanding performer. (Young is currently the women's track and cross-country coach at Yale, and apparently he still carries his captain's role with honor. A few years ago, when I stopped in New Haven, a couple of his runners were impressed to learn he had once been "on Frank Shorter's team." To which Young kidded,

"No, Frank was on *my* team!") Though Young didn't berate me after the 2-mile that day — after all, I had not been expected to score well — I felt he was more upset than I over what happened. I suppose he felt I'd embarrassed Yale — before Harvard, yet. Gieg, though as proud as could be over my eventual successes, would say years later: "He won an Olympic gold medal but couldn't get me a second in the two-mile against Harvard." It was an unsettling experience, and I vowed to myself that I'd never drop out of a race again, and I haven't — except for injury.

I have succumbed in road race competition. On two occasions, they were marathons most people in the sport probably don't know that I ran. And in both, the circumstances of my failure were different from those of the Harvard 2-mile because they were purely physical. In May 1973 I competed in a marathon in Korso, Finland, near Helsinki, and was sailing along, out front at 5 minutes per mile, when an ailing left foot just "popped" and I was forced to stop. I had a stress fracture. A cast was put on it and I couldn't run the entire summer. It probably would have healed without a cast, but then, without a cast I probably would have been foolish enough to run with the injury — and make the whole thing worse. That I was limping about in early summer and was able to run well the following fall and winter showed me I had good recuperative powers.

I also dropped out of my first marathon, which was not, as the running press has stated, the 1971 AAU national championship in Eugene, Oregon (in which I placed second, about a minute behind Kenny Moore). That was the first marathon for which I'd seriously prepared. Three years before, rather impulsively, I ran in the 1968 U.S. Olympic Trials Marathon in Alamosa, Colorado, which was held the August after my junior year at Yale.

With school out, I'd returned to my family in Taos and gotten a job, the only one I could find, laying pipeline for the gas company in northwestern New Mexico at $2.50 an hour. While working, I was living in the town of Aztec with the family of Ken Levan, who also worked on the pipeline and was engaged to my sister Susan. Every morning we'd get up at five, pack a lunch, hustle over to the company, and wait and see if we were needed. I did this for a month, continuing to run, though never more than 12 miles at one time. Still, I thought I was in good shape, and when I realized the marathon trial was coming up, I decided to go just to be in it; also, I thought I could run 26 miles.

I enlisted my younger brother Chris, then eleven, to accompany me. We took the family pickup and drove the 120 miles to Alamosa. I signed up, got my physical, and was all set. I met Buddy Edelen, who'd broken the world marathon record with a 2:14:28 in England in 1963. (By this time, the record was down to 2:09:37, by Derek Clayton of Australia.) And I knew Amby Burfoot would be there because he'd won the Boston Marathon that April. All of the celebrities turned out: Billy Mills, the 1964 Olympic 10,000-meter gold medalist, who was trying to make a comeback. George Young, a two-time Olympian who would compete in two more. Kenny Moore, a fine runner from the University of Oregon, who would become a running companion and close friend.

I needed to see Amby to borrow a pair of racing shoes. I had none because I couldn't afford them. And I'd worn out my training shoes, which were an old pair of indoor racing flats. Amby came through — he had an extra pair of Tiger Pintos. There was one problem: Amby has size 10 feet and I'm a 10½. "Just don't hold me responsible," he said. I borrowed the shoes anyway, and Amby had no worries that he was helping an opponent who might outrun him for a berth on the 1968 Olympic team.

I was the puppy dog in the field of a hundred and twenty-nine. I figured I'd just run along with the big shots and

hope that some of their know-how would rub off on me. It
was hot, and the altitude in Alamosa is 6,800 feet, which is
essentially what the Olympic marathoners would be facing
two months later in Mexico City. These conditions didn't
trouble me but I was going to be careful. I asked Amby if
I could run with him and he said, "Sure." We tucked in
with the second pack. Moore, Young, and a couple of others
were running in the lead group. At about 8 miles, a fellow
named Bill Clark, who was just up ahead of me, turned
around, looked hard in my direction, and said, "Who are
you?" His tone was one of privilege.

I said, "Hi, I'm a friend of Amby's."

To that, Clark did not respond. We went on.

It was a five-loop course and I was feeling good, but my
toes were beginning to blister. I was bleeding through the
size 10 shoes. I thought to myself, this is silly, and stopped
after three loops. Amby stopped a half-mile farther down
the road, and the two of us stood there and watched the
rest of the race. Young won, Moore was second, and Ron
Daws was third. Clark, a marine who was second to Amby
in the Boston Marathon, finished eighth. Sixty-six men dropped out; the heat and the altitude killed them off.

With properly fitted running shoes, I think I would have
finished, but probably no better than in twentieth or twenty-
fifth place. I was not impressed, after this, by the marathon.
It seemed an awfully long way to run, and I viewed it the
way everyone else viewed it then: as a way to make the
Olympic team. America had very few marathoners in the
sixties.

Though I was not then anxious to become one of them,
Alamosa was a valuable experience. I learned that the leading contenders were running 20 miles a day, in double workouts. I was running once a day, 7 or 8 miles. Even with
my relatively meager training, I came away with the feeling
that the better runners were not *that* much more advanced

than I, and I concluded that with more substantial training, I might become the best runner in the Ivy League in my senior year. Running with the Kenny Moores, George Youngs, and Amby Burfoots, getting close to them even briefly, enabled me to understand better some of what it takes to become a champion. It also left me with the confidence of knowing I'd run along with them, having quit the race only because of bloody feet.

After Alamosa, I harbored no aspirations to the Olympics, only to the Ivy League. I let my toes heal and finished out the summer in Taos, where the high altitude was starting to have a beneficial effect on my training.

I phoned Gieg to let him know what I'd been up to. He was in South Lake Tahoe, Nevada, at a high-altitude training camp, helping to groom the U.S. team for the upcoming Mexico City Olympics. He was all for the marathon. "It might be your event," he told me. "It might be a good distance for your gait . . . You can run at a 'steady state' and carry an efficient pace . . . It's a good thing you stopped before you took your toenails off . . . Try it again." Gieg encouraged me to take on the training volume common to long-distance runners. He advised me to run 20 miles every Sunday and train twice a day during the week, with an early morning run of 10 miles. Gieg's always kidded me about my aversion to running at daybreak. "A quarter to noon's an early run for Frank," he says.

I didn't run more mileage right away, but my attitude had changed. The knowledge I'd acquired — that high mileage was essential for cardiovascular fitness and to facilitate interval running — was an emotional boost that I held on to like a secret weapon. It reinforced what had started to become apparent to me during my junior year, when I was fairly competitive but not yet very focused on my running.

I had also belonged to a singing group as a junior. Perhaps it was eccentricity that propelled me into the Bachelors, one of the undergraduate groups that provided the talent for the famous Whiffenpoofs. Because I had attended the choir school in New York City, organized singing was not new to me. Also, I could sing first tenor. I'd do my running at three, then join the Bachelors at five for a few practice tunes. Gieg wasn't thrilled about this, and he'd chide me every chance he got. Especially that spring, when the track team took its annual bus trip down south to train and compete. I didn't accompany them. I went south with the Bachelors.

We were scheduled to appear in Palm Beach for the society folks, and I figured going down to Palm Beach to sing and lie in the sun and drink beer was a better deal than being holed up in university dorms with the track team. Besides, I enjoyed the singing. We were good. And I would still do my running. The day we left, when the bunch of us Bachelors piled into our van and began making a dent in our beer supply, who do you suppose we saw in the adjacent lane when we pulled onto the Connecticut Turnpike? Right. Gieg and the track team. I toasted them as we drove off. Gieg was furious.

Later that spring I gave him the chance to chew me out. I went up to Gieg one afternoon out on the track before practice and asked him, "Just what do you think my potential is? How good do you think I could be?"

Gieg looked at me and said, "If you train hard and make a commitment, you could probably make the Olympic team. But you'll have to give it all your time. And cut out the skiing, the singing, and the sunning."

"Okay," I said, and started to train more. I had such faith in Gieg's integrity that I knew he wouldn't tell me something just to satisfy my ego.

That third year at Yale, then, like the third quarter of a race, was one of transition. My family had moved clear across the country to a somewhat alien environment. I had met the woman I would marry. I joined a singing group for a while. I focused on my studies. I ran at high altitude. I took a crack at the Olympic Marathon Trial. I got the right blend of encouragement and reprimand from my coach. Though my competitive performances were uneven, I'd nudged them along in my own way, and that was good. I felt no pressure to pound away, no guilt at not being fixed on improving my times. When I was ready to push, I would push.

In my senior year, I was ready.

Finishing the summer of '68 after the marathon trial with a daily 7 or 8 or 10 miles in the high altitude of Taos prepared me well for my final cross-country season at Yale. I was in better shape than ever, and the performance that topped off the fall campaign for me came in a meet with Harvard. Harvard and Princeton — the annual HYP meet. It's been going on since 1922, but, again, that's not why it was important to me. I looked forward to running against Harvard's Doug Hardin because he was the best distance runner in the Ivy League, probably the best Harvard had to that time, and for the first time I thought I had a chance to outrun him. The meet was held at Princeton, over a 5-mile course that went down by the river, circled around the lovely campus, and finished on a spread of playing fields. I beat Hardin decisively, winning in course-record time. This so excited me that in practice the next week I was a little overzealous in a workout of interval half-miles and slipped around a turn, injuring my knee. In the Heptagonal meet the following weekend at Van Cortlandt Park, with my swollen knee supported by an Ace bandage, Hardin beat me by 17 seconds.

A 5-foot-7-inch Woody Allen look-alike from Short Hills, New Jersey, Hardin was a Dean's List student majoring in chemistry and the Harvard cross-country captain that season. He was given to the sort of philosophical ruminations about running made popular a decade later by Dr. George Sheehan. In a 1968 profile in the *New York Times,* Hardin said: "Emotional expression through the expenditure of energy is a mystical quality of running. Runners have different words for it, but they all sense it. When they run they're in a different world, a world of sensations, of mute expression. . . ." I just liked the feeling.

I shook the injury and outran Hardin the next two weeks in the IC4A and NCAA championships, also at Van Cortlandt. I placed fifth in the ICs, which was won by Steve Stageberg of Georgetown, and nineteenth in the NCAA, which was won by Mike Ryan of the Air Force Academy. In the latter race, at 6 miles, I was in the top ten with a mile to go when I faded. It was my first NCAA championship run, and as people were passing me in the final mile, coming off the notorious Cemetery Hill and onto the flats for the final drive to the finish, I was telling myself, "You can't hold on because you don't have the base strength. You haven't run enough." For an Ivy League runner, I felt I'd done okay, earning all-American honors. I'd reached another performance level, and each time that happened I'd immediately start thinking differently about my potential and what it could take to reach it. I left New York for New Haven that day thinking, I'm nineteenth in the country, but there are still eighteen guys ahead of me.

Soon I had more time to do the kind of running that would help me get past those eighteen guys. By the middle of the year, with one semester remaining, my course load was light and the only major academic responsibility left was the senior paper. I was still pre-med, with a major in psychology (thinking I might become a child psychiatrist), and I did my paper on child psychology. I finished it way ahead of time in April and, with one final exam left, had little to do but concentrate on running that spring season.

I'd run through a satisfying indoor season, lowering my 2-mile time to 8:45.2 while placing second in the NCAA meet in Detroit. This time I'd made the traditional early spring trip down south, and at the Florida Relays I'd run a 4:07 anchor mile on our victorious distance medley relay team — and that after a runner-up 8:53.2 in the 2-mile. I was giving serious thought to accelerating my training, to finishing my running career at Yale with some distinction and determining where my running might go from there. I set as my goal the NCAA 6-mile in June, my last collegiate race.

☆

I beefed up my training by running twice a day four or five days a week for a total of 80 miles a week. I felt myself getting stronger and stronger and finally won the 2-mile against Harvard (8:58.4) and the Heptagonal 2-mile (8:50.8), then got second in the IC4A 3-mile at Rutgers in New Brunswick, New Jersey. I was beaten by Jerry Richey of Pittsburgh, 13:41.4 to 13:45.2. That showed me how well the accelerated training was working because I'd beaten Dick Buerkle and Art Dulong; and Richey was the class of the East.

I was pleased. I've never been a bad loser. When I'm defeated, I try to learn from it. I try to determine — based on who beat me — exactly what it means in terms of my conditioning. I tend to be an optimist, and I'll usually draw something encouraging, or at least something not terribly discouraging, from a defeat.

Commencement was held during the first week of June, and I officially became a Yale graduate with one meet left — the NCAA Outdoor Championships in Knoxville, Tennessee, three weeks hence. I'd qualified for the 3-mile and 6-mile in Knoxville with my IC4A 3-mile time, a personal best by 13 seconds. Motivated by an instinct that I was ready to run well in this most important of all collegiate track competitions and by Giegengack's faith in me, I used the time left to make sure I was fully prepared.

Two weeks before the meet I decided to run a 6-mile time trial. My family had come east for graduation, and after-

ward we returned to Middletown to visit my paternal grandparents.

It was a steamy weekday afternoon when I ran over to
the quarter-mile cinder track used by Middletown High
School for the trial run. I was training twice a day by then
and had done an easy 5 or 6 miles that morning. The school
is situated in an open area on the east side of town, with
no protection from the midafternoon sun. It must have been
100 degrees out there. I've always been a good hot-weather
runner — I'm not sure why; maybe because I'm so small-
boned and thin — and so the heat did not trouble me much.
There was not another soul around except for my sister Barbara, fourteen, whom I'd brought along to time me. I gave
her a stopwatch I'd borrowed from the Yale athletic department and positioned her at the finish line. All I wanted her
to do, aside from stopping the watch after twenty-four laps,
was to give me my lap splits. It wouldn't be that tricky for
someone not used to reading a stopwatch because this one
had a 60-second face. Not taking any chances, I started the
watch and handed it to Barbara as I began the run. She
missed a couple of splits but essentially was able to tell me
how I was doing. I ran a fairly even pace and my time was
29 minutes flat. Not many collegians were running faster
6-miles in those days — the 6-mile would eventually be re-
placed by the slightly longer 10,000 meters — and I knew
this meant I would be competitive in Knoxville.

When I saw Gieg at the meet, I told him about the time
trial. He seemed impressed and said, "It sounds like you're
in good shape," but I wasn't sure he believed me. I didn't
tell him that it was my kid sister who'd timed me.

☆

I never go into a race thinking that I'm really going to win.
I always know, based on my training, how hard I can run,
and I try and run up to that level. If I succeeded in running

up to what I felt my level was in Knoxville, I thought I would do well.

It was humid and 86 degrees, my kind of weather. There were twenty-four men in the 6-mile, and the early leader was Oscar Moore of Southern Illinois, a 1964 Olympian at 5,000 meters. At 3 miles his split was 14:28. I was 20 yards behind, running the same pace I'd run at Middletown High. I took the lead from Moore with about 2 miles to go and broke away to win by 150 yards in 29:00.2. When I make a break and I'm running free, I'm not afraid to go hard. Rick Riley of Washington State was second (29:23.2). Moore faded to fifth. Donal Walsh of Villanova, who was sixth, collapsed from dehydration and was hospitalized. Only seventeen men finished.

Afterward, I called home to tell my mother how I'd done, the only time I've ever done that. My family was proud but subdued. I received the same reaction after winning the NCAA 6-mile that I did after winning the Middletown Little League home run title. To me, that did not seem unusual or disappointing.

The next day Gieg told reporters that the last time this sort of thing had happened to him — that a runner of his who was not a favorite had won a distance race in grand fashion — was in 1964, when he was the Olympic coach in Tokyo and Billy Mills won the 10,000 meters.

The 3-mile was the last individual race of the meet. I felt rested and relaxed after the 6-mile. We passed 1 mile in 4:33.6 and 2 miles in 9:10.6, and with one lap to go there were four of us left in contention. It was a strange experience. I had to kick, and never having done that before at that level of competition and with a chance to win, I didn't know what to expect. If you're well trained but dead tired and shift into a higher gear and suddenly find a rush of energy, it can be a powerful experience. The last lap of the 1969 NCAA 3-mile was the first time it ever happened to me, and after that I began to develop a faith in my ability to respond late in a race even if severe fatigue had set in.

I came on strongly but did not win. I was second in 13:43.4 behind Ole Oleson of Southern Cal, who won by 10 yards in 13:42. I'd waited too long to make my move, not knowing if I'd have a move. Seven of the starters did not finish, including Jim Ryun of Kansas, who earlier that day had lost his first collegiate mile race ever to Marty Liquori of Villanova. Ryun, in the 3-mile, stepped off the track just before the 1-mile mark. I could empathize with Jim because of my DNF against Harvard, and I hoped he would recover from the letdown.

I left Knoxville a little dizzy. I thought, My God, I can't believe how much better I am with the additional training. I didn't have any delusions of grandeur. I thought of my progress in terms of a curve on a graph, and I saw that the curve seemed to be going up. That was when I made the decision to keep riding the curve.

CHAPTER THREE

Running for My Life

Soon after college, my desire to become the best runner I could superseded all else. I took on the life of a migrant, a migrant runner who lived here and there, earned little money, and survived on the opportunity to excel at running. It was nothing more complicated than that. With significant progress behind me, I experimented, tested myself, ran a little faster, a little longer; everything I did was consistent with the need to get the most out of my running ability.

I lived in Florida to train in the winter and in Colorado to train in the summer. While in Taos, I fought with roughnecks whose illicit hobbies had spilled out onto my running course. I dropped out of medical school because my money ran out and also because there was not enough time to study medicine and train. I attended law school, skipping the semesters that interfered with my Olympics training buildup. I competed all over the United States and in Europe, South America, the Soviet Union, and Japan. What emerged at the end of 1971 was that my best event was the marathon.

I was invited to compete in the Fukuoka Marathon in Japan in December 1971 after winning the Pan-American Games marathon and 10,000 meters that summer in Cali, Colombia. I considered it an honor because the Fukuoka race is the world's pre-eminent international marathon. And

because many of the leading marathoners would be in it, I
knew I could benefit from the experience and trained hard
that fall. Louise and I were living in Gainesville, Florida,
at the time, and for most of the fall I did not race, peaking
for Fukuoka, and I felt fit from the long and hard running
I'd been doing. In late November I went off to San Diego
for the National AAU Cross-Country Championship, where
I won the title for the second straight year. From there I
continued west.

I'd been to Japan once before. In the fall of 1969, after
my first running experience abroad as a member of a U.S.
team competing in Europe, I was part of another American
traveling squad that competed in the Pacific Conference
Games in Japan. One meet was held in Tokyo's Olympic
Stadium, and there I ran the 10,000 and was lapped. In the
other meets I ran the 5,000 and got a second and a third.

Japan fascinated me. The gracious people, the fast pace
of life, the imperial architecture — I was anxious to see
Fukuoka. It's always amazed me how athletes can go on a
European tour, fly from hotel to hotel, go to the tracks, run
their races, pick up their "expenses," and be done with it.
I have to look around, figure out what's going on. I have
to feel the rhythms of the culture. Perhaps it helps, for the
competition, to better understand the environment.

Fukuoka is my favorite marathon. In Japan, the runners
come first. The attitude among the Japanese is: We're here
to make everything as comfortable as we can for you so
that you might run as well as possible. In some other countries, I've gotten the impression that the people associated
with an event are being cordial out of duty rather than sin-
cerity and that they're not going to do too much for you
because, after all, you could end up beating one of their
own. But in Japan, there is an honest effort to produce the
best race possible because the people love the event and
what it represents as great sport. I'm very appreciative of

that — that as marathon runners we are respected for what we do as athletes by the race officials, political dignitaries, the press, and by the average Japanese person watching the race.

Even the New York and Boston marathons still don't have that. Probably because of the enormity of their fields — Fukuoka is a strictly invitational race, with about a hundred competitors — but also because of cultural distinctions, New York and Boston have a certain circus atmosphere that at times causes spectators and support personnel to think of the runners more as objects of curiosity than as athletes. The people straining for a look in Brooklyn or Framingham probably don't appreciate what it means when the front-runners go through the first 10,000 meters in 30 minutes. In Japan they do, and they get excited about it. Other than the Olympics and the Olympic Trials, Fukuoka is the only marathon I've ever peaked for.

I flew to Japan with Kenny Moore, who had finished second at Fukuoka the year before. Kenny and I had traveled abroad and roomed together to run the previous two summers. Once in Fukuoka, I was immediately on edge. Kenny recorded my mood in his account of our experience in *Sports Illustrated:* "This is the first time I've started a trip knowing I couldn't be any better prepared," I'd said. "I've done more long runs than ever, I'm effective over shorter distances, and my weight is down. I'm not torn by too much racing like I was last summer. . . . Of course, it's frightening to feel like this. I've followed the program perfectly. If I run lousy there's something wrong with the program."

I couldn't wait to race. I could muster little appetite and would need a beer to relax. We trained regularly in the lovely parks in and around Fukuoka, always nailed for autographs. It was an anxious week, with too much time for contemplation. I was not the only competitor who felt restless. An Australian, John Farrington, a British-educated university administrator, seemed to be wasting nervous energy trying to psych others out.

His primary target was a Finn, Seppo Nikkari, who spoke only Finnish and who incurred Farrington's wrath for, as he saw it, a lack of couth. But Nikkari instinctively zeroed in on Farrington's vulnerable points and worked on them for all he was worth. We'd get into a cab and Nikkari would sit on Farrington's lap, pinch his cheek, put his arm around him. He drove Farrington crazy. I think the Finn realized that by goading Farrington into wanting to beat him even more, the Aussie would likely be too driven, even angry, to put forth a composed effort.

"I will take pleasure in thrashing him by a few minutes," Farrington told Kenny.

At the start of the race, Farrington was first out of the stadium and onto the route, which followed the coastline out to the flat peninsula. Akio Usami, the favorite as Japan's defending champion and national record-holder (2:10:38), then took the lead. I moved up to him at 2 miles and, sharing the lead in a bunch, was urged on by the flag-waving Japanese. At the midpoint turnaround I was trailing Usami but was able to catch him 3 miles later despite a blowing headwind. Once ahead, I ran a controlled race, maintaining a 200-meter lead, and it was this section — with 9 miles to go, then 8, then 7 — that I always remembered. I realized that I could take the lead in a field of this caliber and hold it. I could get out front, concentrate, and keep rolling. I could press and hold on, even into the force of the wind, as I had when I sensed Usami coming back on me with 3 miles to go. Usami, who'd won marathons in Athens and Munich that year, was probably in better physical condition, but mentally I had him beat.

I won the race by 32 seconds in 2:12:51, my fastest time by almost 5 minutes. It was the hardest I'd ever run. I was drained. I'd given everything I had to give and, at the end, I greeted the other runners at the finish, waiting for Kenny.

I preferred to wait for them rather than take a victory lap. Kenny was twenty-eighth, victimized by the remains of a midweek virus. Nikkari, by the way, was fourth; Farrington finished sixth.

I had much to think about. I showed myself I was not afraid to really go out and try to win a marathon. And that's what any runner who hopes to win major races must have — the courage to put everything on the line in the middle of a race, and not be afraid to lose. It forces certain runners into decisions they'd prefer to make later on, decisions to commit themselves before they'd like to. Running out front, controlling the race, has been an effective tactic for me because it suits my personality. It lets me know how *I'm* doing and it lets me know how the opposition will react to it. Being an analyst when it comes to a race, I'll use almost anything about an opponent — or about myself, for that matter — to try to give myself an advantage.

At Fukuoka, I saw that the 26 miles 385 yards of the marathon was a distance congruent with my developing capabilities. I also saw that a number-one-ranked runner in fit condition and in his home country — an Usami in this case — could be beaten. A lot can go wrong in a marathon, and on any given day something is bound to go wrong with a number of leading runners. It doesn't take much. And when I saw how my pull-ahead-and-press strategy worked, that became my style of running the marathon.

All of this translated into an inarticulated sense that if I continued to train consistently with a program designed to have me as fit as I possibly could be by the following summer, I would have a chance to win a medal in the Munich Olympics.

☆

All through college, just like my father, I wanted to become a doctor. I'd been the one in the family who, as a youngster, had accompanied him on his house calls in Middletown. And

I'd gone out to hang around the emergency room at Horton
Memorial Hospital when my father was on duty. As a GP,
my father delivered about a hundred and twenty-five babies
a year in Middletown, a city of 22,000. He's a very service-
oriented doctor, well liked in town. That made an impression
on me. My interest in pursuing his line of work — and, I
would imagine, his unselfish care — was a form of approba-
tion within the family, though my father did not push me
toward a career in medicine. It was not his way. I remember
when we were vacationing in Florida during spring recess
of my senior year at Mount Hermon, when I knew I'd be
going to Yale. Out on the beach one day, my father turned
to me and wondered, "Frank, what are your plans for college?"

Altruism notwithstanding, it was convenient for the son
of a doctor to tell people who asked that, yes, you too had
decided on medicine, because then they would leave you
alone. You weren't forced to discuss your future any further,
a relief when, deep down, you probably were not sure what
it was you really wanted to do.

I applied to medical school at Harvard, Yale, and New
Mexico. Harvard and Yale rejected me. I was accepted by
New Mexico, helped by being a resident of the state.

I lasted six weeks. Two things happened: I ran out of
money, and I ran out of patience. I'd used up my small
savings and couldn't allow my parents, with a family of ten
children, to scrape up the tuition. I wouldn't take a loan
because the idea of being in debt once school was completed
did not appeal to me. Though the craft and challenge of
medicine appealed to me, I left Albuquerque with no regrets
because I felt abused by the teaching attitude there. I viewed
it as the penance syndrome: I suffered, therefore you will
suffer. It was not as important to learn medicine as it was
to learn how to stay up for 80 hours in a row. Right from
the beginning, they expected you to be a monomaniac. I

couldn't take it. I left and returned to Taos to help fix up the family house, which needed brick floors, adobe walls, and a fireplace.

Every day I took time off from my construction chores to run. It was unfocused running, 12 to 15 miles a day, on the dirt paths and back roads near home. One Sunday in November 1969, with less than a half-mile to go in what was going to be my longest run ever, I drifted out onto the main highway and came upon a group of hoods — *pachucos*, as the Spanish call them — trying to drag two girls into their car. I rushed over to the car and warned, "I know who you guys are and I have your license number." Had I first gone for help, the men would surely have overpowered the girls. But my interference and my threat (hollow though it must have sounded) stirred the machismo in these fellows and, intent on proving who the boss was, they let go of the girls and took off after me.

I'll always remember that car. It was a blue 1957 Oldsmobile with a three-part back window, circular taillights, and a rear bumper so low it dragged along the ground. These guys could not let one skinny runner with no shirt on insult the five of them without teaching him a lesson, so they piled back into their car and tried to run me down. I tried to escape into a field and they drove after me, obviously drunk.

In a chase scene worthy of any B movie, the *pachucos* stopped the car, the doors flew open, and out they came, one with a long knife, another brandishing a broken bottle. I had no plans to use the occasion to test my ability in hand-to-hand combat. The situation took on a comic effect because as I ran, I had imagined short people with bellies hanging over their belts, white socks, and pointed shoes trying to corner me as I darted in circles out of their grasp. The reality was just as funny (I can laugh about it now) as I tore away from them across the open land — not unlike games of tag in primary school. Finally I got away by running into a trading post about a half-mile from home and taking refuge there. The proprietors, a Lebanese family named Saad (whom most everyone assumed was Spanish or Indian), knew me and also knew of the *pachucos*. The Lebanese were good people, tough in their own right, and suddenly the odds were five to three. The *pachucos* grouped outside the store, shouting that they would get me; then, after a few minutes, they left. When I got home and told my father what had happened, he said he had a good idea of who they were.

Later that day, when my father went down to the hospital emergency room on a call, I tagged along and got an idea of what would have happened had I been unlucky enough to have been caught by the *pachucos*. A man was brought in, a hitchhiker, with a broken arm and lacerations, all cut up and bruised. Looking at him, I said, "God, they even rolled this guy in manure." My father said, "No, they kicked him in the stomach and spleen so hard that he shit in his pants." It was a shocking experience. And that was not the end of it.

For a time after that, the same *pachucos* harassed us by speeding around our house in the middle of the night, like the Indians surrounding the wagon train. We carried guns, protecting the homestead, if you will. That didn't stop someone from killing a few of our dogs (by shooting them or running them over) or from sugaring the gas tanks of our cars.

When I ran during that time, my father escorted me in the pickup with a .38 at his side. My route went right by the *pachucos'* house (a few of them were brothers), and they were always around, drinking or working on their car. Once, when they noticed me, they ran down their driveway in my direction, cursing in Spanish, and my father got out of the pickup and pumped a few shots over their heads. The *pachucos* retreated. A sort of frontier justice still exists in Taos. After that, I could run without intimidation. Territorial pride is so ingrained in the area that in a situation like that, you're forced to demonstrate that you're willing to match them blow for blow and, if necessary, go down the tubes together before you'll be left alone.

The conflict ended mainly because of my father's standing in the community. We'd been living in Taos for two years by then and had come through the trial period of assimilation into the rather closed nonwhite society of the area. My father had become the doctor the people could most rely on. He was always available, and he was a soft touch. If you had no money, he would accept fruit or preserves in trade. If you had nothing even to barter, he would ask for nothing. The Spanish community there is a very matriarchal one, and the women of the families who depended on my father were strong and effectively put an end to the harassment.

It was a harsh life. Beautiful though it is in Taos, the extremes of weather were hard on people, and the cold ruined the fruit crop almost every year. There was little business opportunity outside of the small tourist industry, and the world-famous artists' colony was patronized by the rich. Most of the poor people were laborers or on welfare.

I continued to run past the *pachucos'* home, proud that we had stood up to them. That's life in Taos, I figured. I've never considered myself a nose-to-nose confrontational type (though my racing opponents might think otherwise), but there comes a time when you have to try to persevere, to survive in a tough environment.

The *pachucos,* I should emphasize, were a small bad element and not at all representative of the community at large. Generally, people took care of each other in Taos. There is a real sense of neighborhood. My youngest brother, Michael, is mildly retarded and still lives in Taos with my mother and attends a special school. His best friends, the boys who are kindest to him, are his Spanish buddies from the neighborhood.

Over the years, however, my father retained some of the

hard feelings engendered by the *pachucos* conflict, and when a *Life* magazine reporter phoned after the Munich Olympics, my father, showing his emotional side, related the shotgun tale. I guess he did it as a release, to let it all out finally, but I felt the story might be exaggerated or misinterpreted and was bound to reopen the wounds if *Life* made something of it. When the reporter called back to interview me, I said I would not talk to him unless he agreed not to use the story. "Sure, don't worry," he said. But there it was, *pachucos* and all, in an issue of *Life*. I was furious.

So were people in Taos. The town decided against giving me a welcome home reception after Munich, saying, in effect, that I might be a hero for America but I wasn't a hero for Taos. Lawrence Santisteven, Taos' mayor *pro tem*, made it a political issue and stated, "Many people feel that the whole town was being blamed for something that a few individuals did."

Some of our family remained in Taos, and my father continued his work at the rundown hospital of the United Presbyterian Church in Embudo. He was a doctor, and there were poor people who needed him. In a way, he needed them too, and so the animosity died.

☆

I needed to train with someone, Jack Bacheler in particular, and the next spring, in 1970, I left Taos to live in Gainesville, Florida, to run with Jack. I'd met him the year before, as a Yale senior on our spring trip to the Florida Relays. Jack won the 2-mile in 8:35.6; I was second in 8:53. Jack was the best distance runner in the U.S. (and at 6 feet 7 inches probably the tallest of the world's leading distance runners). In 1969, he'd won the National AAU 6-mile (I was a distant fourth) and was undefeated that season until Australia's world record-holder, Ron Clarke, defeated him in a 2-mile race in California.

When I met Jack I found him very friendly. He was not aggressive, yet he could become fiercely competitive on the track. That impressed me. I was also impressed by Jack's interest in pursuing both his professional career and his running at the same time. He was working on his doctoral degree in entomology, the study of insects, at the University of Florida, and that was very important to him. He could slide from his studies to his running and do both well. He seemed like the ideal type of person for me to train with. Jack said yes when I asked him, and it turned out to be a wonderful situation. After I'd settled in Gainesville, Jack told me I was the only person ever to train with him who lasted more than two months.

For a while I lived with two other runners behind the equipment room at the university track. One was John Parker, a law student who got me interested in law. The other was Harry Winkler, who became a two-time Olympian — in team handball. At the Munich Olympics I was shocked and delighted to notice Harry one day as I gazed from the balcony of our fifth-floor apartment in the Olympic Village. I called down, "Winkler, what are *you* doing here!" He grinned and said, "Well, I had to get on the Olympic team somehow, so I went with team handball."

In Gainesville, where I lived on and off for four years, I became part of what was to become a little running colony known nationally as the Florida Track Club. In time, in addition to Jack and me, the group included such world-class performers as Marty Liquori, Jeff Galloway, and Barry Brown. Liquori, originally from New Jersey, became one of the world's truly great runners in the mile and 5,000 meters and still lives in Gainesville as president of the Athletic Attic chain of sporting goods stores, which he founded with Jimmy Carnes. Carnes was the head track coach of the university when I went to Gainesville and was responsible for establishing, around Jack Bacheler, the Florida Track Club.

Carnes didn't coach us; we coached ourselves. But he, along with his assistant coach, Roy Benson, helped with travel arrangements, housing, and our competitive affairs. Carnes went on to become not only a successful businessman but also president of The Athletics Congress, the U.S. governing body for track and field, and men's head coach of the 1980 U.S. Olympic track and field team.

Jack, more than anyone, helped me to become a better runner. Through his example and encouragement, he convinced me that I could take on a high-mileage program and avoid injury. He showed me that I could formulate an ambitious schedule that would bring long-term benefits, and that with all the running to be done — morning and afternoon, day in and day out — I could enjoy it. Jack was running about 150 miles a week, and I was running a little less. Much of it was slow, easy mileage; but there was also some rather intense speedwork. Because our habits differed, Jack and I did not run together all of the time, but that also was good because you appreciate each other more, and get along better, by having a certain training autonomy. You need time for yourself. Jack would do his morning runs earlier than I, at six-thirty. He'd run 9 miles at about 7 minutes a mile. I'd get out at around nine and run 7 or 8 miles at a 6-minute pace. In the afternoon we'd frequently meet for trackwork or whatever the session called for. Other runners would join in. I acquired a reputation for taking very short rests, 45 seconds or less, between the fast quarter-mile repetitions of an interval workout. Jack was a little less intense about his speedwork. So relaxed was he in general during training that in the middle of a run, he could stop suddenly to pick up a butterfly specimen, slip it into his shorts so as not to damage it, and continue running with it secure in his jock.

Jack was such a gentle soul, I sometimes wondered how he could be such a fine competitor. But one day that spring I saw that beneath Jack's calm exterior lurked an aggression he could channel. A bunch of us were running at dusk on our 7-mile loop through the streets when something — it might have been an egg — came flying in our direction from a passing car. It didn't hit anyone, but the car, unfortunately for its occupants, was forced to stop at the next corner for a red light. When Jack saw this, he took off and, like sheep, we followed. There were four or five of us, and we had no idea what Jack was going to do, only that we were going to do it with him. Jack ran to the back of the car, up onto the trunk, over the roof, and down the hood without saying a word. And we followed him, one by one, like steeple-chasers taking a water jump, and sped away, not anxious to test our courage any further. The people in the car must have been so flabbergasted that they weren't able to retaliate, for they did not come after us. Perhaps they were plainly intimidated by the extraordinary exhibition of impulsive aggression.

That incident as well as our performances made the papers, and word spread that some serious running was going on in Gainesville. Running was about all I was doing, and since I paid no rent, I needed little money. Which was a good thing because I only had a little. One way for a runner to pick up some money was to exchange a plane ticket sent to you by a meet promoter for a reduced-fare ticket, pocketing the difference. (Today's top runners, operating in a more liberal financial climate in terms of the amateur rules, have made this procedure an art form.) Once I was recognized enough to receive invitations to compete in Europe, I could take better advantage of the opportunities to make some money on the track circuit. But before notice came my way, I was fortunate to benefit from Jack's generosity. I went on my first two competitive trips out of Gainesville, to the Texas Relays in Austin and Drake Relays in Des Moines, on funds from Jack, who'd put his expense allowance, without hesitation, into a Florida Track Club pool.

Because of the low tuition for Florida residents, $240 a quarter, I was able to enroll in law school, which I pursued more for the intellectual exercise than out of any burning desire to become an attorney. I started school in the spring of 1971 and finally earned my degree in 1974. I passed the bar and am licensed to practice law in Colorado, where we've been living since leaving Gainesville in 1974. However, concentrating on my clothing business, I have never really practiced law. Louise joined me in Gainesville following her graduation from the University of Colorado. We'd been married since June of 1970.

Being able to train with Jack, keeping up with him, gave me the confidence to know that my best years of running lay ahead. That spring of 1970, tagging along with him in competition, I improved my best times, and in the National AAU Championships in Bakersfield, California, in June, I won the 3-mile in 13:24.2 and intentionally tied for first, with Jack, in the 6-mile. We'd run 27:24.0 and won by 6.8 seconds.

With my AAU performances, I'd earned a berth on the American team that would face the Russians later that summer in Leningrad, in the annual U.S.-Soviet dual meet. I'd never been to the Soviet Union and was anxious to have a look around. When the United States competed against the Soviets in track and field, there was a lot of "beat the Russians" flag-waving, and I was curious to know why we should hate these people. I did not believe that the Russian people and the government forced upon them were one, and so I sought out people to talk to, hoping to find them engaging and thus confirm my views. However, we were restricted and got to meet only official guides and interpreters — and the athletes, of course, but not until the meet. From the reading I had done, from the little interaction and some sightseeing, I came away with the impression that the citizens of Leningrad, at least, were a tough and hearty people.

Some members of the American delegation were overcome with paranoia. When we were invited to the Russian circus, I had to convince them that it was not to be missed. "This is a major cultural enterprise," I told them. "Their circuses are not like ours." So a bunch of us attended, and George Frenn, a hammer thrower, let his suspicions get the best of him.

"The lions are drugged," George insisted. "I can see it from here. They drugged the animals."

I ran the 10,000 meters in Leningrad. I won the race and had one of those days that come once a year — if you're lucky. Kenny Moore and I were competing for the U.S., Nikolay Sviridov and Leonid Mikityenko for the USSR. Mikityenko, a seasoned runner, had been third in the 1966 European Championships. I led from the start, and when I heard 13:55 for the 5,000-meter split I couldn't believe it. At the time, only Ron Clarke in his world record races had gone under 14 minutes halfway into a 10,000. And what amazed me was how great I felt.

The crowd got behind me because, as in meets in Oslo and Stockholm, when a runner gets free from the field and moves out unencumbered at a good pace, the people roar their approval no matter where he's from. I ran as well as I could possibly have hoped, winning by 27.4 seconds in 28:22.8, my best time. The Soviets cheered, tossing flowers onto the track. It was one of the most uplifting moments of my life.

It was also the first time any performance of mine was highlighted in the press. The U.S.-Soviet meet was accorded great importance then, and I was credited with "beating the Russians," a tag that could not be refused by anyone who in fact had done so. Even *Sports Illustrated* saluted the victory, putting me on the cover.

The Russians finished third and fourth in the 10,000, behind Kenny Moore, and they were roundly booed. Still, Mikityenko came over to me and embraced me. Then he smiled, went over to his bag, and pulled out two little wooden carvings of Russian people. Through an interpreter, he said, "These are from my children to your children."

In Leningrad and elsewhere in Europe that summer (and the summer before), I roomed with Kenny Moore, whom I had met in 1969. After the NCAA meet in June following my college graduation, I ran the AAU 6-mile in Miami. Kenny, a '67 Oregon graduate, was serving a hitch in the army while remaining active as a runner; he, too, ran the AAU 6-mile, as a way of trying to stay out of Vietnam. Had I known it at the time, I would have purposely slowed down on the last lap — though Kenny passed me anyway with 200 meters to go and placed third. He needed to be the first or second American in order to make the U.S. traveling squad for Europe; then he could spend the summer in Stuttgart and London instead of in Saigon. Because a Mexican, José Martinez, placed second, Kenny was in. I made the European team as well since Jack Bacheler, the winner, declined to go because of his studies.

Kenny and I developed an unusual kinship. I think it grew out of our genuine love of running, our aesthetic appreciation of the sport, our respect for one another, and, most important, out of a sense that we had gone far in athletics despite odds that were supposed to have kept us down. Though Kenny came out of the immensely successful program at Oregon, where he received excellent coaching from Bill Bowerman, he was not a heralded prospect. Yet he went on to win two national AAU titles, set an American record for the marathon (2:13:27 in 1969), and to compete in two Olympic Games. I had come out of the Ivy League, which was not exactly a farm system for Olympic medalists. Also, we were both marathon runners. Marathon runners, even if they have nothing in common other than their running, have much in common because of the profound experience of the marathon.

It was Kenny who convinced me to run it. In 1971, having watched me run the 6-mile and 10,000 meters for two years, he said to me, "I think you can carry your feathery stride over the marathon distance." That a fellow competitor, even a friend, was telling me to run *his* event impressed me greatly, and I believed in him. I knew that he meant it for my own good, and beyond that, he said it, in a way, on behalf of the sport. Kenny felt I might contribute to it, and I am indebted to him for that. Kenny joked about it with the press after the Olympic marathon in 1972. He was quoted as saying, "I kept trying to talk him into the marathon. The reason was that he was handling me so easy in the six-mile and on the track that I wanted to get him into my race. Well, now he has handled me in my race."

Kenny became, for me, a *de facto* coach. As Jack Bacheler had influenced me to develop my physical capacity, Kenny helped me to mature as an athlete psychologically, and at a critical point in my athletic life — after college and before my first Olympics — I was fortunate to be around someone like that whom I could respect.

I could tell early on that we would hit it off because there was no jealousy between us. In 1969, our first season as touring roommates, he was clearly the better runner, and it never bothered me. And I know Kenny was happy for me when my success arrived. From what I've seen, Kenny and Jack and myself are the only runners of our generation who related to one another in this way, and the three of us have remained good friends.

I admire the way Kenny always knew he would be a writer when his days as a world-class runner were over. He started writing on a free-lance basis for *Sports Illustrated* in 1971, signed on full-time in 1980, and is now a senior writer, on the track beat. Frequently, on our trips together, he'd be covering the event as well as competing, and I'd find myself mentioned through his stories. For some reason, Kenny finds how I react in situations very interesting, and I've always

found his accounts of my behavior flattering — not in the
sense of a friend cheering a friend, but in the way he has
of bringing out the nuances that are significant in a gathering
of leading runners. He seems to say what I feel, and feel
what I say.

Encouraged by Kenny, I ran my first serious marathon
on June 6, 1971, in the AAU championship race in Eugene,
Oregon. Kenny and I ran together, and at 16 miles I said
to him, "Why couldn't Pheidippides have died here?" Kenny
laughed, pulled away at 20 miles, and won in 2:16:49. I was
second, weary from the wind, in 2:17:45. We'd made the
U.S. Pan-American Games team and would be running the
marathon together again that summer, in Cali, Colombia.

Despite second-place finishes in the 10,000 in dual meets
against teams from Africa and the Soviet Union, I was confident in Cali and won the 10,000 decisively in 28:50.8. Sooner
or later, everybody gets *turista* in Colombia, and mine came
later, 14 miles into the marathon, which was held five days
after the 10,000, on the final day of the meet. It was one
of the few times that I've ever had to stop in a race to
relieve myself. The urge developed at 6 miles and I held
off as long as I could, running with goosebumps over every
inch of my body. Finally, at 14 miles, after the turnaround
point on the out-and-back course, I succumbed and rushed
off into a ditch. Kenny and I were leading along with two
Colombians, Alvaro Mejia and Hermann Barreneche.

"Bye, Kenny," I said. "See you later." Kenny said nothing.

I finished in a hurry and thought to myself that I would
sneak back up on them, but fast. I'd lost about 30 seconds,
and it took me only about 5 minutes, or 1 mile, to catch
up. As I closed in on them, I took advantage of my slight
frame and tiptoed behind them to intensify the surprise.

In tow with one of the Colombians, I called, "Yoo-hoo,
Kenny, I'm back."

The Colombian turned around, his eyes filled with disbelief, and in the next half-mile both of them faded. Kenny ran into trouble himself, from the searing afternoon heat, dropped out at 18 miles, and was taken from the race in an ambulance. I went on to my first marathon victory, in 2:22:40.

The pit stop incident gave me the satisfaction of knowing that given the opportunity, I could use a psychological ploy to my advantage in a marathon. Psyching is part of the competitive process, and among marathoners, it is usually subtle and unplanned. It is advantageous to be able to react to an opening in the midst of a race. But there was a risk. Had the Colombians forced the pace after my return, who knows what the outcome might have been?

☆

Encouraged by my victory in the Fukuoka Marathon in December 1971, I decided to go to Vail, Colorado, in the spring and train for the Olympics at high altitude. I felt I could make the Olympic team. I would train as I'd never trained before — and at an altitude of 8,000 feet, where the oxygen-thin air, I believed, would intensify the effect. I'd been spending the summers in mile-high Boulder and had grown accustomed to the environment. I'd also started to sense, in a vaguely physical way, how the elevation was helping me. And I had not forgotten that when Bob Giegengack returned from the 1968 Mexico City Olympics, where the 7,300-foot altitude played a significant role, he told me, "There's got to be something to this." African athletes from the highland regions won every men's running event, from the 1,500 meters to the marathon. But Gieg also marveled at how the American runners, no matter what their performances were in Mexico City, returned home to sea level and ran very well.

With less oxygen in the air, the body increases oxygen transport to get more oxygen into the blood per breath and more blood to the tissues per heartbeat. Ventilation increases: We breathe more rapidly and take deeper breaths. In time, your system becomes stronger (up to a point) and, from what I've observed and experienced, your body undergoes less stress at sea level, where oxygen is more plentiful, and produces a better performance. Though researchers remain skeptical of its value, I'm convinced that the altitude provides an edge. There's more return for a given effort.

Armed with an instinct about all that, I left the flatlands of Gainesville, where things had been going so well, for the mountains of Colorado. Jack Bacheler and Jeff Galloway thought it was a good idea as well, so after the Florida Relays in April, the three of us and our wives (Jeff was single then) went out to Vail and set up shop in a house owned by Robert Lange, the man who pioneered the plastic ski boot. I'd met Lange through Mary Estill Buchanan, who became the secretary of state of Colorado. When Louise and I were first married, we lived in Mary Estill's basement and babysat for her children in lieu of rent.

Lange's house was big and beautiful, and we had access to a pool, a sauna, and a weight room. We were all set. Vail is in a fairly flat valley, which was ideal because we wanted the effects of living there more than the opportunity to run in the mountains. Also, we wanted to run a lot of high mileage, which was more easily done on flat terrain.

We had two months. Vail was our laboratory, and we were the experiment. We ran twice a day, sometimes three times. Twenty miles a day, sometimes more. There were a couple of 170-mile weeks, which was probably equivalent to 200 at sea level. All we did was run — run, eat, and sleep. I slept 10 hours a day and napped in the afternoon. I knew that the Hungarian soldiers had done it that way in the early fifties, when they were setting the distance records.

On a long run, when we were maintaining the same pace as we had in Gainesville, we derived more benefit because of the added stress. During our interval sessions, which were done on the smooth, even fairways of the golf course, we had to allow more recovery time between repetitions because of the altitude.

The tricky part of the experiment was determining how many days of adjustment were needed at sea level before a competition at sea level, which is where all of our meets would be held that spring, including the Olympic Trials in Eugene, Oregon. At high altitude, as much as you try to maintain your leg speed, you can't. With less oxygen available, you go into "oxygen debt" more readily and can't work on your speed as well. Before a race, you need a certain amount of time at sea level, not so much to adapt physiologically to living there (though there is a lethargy that sets in that you need to get over) as to do some speed training to make sure you get your leg rate back up so you can run aerobically at a faster pace and recover more quickly when you run yourself into an anaerobic state.

I had learned this two years before, when I ran in Southern California after coming down from the altitude of Boulder. I tried a workout of twelve 220s, and I couldn't break 30 seconds on any of them. But a few days later I could run the 2-mile, in competition, in 8:42. And a week after that I could win both the 3-mile and 6-mile (tying with Jack) in the AAU championships, running the last 440 of the 3-mile in 55 seconds. I sensed I needed ten days to two weeks at sea level to be at my best.

Coming down from Vail to run the Drake Relays in Iowa, I was not bothered by my mediocre performance because we'd only been in Iowa for a day or so. I wasn't going to let that happen when it really mattered, and for the AAUs and Olympic Trials we were careful. With four days at sea level before the AAU meet in Seattle, I ran 28:12, my best ever, to place second in the 10,000 meters. I felt strong, but not fast. Greg Fredericks outkicked me. But I felt my speed coming, and with the Olympic Trials two weeks later, I was right on target.

In the Olympic Trials the race, essentially, is for third place. Three people make the team, so whether you come in first, second, or third means nothing. In fact, winning the trials could hurt you for the Olympics — if you have to put out too much to do it. It is almost impossible to be in peak form *twice* in the same season, especially in the distance events.

I felt I was more ready than anyone for the 10,000 in Eugene and decided to take the lead and set a fast pace. I wanted to neutralize Fredericks' kick, and if I was going to win, I hoped to do so with a minimum of late-race pressure to keep some strength in reserve for the marathon, to be held seven days later. It was 95 degrees out, rare for Eugene. I ran the first mile in 4:25.4 and after that had the race to myself, finishing in 28:35.6. The hard pace also helped Jack and Jeff, who moved up into contention for team berths after the pursuers closest to me, Tom Laris, Gerry Lindgren, and Fredericks, fell back. Jeff made it — in second place (28:48.8). Jack didn't; he placed fourth and, adding salt to the wound, was disqualified because of a bumping incident with Jon Anderson in the homestretch. Anderson was third.

I was ecstatic. I was on the Olympic team. It took all the pressure off me for the marathon.

But it wasn't quite that simple. I developed a blister on the ball of my right foot during the 10,000, and it became infected. The doctor said that maybe I shouldn't run the marathon trial. I said no. Luckily, the infection responded favorably to antibiotics and I ran unimpeded in the marathon.

I forced the pace again, and it felt so easy. Running in the lead with Kenny Moore we shook the field, except for Mark Covert, who stuck with us. I could tell that Covert was just hanging on. "I'm going," I whispered to Kenny at

13 miles. We took off and dropped Covert, but Kenny's right hamstring muscle started to trouble him in the second half of the race, and with about a mile to go, he could barely tolerate it.

"My hamstring just went," he said to me. "Go on."

"No," I said. "We'll finish together."

We had the race won, and I knew I could pull Kenny along. We coasted the rest of the way, into Haywood Field on the University of Oregon campus, and tied in 2:15:58. I let Kenny take the victory lap by himself — it was his home-town crowd — and waited nervously for Jeff and Jack. They arrived next, sharing third — but who would get it? As they neared the finish, Jeff eased off, assuring Jack's position on the team. In that briefest moment of sacrifice was all the dignity that our shared perseverance as marathon runners had come to represent.

CHAPTER FOUR

Munich: 1972

I spent the summer of 1972 training with the American Olympic team, which was based in Oslo. I ran 20 miles a day, as always, and competed in one race a month before the Olympics. It was a 3,000 meters in Oslo, and I ran 7:51.4 for sixth place. That was a good time for me, and I knew I'd made an impression on one runner, a man who finished behind me, Rod Dixon of New Zealand. Afterward, I heard him say with disgust, "I got beat by a bloody marathon runner!"

Dixon is a proud and gifted athlete. He would win the bronze medal in the 1,500 in Munich, place fourth in the Olympic 5,000 in 1976, and, in the eighties, become a marathoner himself, winning New York in 2:08:59 in 1983. Fully ten years after our Oslo encounter, in the summer of '82, I recalled his remark as the two of us raced on the streets of my hometown, Middletown, New York, in the Orange Classic 10-kilometer road race. Running better than I was at the time but perhaps a little race-worn, Dixon could not hold my pace, and I defeated him by 21 seconds. This time he was heard to say, "The old man's still tough in the clutch."

In Oslo we stayed at a student hotel on the outskirts of the city, where I took on the lifestyle that had worked for the Olympic Trials. I ran a lot and I slept a lot; I made a totally concentrated training effort. You have to — that's the only way to compete.

Other teams were there, too, Spain among them. I saw Mariano Haro, who the summer before in Oslo had tried to elbow me into the first-row seats in the homestretch of a 10,000-meter race. We came off the last turn together and he purposely swung wide, shoving me into the middle of the track. I beat him anyway, but his tactics so infuriated some of the crew from CBS, which was broadcasting the meet, that they had to be stopped from going after him.

Cabin fever set in after a while, and I talked the men's head coach, Bill Bowerman, into taking the distance runners over to Sogsvatn, a popular winter sports region. It had an abundance of lovely trails for running and, at 4,000 feet above sea level, just enough altitude to provide a beneficial training effect. Louise and I went up, along with Kenny Moore and his wife, Bobbie, Steve Prefontaine, and Bowerman.

We trained well there. We found a track for speedwork, where Bowerman could look us over and help us polish our form. He showed me how to increase my leg tempo with better use of my arms. But unless one asked, Bowerman was disinclined to coach. He knew to leave us alone. His attitude was: You guys are here because you know how to train. If your coach isn't here, I'm probably going to do more harm than good if I coach. But I'll do what I can to make sure you have everything you need.

Here, again, I was fortunate to come under the influence of a wise man. As with Giegengack at Yale, the athlete, under Bowerman, came first. Their training philosophies were similar, too, though Bowerman coached in a different world at the University of Oregon, where he produced numerous champions and left a legacy of remarkable distance running success that has been carried on by his successor, Bill Dellinger, who ran for Bowerman and was himself an Olympic bronze medalist in the 5,000 meters in 1964. Gieg and Bowerman differed when it came to the rules: Gieg followed them and Bowerman didn't. Gieg was a member of the IAAF Technical Committee and usually went by the book. Bowerman, a maverick by nature, would break a rule just because it was there.

Gieg, who was in Europe to attend the Olympics, came out to Sogsvatn for a while. I recall an afternoon on the track when Kenny Moore and I were doing our preferred interval workouts separately. Kenny did repeat 300s and Bowerman timed him. I did 800s and Gieg timed me. In the middle of this, a workman who was pouring sand into the long jump pit with a wheelbarrow cut onto the track, forcing me to swerve around him and holler some good sense into him. It happened again. Out onto the track and into my path walked the Norwegian and his wheelbarrow. I stopped running and Gieg and I both exploded with uncharacteristic venom. Kenny's laughter, meanwhile, could be heard from the other end of the track.

Through the summer, the rumor mill was working overtime. We'd learn of the performances of the distance runners competing in pre-Olympic meets throughout Europe. But readiness is something else. Who was really fit? Who was injured? Who'd peaked too soon? It was hard to know, perhaps better that we didn't. I liked to see for myself before making judgments, and one contender I did get a look at was a developing twenty-three-year-old runner from Finland named Lasse Viren. He ran the 10,000 in the same meet in Oslo in which I'd run the 3,000, winning in 27:52.4. And what a runner! He did it with "negative splits" — running the second half (13:52.2) faster than the first (14:00.2). He had a very smooth stride that essentially did not change as he accelerated in the final laps. Unlike most distance runners, he did not switch to a sprinter's gait in a furious drive to the finish. Somehow he was able to maintain his form in a controlled fashion and simply run faster. It was all in the rpm's — his leg rate quickened, which made his speed deceptive. It was something to see.

The man was ready, all right, and I would be facing him in the Olympic 10,000 a week before the marathon. I told myself, "The only thing you can do is stay as close to him as possible, because he's going to win."

This didn't psych me out, just opened my eyes a little. When we left Oslo for Munich, I was excited because I knew I was in good shape. The line for the marathon had Ron Hill of Great Britain at 3 to 1 and Derek Clayton of Australia at 5 to 1. In most circles in Europe, I wasn't given much of a chance. But I truly believed neither had been doing the quality training I had. I felt no pressure. From then on, it was just an adventure.

☆

Who could have predicted the tragic events that would disrupt the Games in Munich? At five o'clock one morning Louise and I were awakened by hard, crashing sounds. *Boom! Boom!* It was like a giant door slamming. We were sleeping on the terrace of the fifth-floor apartment in the Olympic Village that we were sharing with Kenny Moore, Jon Anderson, Steve Savage, and Dave Wottle, the 800-meter gold medalist. Dazed, I assumed someone was drunk and was going around slamming doors. But it struck me that I hadn't heard a noise quite like that all week, and I got up to see what might be happening. People were gathered below and looking toward a fourth-floor apartment across from us, a good hundred yards away. It was, we soon learned, the Israeli dorm.

Something was wrong. Word quickly spread that people were killed, Israelis. Rumors came and went. We did not know how many had died or what was transpiring. The day was like that. Just before dusk, we found out that there had been a negotiation and that helicopters would be coming to take the terrorists and the hostages to the airport. When they arrived, we went to the balcony to watch. "You know," I told Kenny, "I don't think it's over."

In the morning, learning the tragic outcome, I was numb with shock. There was so much to think about, to grieve over. What kept gnawing at me was the obvious: man's inhumanity in the name of nationalism or religion. I didn't associate the murders with the Olympics. It had to do with human nature.

We heard that the Games would be postponed for one day and that a memorial service would be held for the slain Israelis. There was a good deal of discussion among the athletes as to whether this was the right thing to do. Ron Hill, the British marathoner, didn't think the postponement was right. Two days before the marathon, now to be run on September 10, I bumped into him in the dining hall. "They should not disrupt it at all. We should all go along according to schedule," he said insistently.

"You've trained your whole life for this," I said. "One more day is not going to make any difference."

I took Hill's attitude to be a lapse in his mental preparation, and it made me feel he would not have a good day.

I did not attend the memorial service. I'm not sure why. It wasn't that I didn't consider it a proper gesture; I just didn't go. I don't attend events — I didn't go to the closing ceremonies, either. It was better for me to stay back at the Village during the service, with nobody around, so I could be by myself and think about it.

☆

Only three of the marathon contenders also ran the 10,000 — Akio Usami of Japan, Karel Lismont of Belgium, and me. I was the only one to make the finals. That the marathon was waiting had no effect on my outlook toward the 10,000 or on my performance. I didn't consider it an especially tough double, as the marathon came ten days after the qualifying round and seven days after the final. I had done it in the U.S. Olympic Trials and had learned to organize myself accordingly. The week between races was good for relaxed running and settling down; the hard training had been done. Running a second event forced me to take it easy before the marathon, and so I ended up going into it well rested from having run barely 5 miles a day the previous four days, my lowest running output in years.

I followed my plan and did whatever Lasse Viren did. Up to a point. On the last lap of my trial heat, I was running along with Viren, Haro, and Mohamed Gammoudi of Tunisia, the 1968 Olympic gold medalist in the 5,000. All four of us were certain to qualify, yet Gammoudi, and Haro to a lesser extent, sprinted to the finish. It was silly. I strode in third, feeling uplifted because I'd run 27:58.2, an American record, and hadn't gone all out. Viren, running well within himself, loped in behind me.

Three days later the real fun began. Midway into the final, on the backstretch of the twelfth lap, I was running on Viren's shoulder and almost went down with him in his Famous Fall, which would have been tragic had it not led to his Remarkable Recovery. We were a bunched group. Viren was on the inside, hugging the track's curb and shadowing Emiel Puttemans of Belgium, just ahead of him in the lead. So tight were Viren and Puttemans that contact was made and, to brace himself, Viren pressed a hand into Putteman's back, slowing down and being tripped by the oncoming Gammoudi, running behind him. For a moment I thought Viren might smack into me and I extended my left arm, but it was not necessary. It might have appeared from pictures that in the web of arms and legs I pushed Viren, but we never touched.

Viren went down hard. Oh, no, he's out of it, I thought

as I hopped over him. But he wasn't. He lay off the track for a moment, got up, and rejoined us before the lap had expired. Gammoudi, on the other hand, who'd fallen over Viren in the tangle, recovered more slowly and ran another lap and a half before dropping out. He had no fight left. I've always thought the responses of the two men reflected on their character. Gammoudi, though an Olympic champion, seemed the type of person who didn't think he could win unless everything went according to plan. Viren was going to win no matter what.

And he did. With 600 meters to go he took off, stringing the four of us left behind him. Haro and I fell back. Puttemans and Miruts Yifter of Ethiopia wouldn't let go. With one lap remaining I was broken, with no chance for a medal, and watched for the drama of the finish. Viren accelerated at need, just as he'd done in Oslo four weeks before. His winning time was 27:38.4, breaking Ron Clarke's world record by 1 second. Puttemans was second in 27:39.6, Yifter third in 27:41.0, Haro fourth in 27:48.2. I was fifth in 27:51.4. "No other distance race in history ever produced such outstanding marks," beamed *Track & Field News*.

I was disappointed. Though I'd improved my U.S. record by 7 seconds, I wondered what it would take to beat the Europeans and the Africans at 10,000 meters. It was a letdown, but it did not give me pause for the marathon, which was a different event with different contestants.

The 5,000 final and the marathon were held the same day. In the 5,000, Viren again prevailed, outrunning Gammoudi with another controlled last-lap acceleration. This time no one fell. I was glad to have been in the marathon.

☆

I spent the morning of the marathon in thought, waiting. There's a certain abstraction to the Olympics, as though they are more of an idea than a thing, and it was comforting to know that at last the day had arrived when I would be running the marathon. Earlier in the week, after the murders, there'd been talk about canceling the rest of the Games. I was against it. The primary motive of the terrorists was to disrupt and possibly halt the competition. To shut down the Games would have been a submission to them.

After a big breakfast I leafed through magazines to pass the time. I thought about the U.S. basketball loss to the Soviets and how precarious it was to be in a team sport, in which judgment calls could determine the outcome. But then, Jim Ryun was a victim of official intransigence after his fall in the 1,500-meter trials. Though there was an equal accomplice to the mishap, the Olympic jury turned down Ryun's appeal. It was a terrible shame; I think he might have won.

I was almost put into a position of appeal. The marathoners had to take a physical, and we were to report to the Olympic Stadium for the test three days before the race, between nine and twelve-thirty. But when the day came, we'd all forgotten about it. At noon Ted Hayden, a U.S. team manager, hurriedly rounded up Kenny Moore, Jack Bacheler, Jeff Galloway (the alternate), and me, and we ran the half-mile over to the stadium testing room for what was a cursory exam to make sure that no competitor was ill. So quickly did we make it over to the stadium that we wondered whether our elevated heart rates would alarm the medics. We were probably the last runners to report; had we not gotten over there at all that day, it would have been grounds for disqualification. I considered, on the morning of the marathon, how lucky I had been and how fate can intervene, as much as you try to structure things so it doesn't.

It made me feel a little sympathy for Stan Wright, the U.S. coach who was blamed when Eddie Hart and Rey Robinson missed their 100-meter heats. Hayden, who drove over for the physicals, observed that after the sprinters missed their race, there was talk that "it could happen to anybody," but he didn't expect it to be proven so soon.

Thoughts drifted into my mind . . . drifted out . . . drifted in . . . I felt good, rested, but not *too* good. Feeling *too* good can be bad. When I think I'm feeling great, I tend not to run that well because, I suspect, it indicates that perhaps I'm a little too keyed up. I don't want to be keyed up; I want to be relaxed. When I'm relaxed I'm also a little lethargic, and a little lethargy is good.

I was not afraid. I was ready to run and had learned by that time that worrying about it does no good. I thought about the marathon, the 26 miles 385 yards of it, and how such a distance in these circumstances requires as much relaxation as possible in the early miles. I did not want to run aggressively from the start. Therefore, I didn't want to build up any aggressiveness while I waited.

Mentally, I reviewed the course. I'd trained over parts of it during the week and felt that if someone managed to enter the English Garden, 18 miles out, with a lead, he would likely win. The 4 miles through the park were of gravel, and the path curved like the S-turns on mountain roads. With difficult footing and places to "hide," it would serve as a buffer zone. A lead could be protected there.

Historically, the marathon has had a strategic pattern. For the first two-thirds of the race, you bide your time. Then someone would pick up the race to try to pull away and go on to win. This time I was not going to let that happen because the wait-and-kick tactic did not play to my strength. I decided that I would try to be the first man to make a break, and that it would be made well before the English Garden.

It was a few moments before three when the seventy-four marathoners were herded from a tiny room next to the tunnel through which we would finish and out onto the Olympic Stadium track. I looked furtively from runner to runner, trying to spot the men whom I expected to be in contention: Mamo Wolde of Ethiopia, the defending champion; Derek Clayton of Australia, the world record-holder (2:08:34); Hill, 1970 champion of the Boston Marathon and

Commonwealth Games marathon; Usami, who fought me at Fukuoka the previous December. I did not want to talk with anyone or even make eye contact. I wanted to watch, as though from behind a tree, to draw any indication of their state of mind that I could possibly use to better my chances. I saw Hill, dressed in a shiny silver outfit to reflect the sun. His shoes were made of the same material and he had taken the tongues out to make them as light as possible. My God, I thought, he's wearing a space suit. I thought that was being perhaps a little too precise, too compulsive. But then, Hill, as Kenny Moore has put it, "occasionally seems possessed with the scientific method."

My method is more intuitive. I didn't run that morning; the morning of the marathon is the only morning I don't run — the marathon is enough. I jogged a mile on the warmup track adjacent to the stadium and then, once inside, lubricated my feet with Vaseline and taped them, taped my nipples to prevent bleeding, changed to my racing shoes, and went out to the track wearing my USA cap. If the sun was out, I thought, I might wear it. I saw Usami wearing his hat, but at the last moment I decided against it and put it down on the infield. "That's the last I'll see of that," I said to myself. I was right, but it didn't matter.

My shoes, like Ron Hill's, were creatively light. That was my concession to science. I was wearing Adidas then and had an Adidas shoemaker in the Olympic Village construct a pair of racing flats for me. He simply put a new sole on my lightweight spikes. In test runs, after some modification, they felt right.

Grouped at the start, I had a position on the inside of the front row, next to Hill. We said nothing. The time, had come.

☆

We ran the first half-mile in the stadium, then up a slight incline through the tunnel and turned right, toward the

Olympic Village. Up near the front, I felt comfortable and took it as a sign that things might go well. Quite often I can tell in the first quarter-mile of a race whether or not I'll have a good day. This day felt good. I've learned I can't talk myself into this feeling. It's either there or it isn't.

Ahead, the course took us across a bridge over the autobahn and, off it, we turned right again up a dirt hill and around a long chain link fence that had been put up for security reasons near the Village. We'd not even gone a mile yet. The course bus carrying the photographers was within spitting distance and starting to get in the way, causing the field to swing wide to its left. I saw some daylight between the bus and the fence and tried to shoot the gap. It was a chance to try and surprise a few people and save a few yards. It didn't work. As I moved for the hole, the bus closed it off — reacting to the runners' calls for it to move over — and I got caught between the bus and the fence. I stopped dead in my tracks, swore a little at myself, doubled back around the rear of the bus (not without smacking it), and accelerated to regain a position up front.

There were about twenty-five men at the head of the field, and no one seemed to miss me. Soon enough I was back with the group, and we continued along at a safely controlled pace, content to conserve energy and talk a little. Conversing like that helps me relax. The bus incident had no effect on me, and I felt fine when we reached the first checkpoint, at 5 kilometers (3.1 miles), in 15:51. I wasn't wearing a watch and paid no attention to the split times. I felt it would do me no good to learn whether I was running slowly or over my head. In no way, for me, was this a race for time. It was a race against other people: I had to react to them (and they to me). And to the distance: With each passing 5-kilometer point, I would tell myself, "Okay, only thirty-seven . . . or thirty-two . . . or twenty-two kilometers to go." This is the way I run the marathon: I think of the 5-kilometer segments as "laps."

The relaxed pace gave me a chance to scout some more. I got a look at Derek Clayton, who was doing a fair share of the leading. He didn't seem to be running that easily. He was tight in the shoulders and jaw, and his tongue would roll in and out of his mouth. At 6 feet and 160 pounds, he's big for a marathoner, and since I'd never run against him before, I thought that maybe that was just how Derek Clayton ran — though the more I watched, the more I believed he was in trouble.

Apparently, Clayton was taking an interest in me as well. I'd later learn he didn't consider me "a natural marathon runner" because my leg action was "too high." As a matter of fact, Hill was not much impressed with me, either. Though I had "a very good record," as he'd put it, I'd never broken 2:12 and "should be fairly tired after running the heat and the final of the ten thousand." Still, in his mind Hill had devised hypothetical racing situations in which he would outkick this runner or that, myself included, at the finish.

Though Hill was well known, Clayton was something of a mystery man. He was the first to run a sub-2:10 marathon, winning at Fukuoka in 1967 with a world record of 2:09:37. In May 1969, in Antwerp, he lowered his record to 2:08:34; however, in some circles the course was thought to be short. I figured that even if it was short, Clayton still had run under 2:10, which made him a threat. Clayton also was rumored to have undergone a punishing training regimen, consisting of long runs at racing pace, in preparation for Munich. I thought, perhaps too pragmatically, that if he fulfilled his potential he would beat me. But I also knew that some people in this fast crowd, on percentages alone, would blow up, and maybe Clayton would be one of them. In any case, I felt I was improving and didn't know that *I* couldn't run 2:08.

Our pace had grown faster. I felt it, and as we came to the 10-kilometer mark inside Nymphenburg, a large park, 50 yards separated the leaders, Clayton and Hill, from me.

I'd allowed myself the luxury of trailing, and a number of men had drifted ahead of me. Seppo Nikkari of Finland and forty-year-old Jack Foster of New Zealand were third and fourth. Usami was next. I was back enough to control the urge to be aggressive, yet close enough to see to it that no one would get away from me.

We reached the first of several aid stations, where plastic bottles marked with our race numbers were filled with our own special drinks. Kenny and I each had defizzed cola waiting; we wanted the liquid for its caffeine, sugar, and water but not the carbonation, which could produce stomach cramps. I'd started sipping this cola the day before to make sure my system would be accustomed to it. But when I reached for my squeeze bottle, Lengissa Bedane, an Ethiopian just ahead of me, grabbed it first. Reflexively, I took the one next to it, which turned out to be Kenny's. "I can't drink this — it's Kenny's!" I said to myself. I was mad. I couldn't give it to Kenny for fear of "aiding" him, which was against the Olympic rules. I threw the bottle down, ran up to Bedane, said, "That's mine," and snatched it from him. I only gulped a little before tossing it aside. Kenny soon came up to me and said, "Next time I'll thank you not to take my drink." I apologized, hoping I had not hurt his chances.

The pace grew faster still as we neared 15 kilometers, a little over 9 miles. We ran down the side of a canal in front of the Nymphenburg Castle, crossed the canal, and went back on the other side of it, in the direction, briefly, from which we'd come. When we made the turn to go up the back side of the canal, a short distance before the 15-kilometer point, the pace suddenly and inexplicably slowed. Clayton was leading, and when the pace changed, those of us running close by gazed around for an instant, waiting for something to happen. I found myself moving up on Clayton and realized that if I didn't purposely slow down I was going to have the lead. I told myself, "Okay, you've got this momentum. Let it carry you."

And I pulled ahead. So fast was my move that by the 15-kilometer marker I already had a 5-second lead. I'd committed myself. This was it — the break. I told myself to get as far ahead as I could because if I got far enough ahead, I honestly thought no one would catch me. I'm not sure anyone but me considered my move a break at the time; a 5- or 10-second lead is not unusual in a marathon and certainly not much with 16 or 17 miles to go. That the break came fairly early helped me to make the most of my front-running strategy because the opposition, assuming I'd fall back before too long, was content to let me take on the pressures of the lead and risk blowing the whole thing.

I pressed on. Once you make that kind of commitment in a marathon, you have to carry that intensity, the mental intensity, to the end. Otherwise, the break is useless.

I knew I could continue to run hard for a while, but also knew I could not keep it up for the entire race. I'd used up a certain amount of energy in making the break and working on it and eventually I'd pay for it. I needed to be far ahead because once I slowed down, those who'd been conserving their energy would be coming after me.

I never lost respect for the distance. I never stopped thinking. I never looked back.

The course weaved, and I tried to lose myself around the blind corners. Out of sight, out of mind. Psychologically, it's very tough on the people behind you. I played the turns. When I sensed I was hidden, I pressed a little harder to be farther ahead when I reappeared. If I could get away, I hoped, the others would start running for second.

I drew farther ahead, the press bus my only companion. By 20 kilometers, I later learned, I had a 31-second lead. I felt right, in control, and was running to get to the English Garden. At the 25-kilometer aid station, Louise was waiting for me. "It's not there," she yelled. The two squeeze bottles with the defizzed Coke and the number 1014 on them weren't there. I'd provided two bottles for this station, one for the others. I considered this the most important aid station. I grabbed plain water instead, took a few sips (I never pour it on me; I don't like the feeling), and went on, wondering — to this day — what could have happened to those bottles. Sabotage? Nah. Well, West Germany did have a contender, Lutz Philipp, who came into the Olympics with the fastest marathon time (2:12:50) among the entrants that season. He would finish only thirty-second. Maybe he didn't like defizzed Coke.

It was all working. I reached the English Garden and had just the lead I wanted. Three times during the race I was told what my lead was, and this time, the first time, was most important. A journalist on the press bus who spoke English called out that I had a minute. It was a tremendous boost for me. Sixty seconds. I started figuring: Since there were 8 miles to go, they'd have to run roughly 8 seconds per mile faster than me to catch up. If I continued at a 5:05 pace, they'd have to run 4:57; if I ran 5:08, they'd have to run 5 flat. I knew it would be very difficult for anyone to run 5-minute miles at that point, given the winding nature of the path through the Garden. What's more, the footing was rough on the gravel surface, which had inspired quite a debate before the Games as to its appropriateness for an Olympic marathon course. I didn't care. If it was a disadvantage, it would be so for all of us.

I decided to try and preserve my cushion by backing off my pace just a bit. I didn't want to be running on the edge of the physiological breakdown that is always possible in the latter stages of a marathon. The records show I slowed by 3 seconds per mile in the next 5 kilometers. Here, Fukuoka came to mind. Nine months earlier, in Japan, I had a 30-second lead on Usami just past the halfway marker, and I beat him by 30 seconds.

"If I don't die badly," I said to myself, "I'm going to win." I could suffer a little and still win. I could relax a little and still win. Whether I would soon suffer or relax was hard to say, but I did not see peril before me. The rest, to be sure, would not come easy, but in one sense the hardest part was over.

If there is a peak experience to be found in running, I came upon mine in the English Garden. More satisfying than victory itself is the anticipation of it. Not of the glory or reward, but simply the feeling of . . . doing it. To run with a kind of hypnotic rhythm, to be ahead and confident of winning while in a state of physical intensity at that level of competition, is the most satisfying feeling I've ever had.

☆

Leaving the cover of the English Garden and heading back toward the stadium for the final 4½ miles, I felt my spirits start to sag. A fatigue had settled in. My hard running in the middle of the race, sometimes at better than 4:40 per mile, was coming back on me, and I knew it. Bad patches, the English call them. You feel bad all over, helpless, as though under a spell. If you're in shape and didn't overdo it earlier, the feeling eventually goes away. Physiologists associate the condition with the transition of carbohydrates to fats as a source of fuel in the body; at its most severe, it is known as hitting the wall. In a sense, it gives you something to do because you must concentrate on working through the discomfort.

I talked myself through it. "Okay, you're past the twenty-mile point. Everybody feels bad; everybody slows down. Just maintain your momentum." Though I slowed only a few seconds per mile, I felt as though I were running much slower, and I had to convince myself that I wasn't. As tired as I was, nothing *hurt*.

It was no small comfort to learn, at this point, that my lead had grown to a minute and a half. Get me to the sta-

dium, I thought. Just get me to the stadium. I summoned
up an old training technique. I set an achievable goal that
would make me feel better when I got beyond it. Sort of
intermediate-step psychology. I just wanted to see that stadium. I visualized it — not the finish line, only the stadium.
With the lead I had, I knew I could run a 7-minute mile
at the end and still win. Thinking like that pushed me on.

In the shadows of the stadium, I hit the ramp that would
take me into the tunnel that led to the track, and I knew
I had it won. But I couldn't dwell on that. My attention
was diverted to the huge roar that had erupted inside the
stadium. I knew the high jump was scheduled for the afternoon. Had the winning jump just been made? Was that roar
for a new world record? I wondered for a moment who
might have done it.

Inside the tunnel, which muffles the outside noise, I braced
myself. "Okay, here it comes. The roar that greets an Olympic marathon champion running into the stadium." And I
got onto the track and it was silent.

I made the right turn for the lap-and-change to the finish.
Someone waving an American flag yelled, "Don't worry,
Frank, we love you," and I thought, Why should I worry,
I'm winning. Still, it felt good to hear some acknowledgment.
With about 200 meters to go, I glanced across the infield
and saw some confusion at the finish. It didn't hold my inter-
est. Suddenly it dawned on me that I'd actually done it.
As I crossed the finish line, I felt a great sense of relief.

I felt awful. I felt wonderful. I was swaying: spent and
achy, then flushed with joy. I knew I'd run 2:12:20, my best
by 3 minutes, but that had nothing to do with it. It had
not even occurred to me to try and speed up at the end
for the Olympic record, the 2:12:12 by Abebe Bikila of Ethiopia, set in 1964. The race had been won outside the stadium.

I jogged a victory lap. I heard whistling, the European
equivalent of booing, and thought, I know I'm an American,

but give me a break. I knew nothing. At the finish again, I
felt awkward. No one told me what to do. How should I
act? I hung around, waiting. I wondered where Kenny was;
I'd heard late in the race that he was in third place.

I saw Karel Lismont of Belgium finish. I saw Wolde finish.
Then Kenny came in, about 30 seconds behind Wolde, limping. I went over to him at the line and he fell into my grasp.
"Well, I won the darn thing," I said. I knew he was happy
for me but bruised with hurt and disappointment. He said
nothing.

Kenny would write of it: "I tempted my twinging thigh,
forcing the pace, frantically trying to get back up to third,
but as I approached the stadium Lismont was out of sight
and Wolde still had me by 200 yards. . . . Around the last
curve, when the crowd buoys you and you sometimes experience a perverse desire that the race not end, I felt only a
great weight."

We walked arm in arm, photographers snapping away.
Hill was sixth, Usami twelfth, Clayton thirteenth. Jack
Bacheler was ninth, making the U.S. the only nation with
three men in the first ten. It was the best U.S. team showing
in the marathon since the early days of the Olympics, and
I was the first American since Johnny Hayes, in 1908, to
have won it. I was proud of that, of "winning for America."
I felt I'd earned some respect for American distance running,
which was considered inferior in the international athletics
community. The victories by Bob Schul (5,000 meters) and
Billy Mills (10,000 meters) in the 1964 Tokyo Olympics were
thought to be more of a fluke than a breakthrough. I'd dem-
onstrated that an American could succeed by doing something that was essentially European in nature — that is, ad-
hering to the training discipline of marathon running. People
with athletic inclinations in the United States grew up wanting to be quarterbacks or pitchers, or perhaps sprinters. Distance running was for the British, the Russians, the Africans,

the Japanese. Not for a moment, though, did I think that my victory would change any of that. I thought only that I had proved a point — that it could be done.

Kenny found Bobbie, and I searched for Louise. I couldn't find her and stalled for time by sitting on the track and peeling the tape from my blistered feet. Skin peeled with the tape and blood rushed out, spilling onto the track. It was a mess. The officials were getting impatient with me; they like to clear the track after a race. I was asked to take my self and my ugly feet to a room for the doping test.

I saw Louise. She'd worked her way to the lower seating, to within 15 feet of me. It was strange. I was still part of the show, she was still part of the audience. We could not join. I was pulled to the doping test.

On my way, someone called, "What do you think of the guy who came in ahead of you?"

"What guy?" I said to myself. Then it hit me; it all fell into place.

An imposter. A perfectly absurd ending to an absurdly imperfect Olympics. I considered it a quirk of fate. He stole my entrance, all right, but that really didn't matter much. These Olympics were so battered by the bizarre and the tragic that I couldn't get worked up over an imposter. I knew little about it until that evening at dinner, when Erich Segal, the author of *Love Story* and a professor of mine at Yale who was doing the TV commentary for the marathon, told me more. It was a harmless prank, but I was pleased that the journalists, for the most part, had agreed not to publicize the guy's name. Unfortunately, a few track and field journals did print it — the statistics nuts had to know.

In the doping room, I was watched while I filled a bottle to make sure I couldn't slip in a vial. I had no trouble providing a specimen. Kenny had trouble. I remember that.

Then I was treated to the medal engraving before the awards ceremony. It was a kick, seeing my name etched onto the gold medal. The man who presented me with my medal was none other than Avery Brundage, the president of the International Olympic Committee. An American, Brundage was a 1912 Olympian and a staunch defender of the amateur ideals. In later years, considering my role in the changing lot of the "amateur" athlete, it seemed ironic that it was Brundage who'd handed me the medal.

Before leaving the arena, Lismont, Wolde, and I were led to greet Abebe Bikila, who was seated on the edge of the track in a wheelchair, the victim of an auto accident in 1969. I hadn't known he was there, watching the marathon finish. It was tragic to see him that way. Lismont and I shook his hand, but it was his countryman Wolde whom Bikila was most anxious to see. Had Wolde won, he would have equaled Bikila's feat of winning two straight Olympic marathons. When it was Wolde's turn, he greeted Bikila with a shrug of the shoulders, as if to say, a mite embarrassed before his country's hero, that his best effort had fallen short on this day.

Finally, after meeting with the press, I got to share the moment with Louise. With no duties left, we departed the stadium for the Village. Outside, we realized we had no transportation and so walked to the nearest bus stop, where we came upon Gieg and his wife, Lucy. For once in his life, Gieg was speechless. His eyes were moist. The bus came and the four of us filed on, the last people aboard. There were no seats left.

It was less than an hour since I'd crossed the finish line, and as the bus pulled away, it started to pour. Standing there, clutching my medal, I thought about how badly I run in the rain.

CHAPTER FIVE

Montréal: 1976

Though by the time of the 1976 Olympics people in large numbers had started to take up running, investing in the sport a prosperity that would soon improve the lot of the world-class runner and, indeed, change the way of life for millions of Americans, I saw little evidence of that when I returned home from Munich, an Olympic champion, in the late summer of 1972. The idea that my victory might carry some significance had not even crossed my mind. I got to see a TV replay of parts of the marathon in the Olympic Village and assumed that viewers would take little interest in it, in keeping with the American attitude that anyone from the U.S. who ran long distances did so because he couldn't do better at something else. Twenty-six miles 385 yards was a funny distance, to begin with, and marathon runners were not to be taken seriously. They were nonconformists with strange daily habits.

I was an Olympic gold medalist, but there were other Olympic gold medalists. And in no way did I consider myself the brand of hero that Mark Spitz, the swimmer, and even Dave Wottle, the upset winner in the 800 meters had become. I figured, as far as Americans were concerned, I might as well have won my gold medal in archery, cycling, or Greco-Roman wrestling. Besides, so much went wrong in

Munich — the Israeli massacre in particular — that most people wanted to damn the Olympics or just forget about them. Any recognition I might receive, I thought, would come from abroad — from Japan, Oceania, Europe, or Africa, where the marathon was understood and appreciated.

This notion sat easily with me. I had not sought recognition, riches, or a platform of any kind. Basically, I just wanted to have the support that would enable me to continue running, to live the life of an athlete for as long as I could compete, to realize my potential in the marathon.

I considered my Olympic victory a foremost personal achievement, the result of hard work, planning, and whatever talent I've been born with. But it was over with and there was more work to be done, more races to run. I knew I could run the marathon a lot faster; there were championships and the next Olympics to plan for. I was not going to allow myself to attach any more importance to winning the Olympic marathon than I thought it deserved. I had had a good day in Munich. Others didn't. I'm not minimizing it. It was wonderful. But I don't dwell on victory. I use victory to fuel my desire to try again, so when I returned from Munich I was anxious to resume law school and train. I didn't want the gold medal to change the kind of person I was.

I saw what could happen. I saw how Mark Spitz, with his seven gold medals, became a cottage industry. People were all over him in the Olympic Village, waiting to sign him up for something or just to be around him and feed off the aura of his sudden and dynamic superstardom.

I wanted none of that. (Not that people were waiting to sign *me* up for anything.) I wanted to go right back to law school in Gainesville as quickly as possible so that, with my studies and my running, I would be occupied immediately. I could accept congratulations. But I didn't want people hanging around me telling me how great I was. There's always the chance that you'd start to believe it. I received

one congratulatory phone call from the States in Munich
after the marathon. It came from the office of Louis V. Mills,
the chief executive of Orange County, New York, where
Middletown is. They wanted to celebrate my victory and
asked if I would stop there before heading down to Gainesville.

Middletown is a small community of 22,000, about an
hour's drive from New York City. It is a little too far north
to be a suburb and a little too far south to be upstate. It
has no industry of note; it's quiet. Though my family left
Middletown for Taos in 1967, my maternal grandparents still
lived there (my grandfather, at seventy-seven, was still practicing optometry), and my father was still highly respected
and remembered.

It was a marvelous celebration. EX-MIDDLETOWNER WINS
MARATHON! screamed the local paper, the *Times Herald
Record.* The paper covered everything I did during my brief
stay in town, even the case of the missing key to the city,
which was found in my grandmother's house the day after
we left. And not a moment too soon: An appeal was to have
been made to the students of Middletown High and Veraldi
Junior High to aid in the search.

Several hundred people attended a testimonial dinner in
my honor. I was given many gifts, including a portrait of
myself by a local artist, Ruth Mutchler. When I ran, kids
ran with me, and they followed me around for autographs.
One resident was quoted in the paper as saying, "I've lived
in Middletown all my life, and this is the most exciting thing
that has ever happened."

I was a hero in Middletown, and that took some getting
used to. I was overwhelmed by the outpouring of warmth
and recognition and consciously tried not to get carried away
by it. I felt as though I were spinning through the celebration
and the showering of honors, my feet still off the ground.
I was part of the fuss — and, at the same time, apart from

it. Though I was, as the paper put it, "the toast of the town," I was a bit fearful of it all and, as I observed all that was going on, I tried to keep things in perspective in my own mind.

It was not the marathon per se that had excited the good people of Middletown. Not all that stuff about Pheidippides and the punishing 26 miles. It could have been the 100 meters, the single sculls, the pole vault — anything. No one understood the marathon. Not yet. I was a kid from Middletown — who still had family in Middletown — who had won an Olympic gold medal.

I was happiest for my family. My father had tried in vain to call me in Munich. He doesn't like to fly and so drove the 2,200 miles, nonstop, from Taos to be with me in Middletown. When, to a standing ovation, my father was called by Lou Mills "one of the greatest humanitarians I have ever known," I had tears in my eyes. I felt very close to my father then.

By week's end, Louise and I were off to Kansas to see her folks and to get our car out of storage and drive to Gainesville. We were sent off with an editorial in the *Times Herald Record* that beamed, "Thanks, Frank, for bringing out the best in us."

☆

Winning the marathon in Munich made my running, in the eyes of others, legitimate. Suddenly it was okay *to be a runner,* to train for 2 and 3 hours a day. There was a purpose behind it, something to be gained. My running had been looked upon as a diversion, as a peculiar habit for a grown man. After all, it was not done on behalf of a university team. It was not earning me a decent living. It was not even making me look manly, skinny guy that I clearly was.

"What do you do?"

"I go to law school. And I'm a marathon runner."

"A *what?*"

The victory took the stamp of eccentricity off me. I was a real athlete. And, as everybody knows, real athletes have to train a lot. Though I try not to react too drastically to the opinions of others, it was nice to be accepted as a serious person, and this took some of the pressure off me at law school. I was able to comfortably study with less intensity than the other students did because my immediate career goal was to add to my success in running, not to become an attorney. However, I don't think this sat well with some of my classmates; it was a very competitive situation, and despite my priorities, I still managed to do reasonably well.

I had another year and a half of law school left, and I really did not know what I would do with a law degree. What I wanted more than anything that fall of 1972 was to run the marathon faster. The twisting Munich course did not allow for fast times, nor did the circumstances of the Olympics, which favor tactics over speed. I had not let myself get out of shape after Munich and was anxious to try for a fast race. My attempt would come at the Fukuoka Marathon in December. If conditions were right, I'd have a chance to break the world record.

They weren't. It was too windy, and there was no one to push me during the second half of the race. The Fukuoka course is out and back and shaped somewhat like a boomerang. When it's windy, you face a headwind for the second 6 miles and the last 6 miles. I reached the halfway turn-around in 1:03:36, right on target, but could not fight my way through the wind toward the end. I won by a minute and a half over John Farrington of Australia.

My time was 2:10:30. It broke the American record and made me the third fastest marathoner ever, behind Derek Clayton of Australia, the world record-holder (2:08:34), and Ron Hill of Great Britain (2:09:28). It was my fastest marathon by almost 2 minutes. I've never run faster. That day's wind is one reason I'm still running hard. I'm convinced I have a faster marathon in me.

Three out of the four Fukuokas I've run have been like that. The first, in 1971, was windy, but different. Inexperienced at the distance, I ran conservatively and pulled away to win by 32 seconds, in 2:12:51. But in both 1973 and 1974, gunning for a fast time, I hit the turnaround point in roughly 1:04, only to make the return trip in 1:07. In 1973 I won by 2 minutes, in 2:11:45. In 1974 I won by 31 seconds, in 2:11:32. My four consecutive Fukuoka victories are a record. Only one other runner, Toshihiko Seko of Japan, has won three in a row.

It must be remembered that marathon courses differ so and performance comparisons are not very meaningful. Also, Clayton's record carried the stigma of charges that the course on which he'd set the mark — in Antwerp, Belgium, on May 30, 1969 — was short. I was curious to see if I could run under 2:10 and knew my best chance would be at Fukuoka (where in 1967 Clayton had run a 2:09:37), because no other event other than the problematic Olympics was certain to draw such an elite field.

But every time I'd hit that wind, my pace would drop from 4:55 to 5:15 per mile. I'd strain and tire, and there was no one available for support. There was no pack in the latter miles to pull me along, no individual to make me fight for it. I needed to extend myself and discovered that with victory in hand, running at maximum effort becomes very difficult. Something inside me makes me let up — to preserve the win, I suppose.

In a sense, I was a victim of my own ability. If challenged, I could draw everything out of me. But the elements required for a fast marathon — which boil down to the right weather, the right course, and the right competition — form a rather fragile union, and without some company in the difficult miles, the body's mission becomes lonely and dark.

You have to be lucky. The weather has to be cool and calm (and for me, dry). The course has to be mostly straight, mostly flat, and at or near sea level. The competition has to be willing to gamble with a fast pace so that at 15 miles and a bit beyond, there are enough runners still at the front to provide those fittest with a sort of motivational companionship. There's something about maintaining a rhythm that is enhanced by having another runner, even a rival (*especially* a rival?), at your side. Two runners will fall into a common flow — perhaps a flow that is not quite their own — and feed off each other's energy, in effect delaying the onset of fatigue. The photographs published in *The Runner* of Bill Rodgers and me at a 10-kilometer race in Middletown in July 1981 show the two of us synchronized, like dancers or drum majorettes. We don't run precisely the same way, but you'd never know it from the pictures. Much the same thing happened to Alberto Salazar and Rodolfo Gomez at the 1982 New York Marathon. Their styles are dissimilar, but after racing together for a few miles they began to look more alike.

If all of the elements fall into place, setting up a world record opportunity, the man who's fittest will break away near 20 miles and be forced to run against time the rest of the way. This demands extraordinary concentration, of the sort Salazar showed in the 1981 New York Marathon, when he ran 2:08:13 to break the world record.

Because of Fukuoka, I had quite a following in Japan and in 1973 was invited to compete in the race that was designated the Japanese national marathon championship. It was the Mainichi Marathon in Otsu, in March. Louise and I went to Japan from New Zealand, where we'd been vacationing while I raced on the Kiwis' summer circuit. I won the Mainichi Marathon, but not without a tense moment. I led from the start and was followed closely by another American, John Vitale. But the urge to relieve myself developed, and at about 10 miles I ducked behind a building where, apparently, some construction was going on. While I was bent over and in an extremely vulnerable position, I suddenly heard giggling and looked up to find a Japanese course marshal taking my picture. I got up, grabbed the camera, and began smashing it into the ground. I noticed no witnesses to the incident, but as I rejoined the race I yelled to no one in particular, "I want that film!"

All this took about a minute. Vitale was now ahead and I charged after him, feeling very aggressive. It took me only 2 miles to catch him, and I went on to run 2:12:03 to win by a minute 21 seconds over Yoshinobu Kitayama. Vitale finished fourth. News of the giggling photographer had gotten around; at the finish, a race official handed me the film with apologies. The lasting impression of that race is how suddenly aggressive I could become, not unlike the aggression all runners suddenly feel when their concentration and peace of mind are broken by a threatening dog or motorist.

This would have been a perfect little tale to relate to a TV talk show host. But it happened a little too late for that. Earlier that winter, I had appeared on the Johnny Carson show. I was in California for an indoor track meet in Los Angeles, and the meet promoter, Al Franken, arranged for me to appear on the program. It was the Olympic victory that had prompted the appearance; I'd also just been named the Sullivan Award winner as the nation's outstanding amateur athlete of 1972. (Though Mark Spitz clearly deserved it. You can't be given the award twice, and he had won it the previous year.)

That was my first guest appearance on TV. I'd been on camera before but only for sports interviews, of the sort done for the evening news. Carson played it straight with me. He asked about the marathon — how you get in shape for it, what you think about during the race, dietary preparation — things that have since become common knowledge but in 1973 were alien, and perhaps perversely stimulating, to people hearing them for the first time.

To my surprise, Kip Keino of Kenya was in the studio audience that night. A four-time Olympic medalist, Keino also was in town for the meet. They put the camera on Keino to acknowledge him, and Keino, not knowing that was to have been the end of it, proceeded to climb over people and make his way to the stage, where he sat down next to me. Carson didn't miss a beat and chatted briefly with him. It was fun.

That was the first indication that my Munich victory might carry some influence, and it also showed that TV would be instrumental in contributing to that. People had started to come up to me and say that they'd seen the telecast of the Olympic marathon and that they, too, were now running. Various opinion polls in 1973 reported that at least six million Americans were running (or jogging). Though the New York Marathon had only 406 participants that year (and was three years away from becoming a major international sports event) and "only" 1,384 people ran the Boston Marathon, other races were cropping up throughout the country.

I finished law school in August of 1974, taking my last semester of study in Europe with the Overseas Study Program of the University of Florida. We studied trade law at Winding's College in Cambridge, England, and at the Technical University in Warsaw, Poland. While in Europe I ran a few races. In one, a 10,000 meters in Stockholm, I had the race won but misjudged the finish line and was beaten.

The trip from Cambridge to Poland was complicated by my failure to plan ahead. I flew to Britain without arranging to obtain a visa to Poland. When we were to leave Britain, I went down to London and in one day got the visa. I learned later that just isn't done. Louise and I then flew to Berlin for the train ride to Warsaw. We had no German currency and no train tickets. We boarded the train for the ride through East Germany. I am nearly fluent in French (from my studies at Yale) and I struck up a conversation with a man sitting next to me, a Pole who spoke French. I told him of our predicament. In due time, the conductor came by and asked for our tickets. The man next to me told him something in German, showing him his identification, and the conductor nodded and went on his way.

It's not that I'm willing to take big risks but that I like this sort of challenge. I'm a survivor.

The next year I faced a different sort of challenge, and it was my background in law that helped bail me out. In September 1975, I was asked to testify in Washington before the recently formed President's Commission on Olympic Sports. My testimony included some remarks about the moneymaking capabilities of amateur athletes, and because the amateur code was so strict at that time, athletics officials from Eastern Europe took an interest in my testimony and asked the International Amateur Athletic Federation to ask the U.S. governing body, the Amateur Athletic Union, to look into it. The AAU did just that, requesting a "clarification" of my testimony, and for a while my "case" was the talk of the track world. There was the chance I would be declared a professional, suspended from amateur competition for a period of time and ineligible for the 1976 Olympics.

In 1975 I had joined the law firm of French & Stone in Boulder. I had passed the bar that spring and did legal research for the firm. I never represented a client. They knew I was training for the Olympics and could work only part-time. That was the deal. It was a fine relationship, and I'm still associated with the firm.

With shrewd assistance from Joe French, I was able to clarify, in a deposition, all that I'd said before the commission so that the AAU could satisfactorily report back to the IAAF that "he is still an amateur." The AAU was happy, and the IAAF was happy, and apparently the Eastern Europeans were happy. I could sleep through the night again.

☆

The next spring, as I ran 150 to 170 miles a week in Boulder in preparation for the Olympics, I had every intention of running both the marathon and the 10,000 in Montréal, as I'd done in Munich. At the Olympic Trials I won the 10,000 in 27:55.6, but a foot injury that would plague me for two years surfaced then, though I didn't know what it was at the time. I didn't even know I was *injured*. I thought my running shoes were causing the problem. I couldn't get a pair of spikes to fit me just so and didn't realize till later on that the discomfort was being caused not so much by shoe quirks as by a developing injury, one that would ultimately require surgery.

I've always been sensitive to any variation, however minute, in my condition, and I felt that something wasn't quite right. As fit as I was, something about my running wasn't working. I won a 10,000-meter road race in Milwaukee following the trials, and it really wore me out. I decided that day, July 4, that I would not double in Montréal.

This enabled Ed Mendoza, who only finished fifth in the trials' 10,000, to move on to the Olympic team. That qualifying run was quite a race. Craig Virgin, Bill Rodgers, Garry Bjorklund, and I ran together for much of the second half of the race, setting up a dramatic finish. I held off Virgin with a 60-second last quarter. Bjorklund, who'd lost his left shoe at 4½ miles and had fallen back, found some strength and dramatically caught Rodgers in the homestretch for what was ostensibly the third and final 10,000 berth on the team. The thirteen thousand track fans watching in Eugene, Oregon, ate it up. But because Rodgers had never intended to double in Montréal, Mendoza was the beneficiary of my subsequent withdrawal.

I ended up doing race commentary for ABC during the Olympic 10,000. ABC did not use my spot. I never found out why, but I suspect it was because my handicapping of the race was so accurate that the network viewers might have suspected something was fishy. I'd announced,

"They're going to go out in about fourteen-ten for five thousand, then all hell is going to break loose and Viren is going to win." They went out in 14:09 for 5,000, then the accelerating Carlos Lopes shook up the field and with a mile to go, only Lopes and Viren remained in contention. "Viren is going to nail this guy," I said. With a lap to go, Viren took the lead and won going away.

The Americans were not at their best. Virgin, suffering from a stomach virus, did not make the final. Nor did Mendoza. Bjorklund made it but placed thirteenth in the final with a 28:38.1, as compared to his 28:03.8 in the U.S. trial.

It was only the year before that Bill Rodgers had developed, rather suddenly, into a world-class runner. Our first meeting came in February 1975, in Gainesville, at the U.S. trials for the annual world cross-country championship, to be held five weeks later in Rabat, Morocco. The distance was 15 kilometers and I won it, finishing 30 seconds ahead of Rodgers, who placed fourth to earn a berth on the squad. Then, in Rabat, he made his breakthrough with an outstanding third-place run, beating a number of Olympic medalists, including me. I was running in fifth well into the 12-kilometer race when a stomach cramp tightened me up. I slid back and placed only twentieth, about a minute behind Rodgers. He'd run the best race of his life and led the American men's team.

But my sharpest memory of the race takes me back to the middle of it. I hadn't started out very fast and at 3 miles was moving up. I came upon Emiel Puttemans of Belgium, and when he clutched his side with an obvious cramp, I sped away with the parting words, "Too bad." Three miles later, as I struggled to the finish, Puttemans came running by, turned to me, and said, "Too bad." I also remember being passed by an East German in the last half-mile. But at the time I did not know the man's name was Waldemar Cierpinski.

Because the world cross-country meet received little attention in the U.S., Rodgers was not considered a contender one month later at the Boston Marathon. He'd placed only fourteenth the year before but in 1975 proceeded to run the race that catapulted him into a position of lasting recognition in distance running. He won Boston with a time of 2:09:55, which broke my American record by 35 seconds and made him the fourth marathoner ever to break 2:10. Boston is a fast course and there was a favoring wind that day, but if you run that fast you're good, no matter what. After that, life for both of us would never be quite the same.

I heard the news in Colorado and was not surprised, having seen Bill's performance in Rabat. I figured he would provide me with good competition the next year at the Olympic Marathon Trial.

And he did. But first, in 1975, we raced together four more times. In June I defeated him at 2 miles in a meet that inaugurated the Track and Field Hall of Fame in Charleston, West Virginia. In late September I outran him in the Springbank road race in Ontario, Canada — but I was beaten by Jerome Drayton. During the summer we competed in a pair of road races that were prototypes for the major events that eventually sprang up all across the country. One was the Falmouth Road Race, a scenic 7.1-miler (now 7 miles even) from Woods Hole to Falmouth, along the south shore of Cape Cod in Massachusetts. I competed there at Bill's request, on behalf of the race organizers, and won by 15 seconds. The other was the Virginia Ten-Miler in Lynchburg, a race known for its hills and hospitality. There we tied on purpose, though the officials saw a need to break the tie and declared Bill the winner.

Bill Rodgers was the top marathoner in America that year. I'd planned to ease off in 1975 in preparation for my Olympics buildup and only ran one marathon, the International Rice Festival Marathon in Crowley, Louisiana. I took it as a training run and won in 2:16:29. So I could not have met

Bill Rodgers that year in Boston, not that I would have anyway, since it had been my practice to pass up Boston because
of its policy of not paying travel expense money to invited
runners. I could never afford to make the trip. And by the
time I could afford it, my running wasn't going that well.
Once — I think it was in '74 — a Boston official called me
in Gainesville and said they "found someone to pay your
airfare." But that was two weeks before the race and I didn't
go. Looking back, I regret not having a chance to run Boston
when I was in good shape. It's a fast course, and I might
have improved my personal record.

Instead of focusing on the marathon, I concentrated on
the 5,000 and 10,000 in '75 and enjoyed my best season ever
in those events. I won a number of important 5,000s, ran
one of my fastest times, 13:29.6, and was the third-ranking
American, behind Marty Liquori and Steve Prefontaine.

On May 30, Prefontaine, twenty-two years old, was killed
in a car accident in Eugene. That same night, a few hours
before the accident, he'd won a 5,000-meter race in fine
style. I was second. After the post-meet party, Pre gave me
a lift to Kenny Moore's house. We talked about how we
might work to try to change the antiquated amateur rules,
and I know Pre's death provided a lot of the impetus for
me when I took up the issue with the athletic authorities.
I was the last person to see Steve Prefontaine alive.

Pre's death was a profound shock to those who knew and
loved him. He was a great talent and a charismatic figure
who seemed headed for a position of influence in American
athletics. It was a devastating loss. The people of Eugene,
on behalf of the city and the sport, gave Pre a poignant
memorial tribute at Haywood Field.

I won another national AAU 10,000 title that year, running
28:02.2, and in Europe twice broke 28 minutes in key races.
In Stockholm I was victorious in 27:51.8, and at the season's
end, in London, I was a close second in a personal best of

27:46.0 in a race that determined the world rankings for the year. The meet was held in Crystal Palace, and the promoters had arranged for a "rabbit" to put us on a fast pace. But he failed to fulfill his obligation and I wound up doing most of the pacesetting, much to the delight of the other men with a chance to win. On the bell lap, Brendon Foster of Great Britain, running the first 10,000 of his life, went into the lead and I took off after him. The finish came up a bit too soon for me and I was beaten by a stride. Foster ran 27:45.9, and on the basis of that victory was ranked first in the 10,000 in 1975. I was ranked second. Six men, a record at the time, broke 28 minutes in that London race.

It was quite a satisfying season for me. The London meet fell between the Falmouth and Virginia events, so I was in superb condition to go up against Bill Rodgers. The tie-breaking decision in Lynchburg was a case of déjà vu. Years before I'd run a few intentional ties with Jack Bacheler, and this always seemed to confound the officials. To them, it was like breaking army regulations, an affront to the fighting spirit. In Lynchburg, Bill and I were way ahead and decided to run it in together. That is a meaningful gesture and, depending on the circumstances, every bit as affecting as a mad sprint to the tape.

Eight months passed before my next race with Bill. It was the Olympic Marathon Trial and I was in the best shape of my life. But with the Olympic marathon ten weeks later, I didn't want to squander my fitness. It was a delicate equation. I hoped to get through the trial, making perhaps an 80 to 90 percent effort. I couldn't let it become a maximum effort. I could run a hard 10,000 a week before a marathon but not a hard marathon ten weeks before another one. A hard marathon takes everything out of you; you don't even want to attempt another one for a while.

As it developed, Bill and I hooked up with Barry Brown and drew away from the pack, after 8 miles, shedding Brown after 12 miles. We clicked off 5-minute miles through the streets of Eugene, and as we came toward the finish, I would've settled for a tie. But with a half-mile to go Bill's calves tightened up, apparently from insufficient fluid intake, and he slowed down; even at that point I wasn't sure how far ahead we were. I eased off my pace at the end and finished in 2:11:51. Bill eased in second, in 2:11:58. The third spot went to Don Kardong, who ran 2:13:54. Only forty-nine of the seventy-seven starters finished.

Bill impressed me that day. He was good, all right, but he seemed to overstride a bit as he ran. Though Bill Rodgers would not have a good day in Montréal, he would soon establish a reign as the best marathon runner in the world. Since 1972 that honor had belonged to me, but in Montréal, in the Olympic marathon, it would be passed on.

☆

At five twenty-five on the afternoon of July 31, 1976, I sat by myself in the contestants' assembly room in Montréal's Stade Olympique, wondering if my racing shoes would arrive in time for me to run in the Olympic marathon. The other sixty-six marathoners had left the room and were out on the track going through their final warmups. The race would start in a few minutes.

I was waiting in desperation for Bob Newland, a manager with the U.S. team, to show up with the backup pair of shoes he'd rushed out to get from my room in the Olympic Village. On my feet were a pair of custom-made racing shoes, the soles of which had become totally unglued earlier as I jogged my warmup on the practice track adjacent to the stadium. Fortunately, I had another pair of broken-in shoes in my room; in the meantime I taped the shoes up, knowing I would run anyway and the taping wouldn't last, and waited.

Once in Montréal, realizing I hadn't fully tested the pair I would use for the marathon, I'd phoned a friend in Boulder

and asked him to air-freight my Tiger Obhoris. The fellow
was Steve Flanagan, an accomplished runner who is now
an active partner in my retail operation. He was house-sitting
for us and arranged to send out the shoes. It must have
gone through one of the fastest customs clearings in history.
It arrived at the Village with good luck messages from U.S.
Customs officials written all over it.

The waiting was murder, but somehow I was able to stay
calm. "Okay, everybody, out on the track," ordered the
clerk, and I was forced to stay behind as the men filed out
for the Olympic marathon. Nobody seemed to notice that
I had chosen to stay behind. In 5 minutes the race would
begin. I couldn't allow panic to set in. I was going to run,
and I was going to run well; for some reason I possessed
the faith that it would work out. It's an attitude I've always
tried to maintain in a difficult spot. It's as though I somehow
have some control over circumstances beyond my control.

Bob Newland appeared with the Obhoris just in time.
Frantically, I laced them up and dashed out onto the track,
where the field was just about in final formation for the
roll call.

"Oh, no," I said to myself.

It had started to rain. Through the open circle of the roof
it was falling — a steady rain, a quiet, fine rain coming
straight down as though through tubes from the sky. A rain
one could walk in without an umbrella, but not for long.
Luck has its limits.

I don't run well in the rain. I dissipate heat very well
and get cold easily. Rain stiffens me up, tightens my muscles,
so I'm not as loose as I might be. My stride changes; therefore, my form changes. And I'm a form runner more than
a strength runner. I depend on a precise running style —
that is, a rhythm and economy of movement — to carry
my speed over long distances. Running style, among other
things, determines the rate at which the body utilizes oxy-

gen, and oxygen use is a critical factor in marathon performance. Even a minor lapse in form can do one in.

Also, I don't like the feeling of being wet when I run. It
makes me uncomfortable. I rarely splash water all over me
or run under a spraying hose on a hot day.

I studied the sky that formed above the doughnut-shaped
roof. I noticed the puddles on the unprotected part of the
track. Right then, yielding to the elements, I changed my
strategy. I'd been planning to make a break early, since
that had worked for me in the Munich Olympics and in
marathons since. I'd even been thinking of trying to establish
a firm lead right from the start, feeling confident enough
in my fitness to risk such a maneuver. But even in those
brief moments before the gun, the rain was giving me pause,
and I decided to be careful and not make my move until
the halfway point. I was not accustomed to feeling a weakness like this, and it troubled me that I was unable to overcome it.

It was not that I no longer thought I could win the race.
I felt I could, but knew it was going to be harder.

As the marathon got under way, I forgot about the rain,
but not the strategy it dictated. I was going to wait. I would
stay at or near the front and after about an hour of running
would test the men around me with a surge — if someone
had not beaten me to it. Despite the weather I was confident,
more confident than at Munich, and I felt no one was in
better shape than I. My training had gone quite well. I had
the benefit of several years of international experience. I
had won the U.S. Olympic Trials marathon. I had a pretty
good idea of who might be challenging me for the victory.
I was ready.

I was also the favorite, or at least the favorite according
to the media. But it made sense: I had won the Fukuoka
Marathon a record four years in a row, from 1971 through
1974; I had won a good many other races since Munich at

home and abroad at a range of distances; my U.S. trials victory over the up-and-coming Bill Rodgers had been an easy effort; and I was the defending Olympic champion.

I didn't mind being the favorite. It didn't put any extra weight on me. I'd been the favorite in every marathon since Munich, against top fields, and had won them all. My goal was singular, to become the second man, after Abebe Bikila of Ethiopia, to win the Olympic marathon twice.

There is a competitive advantage to being a distinct favorite. The other runners watch you, perhaps more than they should. They think about you, perhaps more than they should. This helps you to control the race, to run your best while forcing others to contour their efforts to yours. When Sebastian Coe of Great Britain broke the world mile record in Brussels in 1981 (3:47.33), he did so as the heavy favorite. When the gun went off, everybody just looked at him as though they dared not challenge him, and he was able to run unencumbered, which is how Coe wanted to run against the clock that day.

Because the marathon is so long, the controlling effect is more gradual. To key off a particular runner is not necessarily unwise — unless, of course, the runner being keyed on falters, throwing your plans awry.

We would run through the wet streets of Montréal on a mostly flat course that would take us north to the Rivière de Prairies, an arm of the St. Lawrence, then back through the center of the city and onto Sherbrooke Street for the final leg, 5 straight miles to the stadium. About a dozen of us were positioned ahead. We passed 5 kilometers in 15:19, 10 kilometers in 30:48, 15 kilometers in 46:00. Among the leaders were those expected to be up there — Jerome Drayton of Canada (the 1975 Fukuoka champion), Karel Lismont of Belgium (second at Munich), Bill Rodgers of the United States (the 1975 Boston Marathon winner); those who had no business being up there — Mario Cuevas of Mexico (who would finish eighteenth), Jose de Jesus of Puerto Rico (who would finish twenty-third); and one man who showed great courage just by starting — Lasse Viren of Finland.

Just the day before Viren had completed the "double-double." He won the 5,000 meters, four days after he'd won the 10,000 meters — four years after he'd won the 5,000 and 10,000 in Munich. No one had ever done that before. No one had even won the 5,000 twice. Counting qualifying rounds, Viren had run two 5,000s and two 10,000s in eight days. And on the ninth day Lasse Viren ran the marathon. He was attempting to equal what is perhaps the greatest performance in Olympic distance running, Emil Zatopek's 1952 Helsinki "triple." The immortal Czech won the 5,000, 10,000, and the marathon. Like Zatopek, Viren had never before run the marathon. Unlike Zatopek, Viren did not have a three-day rest before it.

Because of his success, and because his record was fairly undistinguished between the two Olympics, Viren was rumored to have been "blood-doping," a controversial process in which blood is withdrawn from the body and then reinfused to raise the hemoglobin level. Though recent laboratory tests have shown this technique to be a theoretical aid to performance, physiologists are uncertain about its practical application.

There isn't a runner anywhere for whom I have greater respect than Lasse Viren. I do not believe he blood-doped. He trained wisely — for a time, like me, at high altitude — and peaked for the Olympics. In all four of his gold medal–winning races, he was simply the best man in the field. He has had everything it takes to win — the talent, the intelligence, the determination, the discipline, and an innate tactical sense of his competitors' weaknesses.

But I felt he could not win the marathon. With all the hard running he'd done, he could not have had the physiological resources to produce an all-out effort in the marathon.

His energy reserves — that is, the foodstuffs that fuel the muscles — would have been significantly depleted during the week. He would have also been dehydrated. "Look," I said to myself, "at a certain point the guy's human." So I honestly never considered Viren a threat. Maybe that was naive. But, evaluating his chances objectively, I thought he might win a medal, but not the gold.

Viren's strategy was obvious: He was keying off me. He admitted it. "I would simply follow him as long as I could," Viren explained afterward. "Like a dolphin following a ship." I saw how closely he was watching me during the first part of the race, so at certain times I would play hide-and-seek with him. I'd move up to the head of our lead pack, then purposely drift a few strides back to put another man between us so Viren could no longer see me. Then he would twist around, searching for me.

With my occasional vantage point at the rear of the pack, I got to look everyone over and saw that they all seemed in control. We were running just under 5 minutes per mile. I felt a little tight from the rain (though I was concentrating so hard, it was not on my mind), but had not lost the confidence to stick with my plans for a midrace surge. I was telling myself, "Okay, be patient, wait till halfway before you start to run hard."

As we closed in on the pivotal halfway point, eight of us were still together at the front: Rodgers, Drayton, Lismont, Viren, Goran Bengtssen (Sweden), Shivnath Singh (India), a man I thought was Carlos Lopes of Portugal, and me. I kept thinking to myself, Where exactly am I going to do this? Where will I make my move? Everyone was waiting for something to happen, and because I wanted to be as unpredictable as possible, I did not want to accelerate right at a mile or kilometer marker. We passed the 20-kilometer sign and then, just before 13 miles, boom! — I took off. It was more of a sprint than a surge. I wanted to see who might come with me, and I wanted to set the tone for the rest of the race. Unfortunately, it did not have the bruising impact of the move I made in Munich. People hung on, at first. Farther along, at 25 kilometers, we were still a gang of six, but in the next stretch I surged more convincingly and broke up the pack for good. Quickly I built a 40-yard lead and within a quarter-mile, only one man was running along with me on the sloppy streets of Montréal, the man I thought was Lopes.

Carlos Lopes had run a gallant 10,000 in Montréal, winning the silver medal behind Viren. He was also listed as a marathon entry. Though I'd watched the 10,000, I'd not gotten a close look at Lopes except to notice his compact size — listed as 5 feet 6 inches and 126 pounds. The man still pressing me was obviously European and also compact — 5 feet 7 inches and 130 pounds, in fact. His uniform, unlike others, did not appear to bear the insignia of his country — or at least it was not large enough to pop out at me. The guy was Lopes. Who else could he be?

And that's what I thought for the entire race, as the two of us raced our hearts out for mile upon mile. But Lopes had never started the marathon. He was one of four men listed who did not show; the others were Gaston Roelants of Belgium (the 1964 Olympic champion in the 3,000-meter steeplechase who did not run at all in Montréal), Ilie Floroiu of Rumania, and Charles Olmeus of Haiti. Lopes, burdened with injuries after Montréal, didn't attempt a marathon till 1982, in New York, where he told the press he had never run more than 15 miles at any one time in his life. In New York he did not get much farther, dropping out at 21 miles as Salazar and Gomez began to fight it out.

In Montréal we were similarly engaged, me and . . . Waldemar Cierpinski, an East German. The duel lasted for 6 miles, from my breakaway surge near 25 kilometers to his breakaway surge near 35 kilometers. There were many surges in between as we tested one another for almost 30 minutes.

He was tough. And he was smart. I did all I could to try and get away from him. It was almost like an interval work-out. I'd accelerate, but he'd come back at me. This happened again and again. At one point I might have had 60 yards on him but eventually he even closed that gap.

A lesser man would have been too afraid to gamble, "but," Cierpinski explained later, "I was almost sure if we all let him go right then he would win, just as in Munich. The question was whether I could finish once I set out for him. The key fact for me was that I had enjoyed such good training with no injuries. I knew I was well prepared for this race."

My tightness was hurting me. I did not have the freedom in my stride that would have enabled me to hold my surges longer and keep the pressure on. I just couldn't run as force-fully as I had in Munich. But in Montréal, as the seventeenth and eighteenth and nineteenth miles were being finished off, I was still running really hard, as hard as I could. It was the only way I could win. I had to hit it, I had to tangle with the man I thought was someone else. I knew Lopes was fit. To me, his 10,000 five days before indicated readiness, not likely fatigue. After all, in Munich *I'd* run the marathon well after a hard 10,000.

We did not speak. We bumped a couple of times, almost locking arms in trying to shave the tangents (the shortest distance from one point to the next). I could sense the man was not going to slow down, at least not until the very end.

He sensed he was starting to get the best of me. "It was a wonderful feeling when I came alongside," Cierpinski would say in Doug Gilbert's *The Miracle Machine,* a book about the East German sports system. "I glanced at Shorter as I did so, and looked right into the eyes of the man who was my idol as a marathon runner. I knew all about him. And yet I could tell by the return glance that he didn't know much, if anything, about me."

Reaching Mont Royale, the only significant incline on the course, I resigned myself to trying to rest for a while and push again farther up. The elastic was stretching thin. We ran up the hill and crested it together, but then he poured it on down the hill, through the grounds of McGill University. Right about at 20 miles he spurted, like the rush of a fountain, just as I was falling into a bad spell. His timing was perfect. He had a 10-yard lead, just like that. Then 20. Then 30. Then . . . he flew off the descent and onto Sherbrooke, the thoroughfare that would take us home. He was pulling away and I couldn't do a thing about it.

Down Sherbrooke I was in deep trouble. I was watching the way Cierpinski ("Lopes") was running, and I knew how I felt. I thought, If he doesn't run any worse and I don't start feeling better, I've lost this race. At that stage, after he'd committed himself, it was no more complicated than that. It looked as though he had about 100 yards on me with 5 miles to go. I got over my bad patch and came back on him, closing the gap to about 40 yards with 3 miles left. But before I could entertain any false hopes, Cierpinski turned around to check on me and then took off. I faded again, and that was it.

I really crashed. I'd run myself off my feet trying in vain to get away from him, and when he put the pressure on I was drained of the resources to respond. The rain was annoying, but I was concentrating too hard for it to really bother me. The left foot was, in a medical sense, already injured, but I did not feel it. It was just *me*. I hadn't made any tactical errors. I'd done everything I needed to do. I just couldn't run fast enough. It felt strange; that had never happened to me before in a marathon.

My pace had slowed by about 15 seconds a mile in the last stretch into the stadium. Cierpinski also was biding his time, but the records show he had a 32-second lead at 40 kilometers, with about a mile and a half to go. As spent as I was, there was never any doubt in my mind that I would finish. And I felt my second-place position was safe. I sensed there was no one rushing on from behind and worked my way to the end, disappointed that I'd come so close and not won.

There is a picture of me shrugging, somewhat apologetically, as I entered the stadium, clearly defeated. I was telling the crowd, which I knew had been pulling for me, "I've done all I could do. The guy beat me."

I, however, was the first man to stop running. Cierpinski circled the track and hit the finish but, seeing a 1 on the lap counter, mistakenly thought he had another lap to go. As I completed my lap, there was the winner *behind* me, still running. Cierpinski's time was posted on the scoreboard as he finished: 2:09:55, an Olympic record. I reached the end in 2:10:46 and waited to congratulate the man I still thought was Carlos Lopes.

We shook hands and he said, *"Sprechen sie Deutsch?"* And I said to myself, "That's a funny thing for a Portuguese to say."

I didn't learn it was Cierpinski until he and I and Lismont, who placed third (2:11:12), were taken inside for the doping test. We couldn't discuss the race. He spoke no English and I spoke no German. It would come out later that Cierpinski wore a plain white shirt, not the blue and white of the GDR, to deflect the heat in the event of a sunny day. Uniforms had to be registered in advance, so Cierpinski could not switch when he saw the rain, a rain he would find "both refreshing and relaxing." It softened the blow to find it was Cierpinski, not Lopes, who had won. At least I'd been beaten by a man who was fresh, an experienced marathon runner, and not the man who was second in the 10,000.

Cierpinski's performance was not much of a surprise. Though the aficionados had not predicted he would win a medal, I knew of his 2:12:22 from the GDR trials earlier in the year and that the East Germans had brought only him, and not the more established Eckhard Lesse, to Montréal. The only thing I didn't know about Cierpinski was what he looked like.

Don Kardong finished fourth, only 3 seconds behind him, in 2:11:16, his best race ever. Lasse Viren came in fifth in 2:13:11. Absolutely incredible for a man who'd spent the entire week in competition. For Bill Rodgers, it was a difficult day. He said his legs "started to go" after 15 miles, and he suffered the rest of the way, finishing fortieth in 2:25:15.

My second place in Montréal was quite a disappointment. I thought I'd advanced significantly since Munich and that I was ready to run better than ever. In Munich I felt good and the day was good; in Montréal I felt bad and the day was bad.

What was also disappointing, in view of Cierpinski's victory, was the realization that perhaps my independent method of training would no longer be the approach that produced the best results. The East German's superiority seemed to suggest that training — for the marathon, at least — called for something more than simply getting out the door every day. With a team of specialists behind him, Cierpinski had trained scientifically, according to hard physiological doctrine.

That's why, when asked by reporters if I would continue to train for the next Olympics, I said, "If I can find the right doctors." I had no idea then how much of a foreshadowing that would be.

CHAPTER SIX

Moscow: 1980

When President Jimmy Carter first threatened, in his television address of January 4, 1980, that the United States might boycott the summer Olympics in Moscow because of the Soviet aggression in Afghanistan, I knew right then that that was it. We weren't going. We wouldn't be sending our fastest and strongest amateur athletes to the Soviet Union for the nineteenth Olympic Games of the modern era. With the President's brief but firm announcement, he had backed himself into a political corner from which he could not be extricated.

I immediately came to terms with it. Shocked though I was by the sweep and suddenness of the Carter proposal, I tried to understand the conditions that led the administration to take such an extreme position. I guess I wanted to believe that there was some valid reason for using the Olympics as a political pawn. I wanted to believe that America was right: The tragedy would then seem less hateful and unnecessary.

Perhaps I'm naive in such matters. I tend to give people the benefit of the doubt. I figured, he's the President; maybe, as he'd said, our national security (or at least our national interest) was really at stake; and whether he was right or wrong, the U.S. Olympic Committee would not be able to withstand the pressure. It was broke.

It was a complicated and frustrating time for amateur athletes. The issues of the Cold War and presidential politics merged with the Olympic movement and international athletics and sparked a bitter debate throughout the world. Athletes, above all, were put in an uncomfortable position. If we opposed the boycott, we were putting personal goals over national loyalty; if we supported the administration, we stood opposite other athletes — our comrades, if you will — thereby weakening the strength and solidarity of the Olympic stance.

To be thrown into a political free-for-all was a very uncomfortable environment for the athletes. While politics has always infiltrated sports — indeed, most glaringly the Olympics themselves — athletes, especially amateur athletes, usually exist in an illusionary state, denying life's complications as they go about their training and competition.

As athletes it's amazing what we can achieve. But we find it hard to function in the political arena. We haven't been trained to. Athletes learn fast, but because we're athletes we forget fast. Emotions take over: We can do it. We can do anything we want if we try hard enough.

We can stop the Olympic boycott.

I knew we couldn't.

I was a rebel at heart in my younger days, a quiet protester. Anti-establishment. It was in the air. For a brief time in the early seventies I wore my hair pulled back into a short ponytail when I ran. But I've learned to deal with authority and work within its channels to get somewhere. My attempts to broaden the earnings opportunities for amateur athletes through discussions with the ruling track and field bodies have been successful. Where at one time I might have challenged the people who make the rules, I came to realize that an exchange of ideas is much more effective than name-calling.

The boycott was wrong from every perspective: political, diplomatic, philosophical, athletic. The issue raised many questions: Would we halt Soviet expansion into Southwest Asia? Would we rally support from other nations? Would we "punish" the Russians and ruin their Olympics? Would we be destroying the Olympic movement in the process?

I believe in the inherent goodness of the Olympics. Left alone, the Olympics is the most neutral stage we have. The interaction of peoples from around the world is something to behold, something to cherish. It happens nowhere else. Barriers are taken down. It's a very simple idea. In the Village and out on the playing fields you live with people from different places in a setting unified by the purity of sport. It's an atmosphere that promotes good will. It gives one faith in humanity. It's not perfect. Anyone who saw the basketball finals in Munich knows that.

Since I was convinced the boycott would stick, my allegiance then was not to one side or another but to the practical matter of saving the Games from permanent damage as far as America was concerned. Like all of the athletes, I was powerless in the dispute. And though I suppose there might have been some value in speaking out and being heard, I was not about to join in any showing of rancor. I did not want to see a situation that would spoil things for American athletes after the boycott. For all we knew early in 1980, Carter could have been re-elected in the fall. We were seeing how administration policy was determining our fate, and regardless of who would be occupying the White House during the next Olympiad, we all needed to be on the same side. Amateur athletes, particularly in track and field, had come too far to allow divisiveness to inhibit our progress.

At long last we were starting to win significant reforms in the archaic amateur system. I was working hard at it. After my brush with the authorities before the 1976 Olympics, I became committed to changing the system to enable amateur track and field athletes to make enough of a living

Two early teams: my family (I'm at the top left) and the Mount Hermon prep school varsity cross-country squad, with whom I began my distance running career (I'm seated in the center).

Important influences during my years at Yale: Bob Giegengack, the head track coach, and Louise Gilliland, whom I met on a ski vacation in Taos, New Mexico, and eventually married (this shot is from a later trip).

Three good friends: (top left) loosening up with Jack Bacheler, my frequent training companion, before a 1972 Chicago cross-country race; (top right) Steve Prefontaine beating me out for first place in a 1975 5,000-meter race in Eugene —the very day of his fatal automobile accident; (bottom) Kenny Moore and I intentionally tying for first in the 1972 U.S. Olympic Marathon Trial, also in Eugene.

Competing in the 1972 Olympic 10,000-meter with Lasse Viren of Finland (left) and Mohamed Gammoudi of Tunisia, the key participants in the Famous Fall. Gammoudi eventually dropped out after the incident, but Viren came back to win the race.

Rich Clarkson

At the opening of the 1972 Olympic Marathon, I was one of the leaders (second from the right, on the inside lane), but few people suspected I'd still be there at the end of the race.

Track & Field News

LIFE

The Haywire Olympics

Can they be fixed by '76?

Frank Shorter,
first American
to win the marathon
in 64 years,
was a happy exception
for the battered
U.S. team

SEPTEMBER 22 · 1972 · 50¢

Time Inc.

Running through the streets of Montréal in the 1976 Olympic Marathon in the rain—not my favorite conditions. Number 51 in white is Waldemar Cierpinski of East Germany, the man I didn't recognize who eventually passed me to take over first place. Heading toward the finish line in second place, my disappointment is evident.

With Louise in 1978, sporting a cast for the injured foot I'd ignored too long.

Competing successfully against Bill Rodgers in the 1981 Orange Classic 10,000-meter in my hometown, Middletown, New York. Bill and I have frequently been rivals on the racing circuit.

Jane Sobel/Janeart

On the *Today* show in 1979 with Tom Brokaw (right) and Ollan Cassell, executive director of The Athletics Congress, discussing my ground-breaking promotional arrangement with Hilton hotels. Such arrangements now help amateur athletes survive financially while training for competition.

Training in the Rockies with Cheryl Tiegs for a promotional photograph.

from their sport to be able to train properly. I needed it for myself and I wanted it for others. With more freedom and greater opportunity, we could produce better Olympic teams. You couldn't very well devote your best years to serious training if you had to work forty hours a week.

☆

While I was able to gain some accommodations from The Athletics Congress (formerly the AAU), paving the way for business opportunities that would serve my running, I was no longer able to run with my usual freedom. I was hurt. An injury to my left foot that in all probability began in the winter of 1976, before the Montréal Olympics, got worse, and was finally treated surgically in the spring of 1978. The operation was a success and the rehabilitation was encouraging at first; about a year later, however, I aggravated my back, which slowed my progress and prevented my left leg from regaining full strength. With my left leg weaker than the right, my form was impaired, and I could not run at my best.

Though I'd managed a respectable 2:16:15 in the 1979 New York Marathon, placing seventh to Bill Rodgers (2:11:42), I felt out of tune biomechanically. Before leaving New York, I went up to the Bronx VA Hospital, where tests confirmed the dysfunction in my back and its inhibiting effect on my leg.

I was not the runner I'd been a few years before, and, as positive as I always am, I knew I couldn't straighten myself out in time to make a serious bid for the 1980 Olympic team. That's another reason I didn't speak out on the boycott issue. I couldn't protest for having lost something that I really didn't think *I* would have had. And though I could have cried out for my compatriots, no matter how I went about it, people would have perceived it as a stand for myself. I couldn't feel right about that.

On the other hand, it may be hard to exercise restraint when you feel your one chance at the Olympics is being lost. Fate dealt a hard blow to a number of top athletes who were in peak form at the time. One was Bill Rodgers, the world's leading marathon runner in 1979, when he won his fourth straight New York Marathon and his third Boston Marathon, the latter with a victory over Toshihiko Seko of Japan. In defeating Seko (who would win Boston the next year), Rodgers ran 2:09:27, slicing 28 seconds from his American record. He was all set to gear up for the Olympics when the boycott was called.

MARATHON MAN TURNS ANGRY YOUNG MAN, headlined the *Boston Globe* the weekend before the Boston Marathon. Bill's criticism of the U.S. Olympic Committee and the Carter administration turned up regularly in the papers. But Washington put such pressure on the USOC that it had no choice but to comply with the boycott call. Both the House and the Senate had voted overwhelmingly for it, and so had the American people if one trusted the opinion polls.

The Olympic Marathon Trial was held in Buffalo, New York, thirty-three days after Boston, necessitating a choice. It would have been nearly impossible to run both well. Bill Rodgers' decision to run Boston (which he won for the fourth time) and not the trial, separating himself from the other marathoners, disregarded the need to keep the Olympic idea alive at a time of crisis. I ran the trial, knowing I would not qualify, as a gesture of solidarity.

Ironically, the boycott might have been a blessing in disguise for Bill because, in my view at least, he would not have won the gold medal. A medal — yes, in all likelihood — but not the gold. As outstanding a marathoner as he was at the time, he was not the best. And because he would have gone to Moscow as the popular favorite, to return home with anything less than a victory might have cast him as a disappointment in the eyes of the American public. While the loyal track enthusiast will naturally embrace any Olympian, the armchair sports fan, wedded to medal counts and "us versus them" partiality, is not particularly impressed with silver or bronze. It's gold or nothing, and it's hard to recover from "nothing." The Olympics come only every four years.

Without the boycott, I believe the marathon would have been won by Toshihiko Seko. Japan was one of the fifty-one boycotting nations, so he, too, lost out. Seko, in his run against Rodgers in Boston in April 1979, was just then advancing into Olympic contention under the spell of Kiyoshi Nakamura, the masterly coach who makes marathon training a sacrament and who reportedly became like a second father to Seko. The Japanese are wild about the marathon, and an important international race can have national overtones. Seko ran 2:10:12 behind Rodgers at Boston and then won Fukuoka in December in 2:10:35, clearly an indication of what he could bring to Moscow eight months later. And after winning his third straight Fukuoka title in December 1980, in 2:09:45, and then beating Craig Virgin and Rodgers to win Boston, in a course-record 2:09:26, the next spring, Seko seemed to be the one man who had everything in its proper place to beat everyone in Moscow. He was strong, he was fast, he was smart, and he knew how to peak. On August 1, 1980, with the honor of his country at stake, Toshihiko Seko could most likely have become the first Japanese to win the Olympic marathon.

Tony Sandoval of the United States would have given him a run for it. Tony won the U.S. Marathon Trial convincingly in 2:10:19, and from the late-race speed that he showed, it was apparent that he could have run still faster. His twenty-second mile dipped to 4:44; the twenty-third was 4:48. Tony has a very light stride, and though he does not run aggressively, he's a tough competitor. A medical student, Sandoval had taken time off from his studies at the University of Colo-

rado in Denver to prepare for the trials in Buffalo. Sandoval
had the talent and the temperament to keep himself close.
But not the chance. "I'd love to run in Moscow against the
best in the world," he said in Buffalo. "But what can I do?"
Sandoval accepted his fate with no bitterness and proceeded
to become a physician, intent on eventually returning home
to the mountains of New Mexico to practice medicine.

I felt sad for him. I'd known Tony for some time and
we had much in common: New Mexico, Colorado, medicine,
a light running style. Though, unlike most of the other Olympians, he had the promise of a fine career outside athletics
awaiting him, Sandoval's values were rooted more in the
culture of his people than in any expectations of the good
life. As he said in an interview before the Games: "Whether
the U.S. sends a team to Moscow or not, the hay's going
to grow and someone will have to cut it. People ask me
how the boycott affects me, but when I'm in Truchas I don't
see a boycott. All I see are the willows and cottonwoods."

In Moscow, in a full-fledged Olympics, the other runners
fighting it out with Sandoval for the medals behind Seko
might have been Shigeru and Takeshi Sou, twins from Japan,
and my old friend from the streets of Montréal, Waldemar
Cierpinski. East Germany, of course, was right there in Moscow, providing Cierpinski with the opportunity to achieve
what I failed to do in Montréal — become the second man,
after Bikila, to win two Olympic marathons. I had not heard
much of Cierpinski since 1976, and though he'd won a marathon in 2:11:17 in May 1980, the previous December he'd
dropped out at Fukuoka. It turned out he was on a four-
year plan, watched over by doctors and physiologists, that
was designed to have him peaked for Moscow and not before.
It worked. He won. Much as he did against me, Cierpinski
let others do the early leading, moving to the front with
about 4 miles to go and winning by 17 seconds in 2:11:03. I
have nothing but respect for Cierpinski, but he was lucky.

Without the Americans and the Japanese and the others
in there with him, Cierpinski's feat will always carry the
stigma of a truncated field.

☆

Finishing second in 1976 did not seem to affect my stature
in American running. I'm not sure why. Maybe my victory
in 1972 was considered such a milestone that after that I
no longer had to prove myself.

After Montréal, I was preparing myself for life as a former
champion. I thought about it and realized that it was in
the natural order of sport, in the evolutionary chain, that
someone would take my place. I wasn't dreading the day.
The thought of passing the gauntlet had a good feeling to
it. I would not always have to *be* the Olympic champion.
That was one reason I started my clothing business and took
an interest in TV commentating. Before 1980 I wanted to
settle into a type of work that would enable me to earn a
living while continuing to run and compete.

It was right after the Montréal Olympics that I became
a different runner. The victories I was accustomed to were
no longer frequent. The fast marathons did not materialize.
It was my left foot. The pain would come and go: When it
was there I'd struggle; when it was gone, which was not
often, I'd be my old self again.

A major turning point in my career — and, as we've seen,
for all of running — came at the 1976 New York Marathon.
The event has become an enormous success and grown to
be one of the most influential road races in the world. By
its example as a big-city race that could work — that invited
leading runners and treated them well; that drew thousands
of average runners and treated *them* well; that brought out
great numbers of spectators; that attracted the media, including national television; that promoted a positive image
of the city and its people — the event became the model

for races of such magnitude throughout the world. There is hardly a good-sized city left without a major road race, and in many places it's the premier sports event of the year.

In 1976, there were 2,090 marathoners at New York, including Bill Rodgers and me. Fred Lebow, the race director, was then a one-man band; he even picked me up at the airport himself. He drove me back, too. These days Fred is the one being picked up at airports by race promoters who want his advice on how to put on a successful race.

I suffered more in that New York Marathon than in any marathon I've ever run. I felt as though I was redlining the whole way. It was the first time I'd ever run hard right from the start and had someone pulling away from me. Until then, every time I'd run hard I'd been up with the leaders or in the lead and able to sustain the pace.

At 10 miles, through Brooklyn, Bill Rodgers quickened the pace, and I couldn't keep up with him. He broke contact. I tried to chase after him but had all I could do to hold on to second. Bill's time was 2:10:10. I finished in 2:13:12, 9 seconds ahead of Britain's Chris Stewart.

My feet would just get hot. Though I was still having trouble with my shoes, the experimental lightweight model I wore for New York seemed to work okay. But the bad left foot was causing me to alter my running style. I'd run heavier, tighten up, and overheat. It effected a chain reaction, and all of me turned sour. Looking back on my race, I'm quite proud of how I ran. I beat the onrushing Stewart only on pride.

It was frustrating because I thought in one piece I could have beaten Bill. We'd split two races since Montréal. I'd won at Falmouth and he'd won at Lynchburg. I've always believed that at the end of a race, in a one-on-one duel between us, Bill would crack first. I don't have the same fear of Bill in that situation as I have, say, of Lasse Viren or Rod Dixon.

I think my track experience has given me the edge. I'm better prepared mentally to respond with good speed when a sprint is called for. In a track race I can rely on instinct if I'm still in contention in the final quarter-mile, and that's a quality I can transfer to the road. But first I have to be close. After New York in 1976, I could no longer take that for granted.

When the foot felt better, it would give me a false sense of redemption. So badly did I want to be normal again that I could not deny myself the feelings of renewal that would come from a pain-free run resulting in a good performance. From the stress of running, I would later learn, I had torn a ligament in my left foot, and bone spurs had grown out around it. The tear and the inflammation it caused was giving me the pain. It wasn't a real fracture, and so at first it didn't bring on the symptoms that could make it impossible to use the foot. I might have been better off with something like that, something that would have forced me off my feet and made me face the music a lot sooner.

As the 1977 summer season got going, I was doing great. I won the 10,000 meters in 28:16 at the AAU Track and Field Championships in Los Angeles, arriving at the meet only an hour before my race because of an appearance I'd made in Wichita, Kansas, that morning. When Craig Virgin saw me, he looked at me with large eyes that seemed to say: "What are *you* doing here?" Two weeks later, on the July Fourth weekend, I won back-to-back road races that seemed to attract national interest.

Five thousand people turned out to run the inaugural Chicago Distance Classic, a 20-kilometer event that gave the Midwest its first high-powered road race. After winning, I flew to Atlanta and the next day, in a field of fifty-seven hundred, competed in the Peachtree Road Race. The race officials had also signed up Bill Rodgers, Don Kardong, and Lasse Viren, and so my win there meant something to me.

One year after the '76 Olympics, all three U.S. Olympic marathoners plus the distance running star of the Games were racing 10,000 meters through the streets of Atlanta on Independence Day.

The four of us ran pretty much together at the front, with my trading the lead with Bill in the third mile and then drawing away. I pressed hard in the next 2 miles, and with about a mile to go, Bill moved ahead and tried to get away from me. I came back on him and, feeling in control, went by him with a half-mile to go and won by 5 seconds. Kardong was third.

How, I thought, could I run like that if there was something wrong with me? But I knew there was, something that I could only identify then by its tendency to appear and disappear and reappear — a wicked tease.

My AAU victory had qualified me for the first IAAF World Cup, in Düsseldorf, West Germany, in September, established as a biennial meet in which countries or regions would compete as teams. I left early for Europe, to run, and in a 5,000 in Zürich recorded my fastest time ever, 13:26.6, though my foot hurt like hell. I was running alongside Marty Liquori with less than a half-mile to go; he took off and set an American record of 13:16.0, and I hobbled in ninth. (That was some field: Dick Quax, Miruts Yifter, and Henry Rono were among the other runners ahead of me.)

My ankle was swollen and now visible was a lump the size of a Ping-Pong ball. But there I was in Europe for the World Cup, so I had the swelling aspirated and gave it a try in Düsseldorf. Well into the race I was still among the leaders, but Miruts Yifter of Ethiopia, who would win the 5,000 and 10,000 in the Moscow Olympics, ran over me and won the 10,000 with the wait-and-kick style that became his trademark. His time was 28:32.3; I placed sixth in 28:52.5.

I'd had enough. I went cold turkey. Or as close to cold turkey as I was able to. I decided not to run that fall, but like an alcoholic sneaking a nip, I cheated a little. I even ran part of the New York Marathon. The foot hurt, and I couldn't go on like that. X-rays were taken in Boulder, and when they didn't show anything I just felt confused.

In November, at a race in Phoenix, I met Dr. Stan James, an orthopedic surgeon from Eugene, Oregon, who treated many athletes. I explained what I'd been going through, and he told me to take it easy for a few months and then run the Boston Marathon in April as a test. I took it easy, more or less, still a little too defiant about giving in to the weaknesses of the flesh. Pain or no pain, I wasn't about to run my first Boston Marathon unprepared and, somehow reasonably fit, did it in 2:18:15 for twenty-third place. It felt awful. The pain had gotten so bad, I took an anti-inflammatory drug to reduce the swelling to get me through the race. I'd never done that before.

I went into the marathon weighing 135 pounds and probably finished it at 130. The next day, still on the drug, I weighed 140 after a sauna. The drug was causing me to retain water.

I gave in. I flew to Eugene, where Dr. James, through a three-dimensional X-ray technique known as tomography, diagnosed the degenerating foot condition. Surgery, he said, was necessary. I was glad to hear it, glad to hear that finally, something was going to be done to fix my foot. On April 26, 1978, nine days after the Boston Marathon, the operation was performed.

☆

The opportunity to participate in clinics at road races, which began on a regular basis in 1977, was gratifying to me because I'd worked for them as a way in which amateur athletes could earn a living and continue to run. What I found at these clinics — in Chicago, in Atlanta, everywhere — was startling. I found that a good many people were just like

me. We were all runners. We all experienced the same feelings whatever our abilities: the same thrills, disappointments,
the needs and desires, the fun of it all. We were alike. I
just ran faster, but my autograph was secondary. These people *knew* me, and I don't mean my race statistics. They
knew me because they ran, and it was the same thing. Running is running, 40 miles a week or 140, 8 minutes per mile
or 6. The essential experience is the same.

I couldn't believe it. There were thousands of people out
there whose minds were filled with thoughts about workouts,
races, hills, dogs, diet, and injury. About how much to run,
what to wear, what to eat, about when to speed up and
when to slow down. They were curious about *me*, sure —
what was the Olympic champion really like? But much more
than that, they wanted to know how I did it. How had I
managed my running? How had I figured it out so that I
might do my best, given whatever talent I brought to it?

It was wonderful. People were actually interested in what
I did. It was an honest empathy, and it was touching. We
were all in this thing together. It took me awhile to get
used to it.

I had come full circle. First I was strange ("There goes
that crazy runner again"). Then I was the mysterious loner
(*The Loneliness of the Long-Distance Runner*). Then I was
the perplexing hero ("Now what are you gonna do?"). Then,
of all things, I became one of those everyday folks who ran.
The growing race fields and the clinics brought me closer
to people, and I like to think I gave off a feeling of accessibil-
ity. Olympic medals or not, I still wanted to get out of bed
the next day and run.

Because runners so identify with me and (perhaps foolishly) place such importance in what I have to say, I've had
to be careful about what I'd tell them and how I present
myself. I've learned that when you have celebrity, people
ascribe to you qualities you may not have — talents, abilities,

intelligence. They think you know it all and hang on your every word, especially in my situation, as one runner to another.

I never try to be more than I am. I'm not a doctor, a physiologist, or a health care professional. I'm just a runner. I know what's worked for me. But I won't say there are any secrets because there are none. I've always considered the act of running as something to be developed with common sense, body feelings, and instinct, not with complicated formulas. Still, I've given so much thought to all of running that I have considered opinions on just about everything; my views are strong. But I won't be dogmatic. And just because I believe in altitude training or interval workouts doesn't mean I'll insist they'll work for everyone. Basically, I see myself as an average person who tries hard. Though technical information abounds, the lessons of running are simple ones, and that's what I try to impart to the runners I meet.

Being beaten in Montréal made it easier, I think, for other runners to relate to me. I'd tasted disappointment. In the two biggest races of my life, I'd won — and I'd lost. Runners could understand that and could then hope to understand me. Somehow, maybe because of the defeat, they felt they could trust me more. Had I repeated my Olympic victory, I might have been perceived as being too far removed from the experience of the typical runner. But I'd been beaten: I was human. And people saw that on TV and read about it in the papers, just as they'd absorbed the novelty of my run in Munich.

Likewise, being beaten in Montréal made it easier for me to relate to the other runners. I knew defeat. I knew what it was to run like crazy for years, living the ascetic life, and fall just short of a goal.

The group dynamics of a running clinic are fascinating. The process and the atmosphere rarely change. It's part advice column, part press conference, part adult education course, part standup comedy. What do I eat? How much do I run? What shoes do I wear? *What should I do?* What do I think of this, and what do I think of that? They want to know all about my daily habits, and they tell me about theirs and want to know if I think they're okay.

I try not to get too personal. Basically, I'm standoffish, even shy in small groups, at times uncomfortable among other people. The clinic scene could be a scary one, but as long as I can keep my distance I'm all right. The subject matter enables that. I can be an authority on the topic without revealing too much of myself. I need that shield. I couldn't operate in that environment if it became too intimate.

Others thrive on it. On one summer Sunday morning in Asbury Park, New Jersey, I shared the stage after a race with Dr. George Sheehan, running's leading philosopher and modern Thoreau of the lecture circuit. When one runner went on and on about his bowel movements, George had a field day. You couldn't stop him. Asked for an additional comment, I became embarrassed, deferred to Dr. Sheehan, and made a quick exit.

These clinics have been good for me. I've learned to speak in public and have become less shy about addressing large groups. They've forced me to think more about my running, about what I do, and to exchange views with others. This added to my confidence and helped me in my TV commentating, which I started doing in 1978.

I have worked for two of the three major networks, covering track meets, road races, and an occasional triathlon. My first big assignment was the 1978 Millrose Games at Madison Square Garden in New York, for NBC. There's more hard work and less glamour in it than most people realize.

This is an opportunity that only a short time ago was not available to amateur athletes, not without the threat of suspension. But there had been changes, and at roughly the same time I was able to break ground for amateur athletes in other areas. After the Montréal Olympics, I started a clothing business with a line of running attire that carried my name, and I opened a retail shop in Boulder that sold running gear and other equipment. In time, other stores were added.

And in the spring of 1979, at a press conference at the Waldorf-Astoria Hotel in New York, Hilton International and The Athletics Congress (TAC) announced the first legitimate product endorsement deal to involve an amateur athlete. The arrangement called for Hilton to become a national sponsor of TAC, paying it for the privilege, and for me to become a paid "consultant" to the Hilton hotel chain, which signed me up for commercial endorsements. This fell within the international rules.

Unfortunately, my advances in the political arena were not being matched by my running. Though the surgery had been a success, I was still having trouble. After the operation, in April 1978, my foot was in a cast for six weeks, and it was four more weeks before I was permitted to do any running. During this time, I rode a stationary bicycle for up to an hour and 15 minutes a day to maintain cardiovascular fitness, which was critical to the rehabilitation process. I also did isometric exercises to strengthen the atrophied muscles in my left leg. I continued the therapy when I resumed running and was able to work my way back into some sort of shape by the fall.

Sometime during the rehab period, however, or in the fall when I resumed competition, I developed complications in my back. I'm not sure exactly when it happened or how I did it, though doctors would tell me the back problem was probably caused by my tendency after the surgery to favor my healthy right leg while running, impeding the progress of the left leg and spreading dysfunction up through my back. The back condition, in turn, gave the leg a bad time. At first none of this was apparent to me; since the physical discomfort was tolerable I went on with my running, beside myself because the rehab exercise was not bringing my visibly smaller and obviously weaker left leg back to normal strength. And it should have.

I'd stand in front of a full-length mirror, like a teenager dressing for a date, and look at myself. I'd inspect my legs, which is really all I have. I'd see the right one, fully defined. And I'd see the left one, attenuated. I'd run my hands down each one, feeling the bulges and the grooves and the atrophy, and wonder when I'd have a matched set again.

Maybe I tried to come back too soon — the athlete's favorite lament. By late August, four months after the surgery, I was running 100 miles a week; and I was racing. There was no time to lose. It's hard to lay low when you've been on top, with the memory of what it's like to run with abandon. Friends would try to convince me not to worry: that I was the first, "the Arnold Palmer of running," and no matter what happened, no one could take that away from me. But I wasn't concerned about my place in running history; I just wanted to regain my old form.

I was also concerned with my business affairs and couldn't give my running the attention it needed. I would get it done, however — it was the one structured absolute in every day. It was ironic. Tormented that I couldn't get my running to work the way I wanted, it was my daily running, even in its defective state, that was giving me the balance to get by.

That fall I was fourteenth in the Virginia Ten-Miler, twenty-fourth in the Diet Pepsi national 10-kilometer championships, and twelfth in the New York Marathon. In Virginia, interestingly, I'd finished right behind Lasse Viren, who'd been injured himself. He would also run New York that fall, out of curiosity, he said. He was never in contention and dropped out somewhere in the last 6 miles. I ran it on one and a half legs and finished in 2:19:32. Bill Rodgers' time was 2:12:12, winning New York for the third straight year. There was more interest in the result of the women's competition, for it marked the marathon debut of a twenty-five-year-old schoolteacher from Oslo, Norway, who'd excelled in track and had entered the race at the last minute just for the experience. After Grete Waitz ran New York in 2:32:20, breaking the world record by over 2 minutes, women's distance running would never be the same.

In 1979 I felt flashes of my old self — I even beat Bill Rodgers twice in races two weeks apart in the summer — but I could not put together a good marathon. I ran miserably at Boston, finishing seventy-ninth in 2:21:56, and much better but still far behind at New York, finishing seventh in 2:16:15. Bill won both. The bad leg, apparently, was able to hold up for 6 miles or 10 miles, but not 26. It succumbed from lack of strength, throwing my form off. I could feel it and I could see it. After a race, examining the soles of my shoes, I saw the uneven wear pattern, indicative of the way I'd transferred the forces of my running primarily to the right side. I started to suspect that my troubles were connected to something more than the chronically weak muscles in my left leg.

I was desperate. I went into New York in '79 feeling I could be competitive again in the marathon, though perhaps not quite as competitive as some New York reporters were making it. Writeups of a Rodgers-Shorter showdown made for good copy but were charged more with emotion than reason. I just wanted to be close. I wasn't.

The next day I went to the hospital for the tests that would reveal the disturbances in my back. The doctors gave me more exercises to do and wanted me to stay in New York for a while so they could test me again. I couldn't. I had things to do. Maybe I should have. When you're a full-time athlete, you can hang around New York for two months, being rehabilitated by good doctors. But I had to get going. At least the source of my problem had been located, and I was hopeful that in time I'd be well.

☆

Some weeks later, it all became academic. If the Russians did not pull out of Afghanistan, said Jimmy Carter, America would boycott the Moscow Olympics. Carter stuck to his guns, and come spring, even the most diehard optimists realized the 1980 summer Olympics were in ruins. The debate over the boycott was moot. A new issue rose above it: What should be done for the U.S. athletes? What should be done with the Olympics once the nightmare was over? And a new concern became paramount for the Carter administration: how to get as many nations as possible to go along with the boycott.

The British went to Moscow. So did the French, the Finns, the Italians. Fifty-one nations sided with the U.S. and stayed home, but ninety did not. The biggest miscalculation the Carter people made was rooted in their insensitivity to the workings of international athletics. They assumed they'd have the leverage of the entire Western world behind them. Had they made an attempt to find out, they would have learned that, as the IOC provisions mandate, the Olympic committees of most nations are powerful, independent bodies that are not easily influenced by the political extremes of their governments — not when the Olympics are at stake. This was not the case in America, where the USOC was beaten down by Carter's threats. But it became very apparent elsewhere. Perhaps the best example was our closest ally, Great Britain, where the Olympic authorities voted to go to Moscow, and go they did despite the objections of the Thatcher government.

I took satisfaction in that. It showed that politics didn't *have* to come first. Sport counted, the Olympics mattered,

and what if the Games *were* in Moscow? If you could put
on the Games, if you could provide the facilities and personnel and housing, you deserved them. Munich, despite all
that happened, was a beautiful setting for the Olympics.
Maybe the best solution would be to give the Olympics a
permanent home, as some have advocated. It would make
good economic sense and save all the time and energy spent
in choosing the site. It would scale down the enormity of
the whole process. My vote would go to Helsinki — because
Finland is politically neutral; because being so close to the
Soviet Union, the Finns are experienced in dealing with
the Eastern bloc; they have an Olympic stadium that historically produces outstanding performances; and the weather
for athletics is fine there in the summer.

The British decision to go to Moscow gave the Olympics
Coe and Ovett, which was important for track and field
because it meant there would be two races at least that
would go largely unspoiled by the boycott. Sebastian Coe
and Steve Ovett were clearly the world's finest middle-dis-
tance runners and the talk of track. They'd met in competition only once, two years before, and everyone was anxious
to see them go head to head — twice — in Moscow. Different
in upbringing, personality, and running style, theirs was a
rivalry made in heaven — or at least in the British press.
Coe had broken three world records in 1979 and a fourth
in 1980. Ovett, going into Moscow, had won forty-three
straight races at 1,500 meters and the mile over a three-
year period and had, the month before, tied Coe's record
in the 1,500 and broken it in the mile. In Moscow they settled
nothing. Ovett won the 800; Coe ran like a rookie. Coe won
the 1,500 — he had to.

Any plan for an alternate Olympics was doomed to fail.
The athletes knew this from the start and didn't want it
anyway. There can be no substitute for the Olympics. As
the American decathlete Bob Coffman told Bruce Jenner,

a TV commentator, at a track meet that April: "Where would *you* be without the Olympics, Bruce?"

I had been hired, along with Jenner, to be part of the NBC team in Moscow. Even as the boycott grew, the network held out hope, and I was just as uncertain about NBC's plans as anyone, keeping up with things through the press and the grapevine. My bags, to be sure, were not packed. Finally, NBC took only a skeleton crew to Moscow, primarily for administrative reasons, and the Olympics were not shown in the States.

The Olympic Trials were. Though the qualifiers would be members of a "paper" team, it was important to carry on with the trials so that all of the athletes could complete the cycle. Scores of athletes had worked so hard and sacrificed so much to try to be in peak form in the spring and summer of 1980. If they couldn't have the Olympics, at least they could have the Olympic Trials. To deny them that would have been tantamount to ordering competitors off the track before the end of a race. The trials would also leave those who made the team, especially the young ones, with a taste of the real thing. There's something about going through the experience of the trials, even with little at stake, that makes you grow as an athlete. And a trials without the reward of an Olympics, in a perverse way, may demand even more of an athlete because an all-out effort must be put forth despite the absence of reward.

The track and field trials were held in Eugene again, and I almost competed in the 10,000 meters. I worked the trials for NBC with Jenner and anchorman Charlie Jones, and the TV people had agreed to let me run. I'd tried it the year before at the National Sports Festival in Colorado Springs. There I won the 10,000, then put on my TV hat, apparently no worse for the wear.

In Eugene, during my warmup, my back felt tight and would not loosen up. I looked down at my left leg and saw how weak it still was. The rehabilitation was slow. Then I realized it couldn't work. "Who am I kidding?" I told myself. "You're not going to be able to run with the leaders."

I don't race where I don't belong. And it's a funny feeling not to belong.

I scratched from the 10,000. It turned out to be a wonderful race, one of the best of the entire meet. Craig Virgin, the American record-holder at the time, tore out on a hot pace with Herb Lindsay in tow. Lindsay, who'd become a skilled road racer, couldn't hang on in this test of fine speed and fell away to ninth. Virgin, in control all the way, won in 27:45.61, an excellent time. Greg Fredericks was a distant second in 28:03.14. The third Olympian was a twenty-two-year-old University of Oregon runner named Alberto Salazar.

Salazar at that time had yet to run a marathon. One month before the track trials, the marathon trial was held in Buffalo, and that was the last time American marathoning would not be influenced by Alberto Salazar.

The date of the race was May 24, which also happened to be the deadline for nations formally to enter teams in the Moscow Olympics. Of the 225 men who'd qualified by running 2:21:54 or faster between April 16, 1979, and April 21, 1980, only 164 showed up to run. The boycott issue was all but buried, and there was a marathon to run. All the emotion and politics had been distilled to that: Twenty-six miles were waiting for us.

What was waiting for me? I knew I wasn't physically ready to run well, but I wanted to be in the race to support the trial and I needed to know how far I'd drifted from the level of marathon running I'd known. The evening before the race, watching Louise compete in a women's 10-kilometer run at nearby Grand Island, I told reporters: "If I run 2:25 tomorrow, I doubt you'll see me in too many races. I haven't been running badly enough to retire or well enough to enjoy it."

I ran 2:23:24 and came in eighty-fifth. At least I still had enough of a grip on things to sense what I could do. I was able to stay up with the leaders through 10 kilometers, but after that — pfft! The leg, the back, everything. One minute I was fine and the next minute — my legs wouldn't extend, my stride shortened and I was gone. It was so frustrating because mentally I was still able to push myself hard. I used just as much mental energy running 2:23 as I've used when I've run 2:10.

If I'd been physically whole and run that badly, I probably would have quit right then and there. But I hadn't lost the will; my body was in disrepair. It would get better. I'd been running my 100-plus miles a week but realized that all the training in the world was not going to overcome the handicap that had stricken me. I thought that if I could restore the strength to my left leg, I might be able to run a good marathon again. I felt I had to continue training and racing to see how I'd run once the impediment was gone, if for no other reason than peace of mind. When I do retire from major competition, I want it to be on my own terms.

CHAPTER SEVEN

Getting Fit

Steve Prefontaine was with me in both a workout and a race that illustrate two of the most important principles of successful running.

In February 1975, three months before Pre's death, we were skiing together in Taos, New Mexico. We were also running, and the harsh winter weather made for rather rough going. I recall one day in particular when we were out for a 10-mile run in the mountain trails where the altitude reached 10,000 feet. There was a blizzard raging, and the snow was blowing so hard across our faces we could barely see. Being familiar with such conditions, they came as less of a shock to me than to Steve, who lived in western Oregon away from the mountains. He was jabbering away, complaining. Steve was a great complainer, which masked his courage and belied his success as a runner. He'd even complain about a nice sunny day. It was part of his routine.

In the middle of that workout, at the height of his objection, I turned to Pre and said, "You know, nobody in the world is training harder than we are right now." Pre put his head down and didn't say a word for the rest of the workout.

The previous spring of 1974 had found me ill prepared for a 3-mile race against Pre in Eugene. I was finishing up law school in Gainesville, preparing to study abroad that summer in Warsaw, so Louise and I were in the middle of a move. For about a month my training was curtailed and I did no interval running, which has been the hallmark of my training program. The only element of intensity in my running that month was hill repetitions.

Louise and I left Florida and headed west with two cars, a U-Haul, all of our worldly possessions, and a Great Dane. We were on the road for a week, and all my running consisted of was two 40-minute jogs a day.

When I arrived in Eugene, Pre told me he wanted to shoot for the American 3-mile record, which was 12:53.0, and I agreed to share the pace. It wasn't a great day, either — the wind was kicking up in Hayward Field, and of course I was not in a record-conscious state of mind to begin with, and I told Pre. But I'm not one to back away from a challenge on the track, and we went for it together.

We'd decided that to get the record we'd try to key on the half-mile splits, which would have to be 2:09 or better. In effect, we set out to run half-mile "intervals," sharing the lead and knowing that at the end it would be each man for himself. The meet was called the Hayward Field Restoration Meet, to be renamed the Prefontaine Classic after Pre's death.

The wind was tough. But we were running on target, and it was a wonderful surprise to me as we circled the track in 64 and 65 seconds a lap that I was able to keep up with Pre. Based on my limited training, I should not have been running that well. "This is interesting," I told myself midway. "Let's see how long I can do this."

We sped along, and I actually managed to get 10 yards on Pre with 220 to go. I'd started my kick before he did. But Pre had 3:54-mile speed and sprinted ahead to win in record time, 12:51.4. I faded, but hung on to break the record myself in 12:52.0. The crowd went crazy. It was one of the most thrilling races I've ever run and the most satisfied I've ever been in defeat.

That was the closest anyone had ever come to beating the immensely popular Prefontaine at a distance of more than a mile on his home track, and to think that I did it in an event not my best, and when I had no business to theoretically, is an effort worth contemplating. It suggests a canon of running that has been critical to my success over the years, one that I believe is important for all runners who hope to achieve their potential: mental toughness.

It has to do with attitude and how you approach your training and competition. You have to be willing at times to be in over your head. You have to be able to operate when the odds are against you. You have to have an instinct for survival. In the middle of the 3-mile with Pre, I did not say to myself, "Wow, this is too fast. What am I going to do?" When it comes to success or failure, you have to set out your task and step toward it, not with a foolishly naive optimism, but with a sort of rational willfulness. This is both innate and something that can be developed to a degree.

Mental toughness is manifested in different ways — it is not confined to the midst of a high-powered race — and I consider it to be one of six primary factors in successful running. Another factor, exemplified in the blizzard run with Prefontaine, is distance consistency. We could have quit running that winter's day in Taos, or not started out at all. Would it have really mattered? How important is that 10-mile run when I'm running thousands of miles a year? It was not so much the 10 miles per se that were significant but the idea that we were out running, training, continuing with our scheduled workout, despite conditions of adversity. As runners, no matter what our ability, we are constantly seeking, and then treading, the fine line between running too much and running just enough. In due time, if we're lucky, we learn how much we can take, when we should back off, when we should press on. Running 10 miles in a blizzard at 10,000 feet is the sort of thing that makes me feel I can go as hard as I can when it really matters, that I've got the edge on the guy I'm going to compete against who submitted to the elements. This also brings up the relationship between the physical act of training, which is concrete, and the psychological ability to put that training to use in competition, which is somewhat abstract.

From my experience and observations in twenty years of running, I'd say mental toughness and distance consistency each account for 20 percent of the total running program. The most important factor is speedwork (30 percent); the remaining three elements are general experience (15 percent), rest (10 percent), and nutrition (5 percent).

☆

Running is developmental, and no matter how much talent you bring to it, the results you get will come from hard work more than anything else. This is a physiological fact. Almost anyone can become a runner and achieve success in it up to a point. This is not to say skill isn't involved — it is; only a few get to the Olympics. But for everyone there can be an accessible "Olympics" — the Boston Marathon, the local road race, whatever.

We are privileged as runners to be involved in a sport that provides immediate and constant feedback. Every run, every workout, is a learning experience. Every gain is tangible — you feel it when you're running well, and there's no greater feeling.

Training is both simple and complex. It is simple because essentially it involves one thing — running — sometimes fast, sometimes slow. It is complex because the human body is complex, and to take the body and groom it to run a given distance in a specified time and react to others trying to do the same is an extraordinary task. For all we know about running theory — and, believe me, there are no secrets — we don't know very much. I like it that way because I truly enjoy exploring the limits of fitness for myself. I like the idea that there is much to learn — about oneself as much as training theory — because one of the greatest challenges of my life has been to train myself to run at my best. Though competing well is the goal and is what people associate me with, I'm more interested in the process than in the result. I'm not obsessed with competing or with winning. What I am obsessed with is training; I know that if I'm well trained I'll compete well. My running goals are really training goals. Give me several months of unimpeded running and I'll be my happiest.

I train hard. I've had to because I've never felt I've had any special physiological gifts. It is my persistence coupled with an ability to keep my running in focus and to know how to train that I think has distinguished me from others with perhaps more talent.

It was this view of natural versus applied talent that made me reluctant to participate in the landmark study of distance runners conducted at the Institute for Aerobics Research in early 1975. I didn't think I would score very "high" on the physiological tests, and though they would reveal physiological patterns and not prove anything conclusive, I suppose I wasn't excited about the prospect of finding out, according to laboratory tests, that I wasn't supposed to be beating the people I'd been beating.

But I felt an obligation to scientific inquiry, so I went along with it. There were some good people in on the study, including Kenneth Cooper, M.D., of the institute, who made "aerobics" a household word, and David Costill, Ph.D., of Ball State University, who has become America's foremost exercise physiologist. Twenty of the twenty-four elite distance runners who were contacted agreed to participate in the study, including Kenny Moore, who wrote about it in *Sports Illustrated*. Sensitive to the cynicism that runners felt toward such tests at the time, Kenny wrote an initial letter to us all that stated:

> The experiences of top U.S. distance runners with physiological research in many cases have not been happy. Those of you who were on our last Pan-Am team or the Munich Olympic team will recall that on both occasions blood was taken from athletes under pretense that it was part of the routine physical examination necessary to be admitted to the team. In fact (we learned too late), it was part of someone's private study, the results of which have yet to be made known to those who participated. (In 1971, it was only the last man in line, Marty Liquori, who flatly refused to surrender his blood, was admitted to Colombia anyway, and so demonstrated to the rest of us how we had been taken.) The result of such abuses has been the growth of a very healthy suspicion of all doctors wielding needles. The purpose of this letter is to allay that suspicion with regard to the proposed study at the Dallas aerobics center. . . .

The findings came as no surprise. My resting pulse was 46, average for the marathon group. My body fat was 2.2 percent, lower (that is, "better") than average. Though these two factors do not predict performance, they are associated with being fit. There aren't too many men walking around with 2.2 percent body fat. Most experienced marathoners have less than 10 percent body fat; to have more is theoretically to hamper performance because more fat means more weight to carry and more tissue to fuel.

I was also found to have 80 percent slow-twitch muscle fiber and 20 percent fast-twitch, consistent with my affinity for the marathon. The muscle fiber test is considered a reliable indicator of the distance at which one can run best. The greater the percentage of slow-twitch, the more suited one is for distance running. (In the fiber test, a slice of tissue is excised from your leg, and I've never been excited about that. They tell you there's no damage left when they do that, but I can't believe it.)

In the test that seemed to "count" the most, I had the lowest score. This was the test for maximal oxygen uptake — VO_2 Max, they call it — a measure of how much oxygen you take in while running to exhaustion. When I stepped off the treadmill and was given my rate, I was not surprised. I scored 71.3, well below the average of 74.1 for the marathoners and 76.9 for the entire group of runners. Pre registered 84.4, one of the highest figures ever recorded.

However, even that test is not conclusive in distinguishing elite runners from one another. Other factors are instrumental, such as running "efficiency," and I was found to be the most efficient runner tested. I expend little energy even when I run at a good speed, and therefore I can use a large fraction of my maximal oxygen uptake, as much as 90 percent, for prolonged periods. In other words, this efficiency enables me to run at a fast pace for a long time. It may be why I run particularly well in the heat, too. When energy expenditure is high, the working muscles generate a great deal of heat, impeding performance, and of course this is exacerbated by warm weather.

I don't know if good running form has anything to do with it, but I've been able to train at an extremely intense level for most of my career. When I look over my old training logs, I find that in the decade from 1970 through 1979 I *averaged* 17 miles a day (mostly in double workouts) — even counting the months in 1973 when I was sidelined with a stress fracture in the foot and the months in 1978 when I was recovering from the surgery for a more serious foot injury. That's about 120 miles a week for ten years. That includes a good deal of hard, fast running and frequent competition — cross-country, track, road racing, and marathons.

Runners such as myself have to be able to tolerate this sort of training — because consistency is essential — but

the more intense it gets, the more we have to watch out
for signs of decay. It's ironic. We are tough and strong; yet
as we toughen up we also become fragile. The first time I
ever ran 100 miles in one week, in Gainesville in 1970, my
left knee ballooned, but in only two weeks' time I adapted
to it. Anyone can run to the brink — and for most people
it's a lot less than 100 miles a week — but you also have to
know when to back off. You have to know where the preci-
pice is. That's part of what excites me about running: trying
to hold a fine edge. I want to be sharp enough to compete
well and come as close to peak form as possible without
being stale.

You have to "know your body." It's part of the beauty
of the training process, and once you've determined how
much your body (and mind) can take, you can then begin
to reach your potential. As intensely as I've trained over
the years, I never felt I was training too hard. I always felt
I had a little more to give, even when I was running three
times a day at 8,000 feet to prepare for the Munich Olympics.

I think I've grown to know my body and exactly how it
reacts to running. I can detect subtle changes in the way I
run and feel, which better enables me to gauge the effort
I put in to running and the training effect I might derive.
I know when I'm fit, and why; I know when I'm not, and
why.

In 1975 I participated in a study in Tampa to test a method
devised by the East Germans to ascertain fitness levels in
distance runners. Using a computerized approach, blood
samples were analyzed to determine how much effort was
being put forth to run a certain time. The distance used
was 2 miles, and I felt I could run 8:30 at the time. As part
of the test, I was told to try and run at what I felt was a
75 percent effort for 2 miles on the track; my time was
8:51. The computer, given my blood samples, gave a printout
of 8:52. This showed that I could subjectively know how
much effort was needed to achieve a desired result.

Jogging to shape up, feel better, and ward off disease is one thing. Training for performance is quite another. While the running boom's overall rate of growth may have slowed in the eighties, the segment of the running population involved in competition has increased significantly. This has created a universe of athletes hungry for the training and racing methods best suited to achieving their goals. These people — some talented, some not — are just like the elite runners they come out to see at the big road races. Not many days go by when they don't wonder: How can I train to improve my running?

When I was at Yale and finally getting serious about running, I asked myself the same thing. I also asked my coach, Bob Giegengack, who taught me the sensible things to do. Seeing me as a potential marathoner, Gieg advised me to run more, to add to my mileage base and develop a stronger foundation. But that came toward the end of college; all along Gieg fed us intervals — fast, repeated runs that he monitored carefully to make sure none of us would overdo it. After college, in Gainesville, Jack Bacheler convinced me of the need for consistency, and later, Kenny Moore showed me there's a place for moderation as well. How can I claim moderation when I run 120 miles a week? It's all relative. I remember one workout in Eugene, with Kenny Moore, before the 1972 Olympic Trials. We were moving along at a 6-minute pace, and after 22 miles I stopped and got in the car our wives were driving to give us drinks along the way. He continued to 38 miles. But for the next couple of days he jogged only a few miles; I did my 17 a day.

You have to know yourself — your goals and what works — and then balance the elements. I've not had a coach since college, but my training, in principle, has been largely the same since. I saw that what made sense in theory really worked because I watched over my conditioning carefully and tested it in competition. And I'm not above reevaluation. Preparing to bid for the 1984 Olympic team, I consulted in particular with Bill Dellinger of the University of Oregon. Dellinger, who has worked with Alberto Salazar and other leading runners, won the 5,000-meter bronze medal in the 1964 Olympics, at the age of thirty-one. I figured he knew something about "older" folks doing well in the Olympics.

I'm a creature of habit — most serious runners have to be — and from week to week there's little variation in my training. I run twice a day Monday through Saturday and once on Sunday, when I take my longest run of the week. My morning runs begin at eleven, by which time I feel loose and energetic, and my second sessions, which are reserved for speedwork twice a week, are done in the late afternoon, before dinner.

I run 20 miles on Sunday. Rarely will the pace be slower than 6:30 per mile, and when I'm fit and in the groove I'll run the second half of the workout at close to 5 minutes per mile. At times, when I've been really sharp, such as before the Montréal Olympics, I've run the first 10 miles at 5:40 and the second 10 under a 5-minute pace. I'm a great believer in accelerating the pace in the course of a workout so that the fastest running is done at the end because in competition, late-race strength and speed are frequently called for. Historically, the marathon has been different, but even that is changing, and now we see the top runners actually "kicking" during the last 5 kilometers.

The 20-miler tires me, but I find that the quickest recovery comes after these faster-paced efforts. That's because I have to be terribly fit to be able to run a fast 20-miler, and a by-product of fitness is faster recovery power. It's a wonderful feeling to know the elements are working together in a kind of symbiosis, and as you develop you crave that feeling, both for its own sake and for what it signifies for your racing performance.

Monday is a recovery day. For me that's 7 miles in the morning at 7 minutes a mile and 10 miles in the afternoon at a 6:30 pace. This is a form of rest, and it must follow any intense workout. Hard running demands a great deal of the body, and to get the full value of intensified training you have to balance it with some form of recovery. For some runners that means an hour's jog or even a day off; for me it's a comfortable 17 miles.

On recovery days I rest my mind as well as my body. I free-associate — what sports psychologists call disassociating. I sink into a relaxed pace, put myself on automatic pilot, and let anything pop into my head, as though I were falling asleep. When I run hard I focus on the effort and monitor it.

There are two sets of controls at work here, each representing not only a different training mode but different needs, joys, and personality traits. On my easy runs I escape. It's been my method of stress management ever since college, when I needed a break from the rigors of academia at Yale. Now it's the stress of business. Some people have a three-martini lunch; I go out and run. And when I do I just flow along in the foothills around Boulder. When it's warm and I can take my shirt off and I'm out there getting a tan, lost in thought, it's a happy time, therapeutic, restful, and exhilarating all at once. I feel good because *I feel good running.*

The hard running is different fun. The intense work gives me a feeling of accomplishment. I set goals and try to reach them.

On Tuesday I run 7 miles in the morning at a 6:30- to 7-minute pace. In the afternoon I run fast. To warm up I jog for 2 miles, then stride four 110s at three-quarter speed. I don't stretch. I find I don't have to; perhaps the speedwork keeps me loose. I'll sometimes stretch before a race, but that's only to use up some nervous energy. If I didn't stretch I'd probably run, and I don't like to run too much (not more than 2 miles) before a race.

Typically, my Tuesday afternoon speedwork will consist of ¾-mile repetitions done on a track. I'll jog 660 yards (half the distance of the fast repetition) between each run and, at the mile-high altitude of Boulder, I shoot for times of 3:15, 3:12, 3:11, and 3:09 for the set. At sea level my goal might be 3:12, 3:09, 3:08, and 3:06, and I would shorten the rest interval to a 440. When the repetitions are over I jog 2 or 3 miles to "warm down."

Wednesday is the same as Monday, a recovery day, a total of 17 miles easy. On Thursday I'll resume speedwork. I repeat the morning 7-miler, then hit the track in the afternoon for quarter-mile repetitions. I might run twelve 440s in 62 seconds with a 220-yard jog between them. At sea level I would either speed up the 440s to 60 or 61 seconds or reduce the rest intervals to 110 yards.

Speedwork does not have to be done on a track or as an interval session. Herb Lindsay, one of the country's best road racers, sticks to the road for his speedwork. He's very good, for example, at running hard for 3 minutes, easy for 1 minute, and repeating that over and over again. He can run anyone into the ground in this kind of workout. I've asked him about it. He says he avoids the track because he doesn't like to know how fast he's going. I'm just the opposite. I can run faster when I know my precise pace. I thrive on trying to maintain tempo.

Good form is my most important asset, and if it's not there, I'm giving something to the opposition. When I'm at my best you can see it in the way I run. I look straight ahead, keeping my torso upright and over my center of gravity. I don't tilt my body or sway my shoulders. My arms thrust easily up and back, not side to side, where energy is wasted. I get my knees up but not so much that I overstride. It's a fluid, natural movement, not something I've had to learn. It's the one significant talent I've brought to my running.

Runners can learn to improve their form and increase

their efficiency, and that's where a coach is helpful; he or she can spot errors and suggest on-the-spot adjustments in body lean, arm carriage, knee lift, and the like. There is no one "correct" way to run, rather, certain principles of good form that theoretically apply to different events. "Ideal" running form in the marathon differs from "ideal" running form in the mile. Usually, as your fitness level improves your form improves, because you're stronger and more able to tolerate stress and run in control. Perhaps the best advice is to concern yourself first with getting in good shape and then worry about whether you may be carrying your arms a little too high.

After Thursday's speed session I'm due for recovery, so on Friday I repeat the relaxed running of Monday and Wednesday. On Saturday I might have a race; if not, I run an easy 7 miles in the morning and another 10 miles in the afternoon, jogging 2 miles, running a near-5-minute pace for 7 miles, finishing with a 1-mile jog.

That's 120 miles for the week. At sea level, putting in the same effort, I'd end up running 140 miles a week.

☆

Because I've been able to train that way for months at a time, I've found myself in consistently good shape for competition without having to undergo much additional intensity to reach peak form for major events. There are two philosophies with regard to peaking. One holds that once you're racing fit, you should take advantage of it and compete regularly for the possible reward of victory or faster times. The other idea holds that you should delay gratification and try to win, or do your best, in only a few important races a season. The second approach has worked better for me. I may race a lot, but I'll train "through" many races and peak only for a chosen few.

Historically, the peakers — the real peakers, who pick

their spots — win at the Olympics. Look at Lasse Viren or Waldemar Cierpinski or Kip Keino or Miruts Yifter or even me. There's something about the level of intensity of an Olympic race that's different from all other competition. An athlete must be willing to put all of himself into an Olympics; there can be no holding back. It's easier to fulfill that commitment, both physically and emotionally, if you haven't totally committed yourself too many times before. It's almost impossible for a distance runner to do both — to race frequently in top form in major competitions year in and year out and also fare well in the Olympics.

Ron Clarke of Australia is remembered both for his string of world-record performances — at every distance from 2 miles through 10,000 meters — and his failure to win at the Olympics and British Commonwealth Games. Clarke was a strange bird. He'd smash records in obscure places; he wanted only to run fast. I don't believe he really cared about the Olympics. I suppose he, and others like him, needed the periodic reinforcement of the victory or the record. That type of runner doesn't intimidate me.

I *was* intimidated by Lasse Viren. I remember sitting in the holding room in Montréal before the 1976 Olympic marathon, watching him. There I was, the defending Olympic champion, and what was I doing? Studying Viren, watching him lace up his shoes as though I were waiting for his autograph.

There's nothing I respect more in a runner than mental toughness and control. Clarke may have been out of control. He would train hard, get in good shape, and figure, "Okay, let's go find a race." Viren, at his best, was always in control. He had the peaking process down pat. There's not much difference in physical ability among the top runners. The difference lies, I think, in emotional cunning and tenacity, put to use in the style of preparation and in the competition itself.

It's what makes a good competitor. I've drawn my confidence and competitive readiness from the security of knowing I've trained well and peaked properly. And when I've done well, it's not that I was necessarily in better physical condition than those I beat. Rather, I was better able to respond to the competition. That's why I beat Ron Hill and the others in Munich — and why Cierpinski beat me in Montréal. I was ready to respond in Montréal. Cierpinski was readier.

By the same token, no matter how racing smart you might be, you can't compete at your best unless you're prepared. I remember a workout in the summer of 1975 in Milan in which I ran sixteen 440s in 63 seconds, with only a 50-yard jog between each one. Given such a short rest interval, it was a tremendous workout. I knew I was fit, and that season I ran very well, winning some big races on the European circuit and hitting a lifetime best of 27:46 for 10,000 meters.

Another time, in Oslo before the '72 Olympics, I ran a workout of four 880s in 2:03, 2:02, 2:01, and 2:00, with only a 220 jog between each one. Giegengack was there and commented, "Jesus, you're in shape!" I knew I was. Later in the week I was running in the outskirts of town with two Italians, Francesco Arese, a savvy miler, and Giusepe Cindolo, a marathoner. Arese turned to me and said, *"Tu gagnera le marathon."* "You will win the Olympic marathon." (They didn't speak English and I spoke no Italian, but we all knew some French and could converse during the run.) He was not blowing smoke at me. He'd seen me run in Italy and saw a 3,000-meter race I'd run in Oslo that week. I hadn't won it but showed good speed at the short distance for someone training for the marathon. I guess Arese was impressed, and I used his faith to build my confidence.

Though speedwork has been the critical ingredient in my training recipe, I've come to my best performances by way of varying measures of intensity. In the fall I'd run longer repetitions of 1 or 2 miles on Tuesdays, which seemed to strengthen me for the national cross-country championships, which I've won four times. The meet is held in late November, usually one week before the Fukuoka Marathon, and the strength I carried into the fall and augmented with longer repetitions would be sufficient preparation for Fukuoka. I never really had to train any harder than usual for Fukuoka, though I always considered it my fall peak.

Before the Munich Olympics, on the other hand, I did intensify my running quite a bit. I'd never run as hard as I did that spring and summer of '72 — nor have I since. Jack Bacheler and Jeff Galloway, who also made the '72 Olympic team, were my running companions in my chosen training ground of Vail, Colorado, 8,000 feet above sea level. At one stage in the spring we were running three times a day: 160 miles one week, 170 miles the next, then back down to our normal 130. We were exhilarated with the challenge of riding the line between intensity and excess; and remember, 170 miles at 8,000 feet is equivalent to 200 miles at sea level. And this included speedwork. With it all, I felt in control. Never did I feel I was overdoing it, and still I was convinced that nobody else in the world could have been training that hard. Whether that was true or not, it was one thing that motivated me.

The more running you do, the trickier the process of tapering off before competition. I find I can't cut back too much because my body is accustomed to a certain amount of stress, and I start to feel edgy if I run too little when I'm really fit. I'll cut my mileage by 25 percent before an important race, more before the Olympics because I want the Olympics to feel extraordinary.

For me, every race is a test of will, especially when I *am* fit, because then my personal standards are high and I don't want to disappoint myself. There comes a point in a race — two points, actually — when, consciously or not, you persist or you give in. It first hits you in midrace. If the pace is hard you start to feel a discomforting strain — I won't call it pain — and wonder how long you can keep it up. Your body is closing in on the threshold of "oxygen debt," but I find that if you try to maintain your rhythm and push through it you'll conquer the "barrier," because the pace will usually slow down and the reinforcement of having held on will spur you further. You're outsmarting your body's physical signs of distress. Of course, if you're not fit to begin with, you'll crash. But if you are fit you'll have a built-in margin of performance you can reach for, and that's why, if you're tough enough, you'll be able to pull through this zone.

Toward the end of the race the challenge comes up again. With a few laps to go the tempo picks up and the kick begins, and then you *do* go into oxygen debt, which means you're running "anaerobically" — you're unable to take in and circulate enough oxygen to fuel your muscles. That hurts. Can I do it? you wonder. It happens to me all the time. But mentally I know I can do it — I can accelerate despite the fatigue — because I've done it in training.

Every speed workout I do is basically increasing the intensity to simulate race conditions. That's how a 5,000 or 10,000 is run at the international level; the marathon, too, favors late-race strength. And that's what's called for: *strength.* It's your ability to run fast while in oxygen debt, and that's a function of strength as much as pure speed.

☆

When my running is going well, people can see it in my everyday demeanor. I'm more focused, I guess. But it's not that I'm thinking about running or daydreaming about it; I try not to. I want my time spent running to serve as a reward; I don't want it to take over every aspect of my life.

There's always that danger. As athletes, we can become victimized by our devotion. I try very hard to lead a normal life — to have interests outside of sports and not neglect my business and family — and that's been difficult. But I know I can never be totally separated from my training. Everything I do — eating, sleeping, traveling, going out — affects my training, and that's a good reason to have an off-season, when the urgencies of running can be moderated. But I am still at it year-round, and when you run 15 to 20 miles a day every day, you have to give up things.

I've tried to make the most of my traveling, and when I was a regular on the European summer circuit, I tried to do as much sightseeing as I could. I saw that as a way to balance the compulsions of running. I recall one summer in the early seventies when a bunch of us were barreling around Finland in an old Saab, going from meet to meet. We wanted to experience an authentic Finnish sauna, so a meet promoter, Jaako Tuominen, found one for us in the woods. Steve Prefontaine and Ralph Mann (an intermediate hurdler) and Jere van Dyk (a miler) and I hiked a mile or two into the woods, where we were treated to a sauna that was heated by a wooden stove and built over a lake. It's customary to jump into the lake after a sauna, and that we did. The Finns believe that the cold right after the heat is good for you. I agree, and I'll try anything Lasse Viren does.

☆

When it comes to children and running, I believe it's not in a child's best interest to train too hard before total physical maturity. There are mental scars left when a young runner does too much too soon and, according to some of the medical experts, the potential for physical damage as well. Parents should encourage their children to do a bit of running at an early age, but only to develop an interest in the sport for health reasons.

The attention given the competitive performances of children is disturbing. Success as a young runner probably is a function of how fast one matures and does not indicate any real talent. If children enjoy running, there will be plenty of time eventually for them to train and be a part of the sport. Let them enter races at an early age to acquire a sense of competition and pacing, but only at its most basic level and for the fun of it. We all go through a self-selection process, and it's best for children to try different sports; when they're ready they'll choose what they feel they're best at, based primarily on body type. Pushing a child into intense running and hoping for future success when you don't even know his or her physical predisposition makes no sense.

More and more distance runners are now experimenting with weight training, and I'm one of them. I've come to believe that high repetitions with low weights, if done sensibly, can be beneficial to performance. I work on my upper body and find that the weights help my finish in a race by giving my arms more power so I can drive better in what is my version of a sprint. It can make me 2 or 3 seconds faster over the last 400 meters. Upper body strength also helps my training because it enables me to do my speedwork at a faster pace.

I don't work on my legs much (except in a therapeutic sense, to correct a muscle imbalance) because I have a tendency to aggravate my muscles by overdoing it; besides, my lower body gets enough of a workout from running.

I use the Nautilus system rather than free weights, which are probably just as good, except I can never be sure I'm using them properly. The Nautilus routine is structured and, on stationary apparatus, safer. I do the full Nautilus circuit except for the legs: the arms, shoulders, back — the entire upper body. I'll do this two or three times a week, and I'd recommend it to any runner looking for that extra edge.

Which brings us to the subject of food. I must say that

reports of my unorthodoxy have been grossly exaggerated. Contrary to what has been written, I don't eat a lot, I don't drink a lot, and I don't eat much junk food. I'm conservative when it comes to nutrition. I don't subscribe to any exotic theories; I don't even eat that much when it comes to carbohydrates. I try to maintain a well-balanced diet. I enjoy an occasional snack and a beer. That's it. I do believe nutrition is important in running and that once you arrive at the kind of diet that works best for you, it should become an extension of your training program in terms of consistency. It helps to eat the same kinds of food from one day to the next.

Because my first workout is at eleven, I'll eat an early breakfast that might include cereal, fruit, toast, and coffee. Lunch is light because of my second workout and generally includes a few cookies, and a little bread and cheese or peanut butter for protein, as opposed to any kind of meat, which is difficult to digest. I never have a salad for lunch because I don't digest it well. I don't know how weight-conscious runners have a salad for lunch and then run later on. I eat a full dinner — mostly with chicken, occasionally fish or veal, and once in a while steak — including dessert and a couple of beers. I like pasta, but I'm not a fanatic about it. I do increase my carbohydrate intake before an important race, especially a marathon. Aside from stocking the fuel supply, I find that with tapering my running I get nervous; when I get nervous I get hungry, and carbohydrates are easiest to digest. Actually, I prefer rice to spaghetti as a starch. Altogether, I probably take in less than 3,000 calories a day, which is not much for the running I do but seems to be enough for me.

My weight is a fairly stable 132 pounds, and at 5 feet 10½ inches I'm obviously an ectomorph. But many runners aren't, and there is a real danger in trying to become one through heavy running and uncompromising dieting. Don't try to be something you're not; it's not healthy.

When it comes to food, many runners have unconventional habits. Jeff Galloway comes to mind. In Vail, during that intense training period in 1972, Jeff ate almost nothing but liver. We asked him why, but he couldn't say. But he made the Olympic team. To this day it's the only red meat he ever eats.

The Italians, not surprisingly, are the biggest eaters on the running circuit. I was always amazed at how much a guy like Franco Fava could eat. An old friend of mine who was eighth in the 1976 Olympic marathon, Fava is now the director of the Rome Marathon — and a chain smoker. He and the other Italians could eat a three-course lunch, nap, run, and come back for a full dinner. They'd train as I did but take in twice the calories. But that's a part of their culture and it works for them. Fava would have gone crazy on peanut butter for lunch.

☆

As I said at the outset, the principles that have guided my running can be adapted to almost any runner's program. I'd like to make a few last recommendations for runners of different ability and commitment — and bear in mind that men and women can train in the same fashion.

New runners trying to get in shape

If you haven't been active, get your doctor's approval before starting out.

Buy a pair of running shoes from a reputable retailer. (I can't suggest one brand over another.) Don't believe anything you read about shoe "ratings." We're all different in the way we run, and an experienced salesperson will know how to fit you according to your body type and level of running. After that it's trial and error.

Gradually work yourself up to the point where you can

run for 30 minutes three times a week. To develop your heart muscle and for an overall training effect, you should get your pulse rate up over 120 beats per minute — but that should happen naturally because you'll be unfit to begin with and your pulse will be high.

Give yourself two months, then decide if you like to run. If not, consider a different aerobic activity to improve your fitness, such as swimming, biking, or walking.

Novice runners hoping to compete
After three to six months of running, during which time you've progressed from three days a week to five and are putting in 20 miles a week, you're prepared to run your first race.

The distance should be no longer than 10 kilometers (6.2 miles). Run it safely — just to finish.

Consider it as just another training run, only a bit longer. You'll see how your excitement makes the effort easier than you expected.

Experienced runners hoping to improve their racing times
At this point, which should come after at least six months of running, you need to increase your distance to 25 miles a week and add a small dose of speed to your program.

All the speedwork need consist of is a weekly foray to a nearby track. Jog a mile. Run one fast quarter-mile lap, then one slow one for recovery. Do that three more times for a total of four repetitions. You want your pace to be a little faster than your goal pace for 10 kilometers. If you're racing the 10K at an 8-minute-mile pace, make sure your fast laps are better than 2 minutes; say, 1:45 to 1:50. Jog a mile to finish up. That's your introduction to speed training, which cannot be done effectively until you've acquired an aerobic base.

Competitors trying to run their first marathon

Make one of your weekend runs at least 10 miles so that your weekly mileage climbs to 30, and gradually increase that long run to 15 miles and do it once a week.

Continue to do the weekly speed session — on the track or roads or a golf course — wherever it's possible.

Add a sixth day of running to your week, and take one of your runs at a sustained stepped-up pace — roughly the same pace at which you hope eventually to run the marathon.

All this will now give you three days of accelerated running a week; they should alternate with three days of slow recovery running.

Add a few miles here and there to your schedule so that you're running 50 miles a week for a month before the marathon.

Race more regularly for the experience.

Your first marathon should not come until you have at least one year of running under your belt.

Marathoners hoping to run well below 3 hours and to lower their other racing times as well

Depending upon your specific goals and ability, gradually advance to 70 or 80 miles a week and generally intensify your training.

Add a second interval workout. Do one session of long intervals (a mile or mile and a half) and the other of short intervals (440s or 880s).

Try not to run less than 10 miles any day you run. Decide whether you can manage to run seven days a week.

Advanced competitors hoping to reach national-class caliber

Keep the same mileage, about 80 a week, but increase the intensity of the speedwork.

Your weekly long run should be a steady 15 to 20 miles.

Your weekly sustained run of 6 to 7 miles should be close to your 10-kilometer racing pace.

Shorten the recovery time between your fast repetitions, and since the intensity of the intervals is the key element, be sure to run comfortably on the easy days.

Top runners trying to become world class

Do my workouts, or a reasonable facsimile.

The essential difference between the training of national-class competitors and that of Olympic contenders is that the Olympic hopeful is running twice a day so that his mileage is up over 100 a week while he is also doing a healthy amount of fast running of significant intensity.

☆

What fascinates me most about the sensation of running is how it seems to compress time. If I run a hard interval session, it feels as though it's over in no time. A 45-minute run on the road feels like 20 minutes (while a 45-minute session on the exercise bike feels like an hour and a half). A hard marathon, especially if I've run it well, seems to fly by, and subjectively the elapsed time feels like 30 minutes, even though it takes more than 2 hours.

It's an odd feeling, and I think it comes from the powers of concentration that go into a hard effort. You're so intent and tuned in on the act that you forget you're doing it . . . and suddenly it's over, like the quiet you feel when a dripping faucet has been shut tight.

It's a powerful consciousness. I marvel at the body's ability to undergo an altered perspective when put under a great effort. What I do when I'm running hard should feel harder to do than it does. However, when I'm watching someone else do it, none of the same feeling exists. If I watch another

runner do sixteen quarters on the track, it seems awesome.
I remember watching Steve Prefontaine run 13:22.8 to set
an American record in the 5,000 meters at the 1972 Olympic
Trials and saying to myself, "How can anyone run that fast?"
Then I reminded myself that *I* could run that fast.

Realizing that meant a lot to me.

CHAPTER EIGHT

Getting Hurt

The physical disabilities that have nagged at me for years have as their origin an indoor workout on a Tuesday afternoon in February 1976. The Montréal Olympics were less than six months away. I was full of hope and confidence, buoyed by a productive period of training in which I'd advanced from my track success of '75 into the months when I would try to become as fit as possible in preparation for the Games.

Everything was fine; then — pop.

Usually, that's how it happens: unsuspectingly. You feel good; then suddenly something hurts. The body has its way of dropping hints, but committed runners frequently miss them. And when we do see them, we like to look the other way. It's denial, pure and simple.

I think I've finally outgrown it. In time, most runners do. But on that fateful afternoon, there was little to suggest that I'd eventually come apart over the next two years. I felt only a tremor. Not even a pop, really. No snap, no crackle. Just a little pain.

It happened during my second workout of the day. After a 12-mile run in the hills that morning, I went over to the

University of Colorado in the afternoon for speedwork. The university has a 220-yard indoor track with a synthetic surface, fine for the sort of anaerobic running I like to do at least twice a week. For a warmup, I jogged the 2 miles from my home, then jogged some more once inside. The speedwork consisted of six repeat 880s with a 440-yard jog between each one. I'd been doing that kind of workout for years, and I'd try to run each succeeding 880 a drop faster than the one before. I had some short indoor track races coming up and needed to have that ability. I ran the first 880 in 2:12. On the second I hit 2:11. Then 2:10, 2:09, 2:08, and 2:07.

On the third repetition, my left foot started to hurt. I felt it on the inside of the foot in the middle of my ankle. It was a pulling sensation, pronounced, but more like a cramp than a sharp pain. It was the type of ache you'd feel if you jammed your toe up against the front of your shoe. I don't know what caused it. I didn't do anything differently that day. It was my customary Tuesday afternoon workout. I warmed up and felt loose. I was not overtraining or overracing. I wasn't ill. I wasn't wearing new shoes or trying anything novel. On that third 880 I didn't plant my foot wrong or break stride or step on anything. I felt in harmony with my body.

It just happened. Injuries can be that way. They can creep up on you and turn your training world upside down. The body, for all of its strength and resilience, is an organism just waiting to get injured. The cumulative effect of years of running can cause some dysfunction in the body's systems, and there you are one day with a pain in the left foot.

It's like the sound wave built by a tuning fork: It starts out as a little hum, then vibrates harder and harder until something cracks. Only you don't always feel the vibrations building within your body.

Doctors and physiologists are now finding ways to predict

the onset of injury. It's an inexact science. You need to be tested regularly so they'll know when a certain variation — say, in blood composition — constitutes a reason to stop running for a while.

The pain in my foot, though medically severe, was not so severe that it immobilized me. I continued my workout unimpeded and jogged home from the track with nothing more noticeable than a mild discomfort.

I did nothing to treat it because the pain went away. The problem was that the pain came back.

☆

Two years later only surgery could take it away. Because the injury would go into remission, modulating its impact on my running, I didn't feel the need to curtail my training or find medical help. After all, I was running well, and winning — though not winning enough: *second* in the Montréal Olympics; *second,* three months later, in the 1976 New York Marathon. I suppose the sensible thing to have done, by late '76, would have been to back off and direct my energies toward clearing up the problem. But things were happening so fast in the sport that I couldn't let go and spend time hunting around for the right doctor. And I couldn't face the fact that something was really wrong. It was easier to hope it would go away. It *would* go away but never stay away. The pain would recur on the side of the foot and migrate up to the mid-arch area, in the region of the joint that lies just in front of the ankle and slightly to the inside of the foot.

Dr. Stan James called this spot the talonavicular joint, part of a series of three joints in the hindfoot that adapt the foot to the surface on which it's placed. James is an orthopedic surgeon from Eugene, Oregon, who specializes in treating runners. I had known of him as a figure in sportsmedicine, and we met in November 1977 at a road race in

Phoenix. By that time, the condition had deteriorated considerably and I could not run the race; I'd dropped out of the New York Marathon the previous month. Still, the race director in Phoenix implored me to help promote the event and participate in a clinic, in which James was also involved. He examined my foot briefly in Phoenix and found tenderness over the talonavicular joint. I told him that the pain on the side of the foot had grown worse that summer and while competing in Europe I had been treated for it; after that, as he found, the pain seemed to localize more in the joint near the ankle.

He advised me not to run for a month and then start again gradually. I agreed. By early February 1978 I was able to run for almost an hour without pain and even managed to place seventh in a 15-kilometer road race. A month later I was up over 100 miles a week again, but a short time after that the foot pain began again spontaneously. Uncharacteristically, I took an anti-inflammatory medication, to allow me to run the Boston Marathon in April. I placed twenty-third in 2:18:15. My luck had run out. The next day I called James and a week later flew out to Eugene. The day after that, April 26, I had the operation.

I was a desperate man when I arrived in Eugene. Something had to be done about my foot. The pain was worse than ever. For months I'd worried that my career as a world-class athlete was in jeopardy. Now it was apparent I might not be able even to jog anymore unless a solution were found.

When James examined the left foot, he felt tenderness over the top part of the arch in the area of the talonavicular joint. He said, as well, that there was roughness and irregularity over the area with a slight grinding sensation. X-rays of the foot revealed bone spurs on either side of the joint. Earlier X-rays had not exposed the bone spurs, but James used a three-dimensional X-ray technique known as tomography, which provided a more detailed look at the joint.

Though injuries to the midfoot are common to runners, they are not as common as injuries to other parts of the body, such as the heel, lower leg, and knee. The forces of running, though they originate in the foot, are driven up through the leg with considerable power, and if injury is going to occur for one reason or another, pain will tend to locate *above* the foot. This is true even when an abnormality in the foot is the root of the problem. Similarly, bone spurs — excess pieces of bony matter that can be caused by continued pressure on an area of irritation, sometimes a result of nature's misdirected attempt to heal an injury — are not uncommon in runners but far less likely to occur than, say, tendinitis. To have bone spurs in the midfoot was to have a fairly unusual running injury. James told me he hadn't seen precisely this injury before and that he could not pinpoint the reason for it because it had developed over a period of two years. He postulated that initially it may have been a ligament tear with "continued insults," eventually causing chronic inflammation and ligament degeneration, with spur formation on either side of the joint. In other words, I hurt my foot and didn't take care of it.

James told me surgery was probably the only answer. I knew he was right. Time was running out, and I had visions of never running again. I knew the surgery would be risky; James himself said so. But I knew he was good. He'd treated Alberto Salazar and Mary Decker and other runners whose futures depended on the normal working operation of their legs and feet. He was a skilled surgeon and his usually conservative approach impressed me. Also, as an athlete himself — he skis cross-country, lifts weights, and runs up to 60 miles a week — he could be sensitive to the emotional trauma I was going through. He knew what it meant *not* to run.

Anytime you do surgery, James said, there's always the chance that you'll never come back fully. He made no promises, and I asked for none. But without the surgery, I knew there was the possibility, given the likely progression of the injury, that eventually I wouldn't be able to jog around the block without pain. More than any other motivating factor in my running success is that I simply love to run. That underlies everything — the great feeling I get from the act of running. Above all else, I needed to have that.

The wait-and-see approach initiated by James the previous fall in Phoenix matched the view of medicine I'd seen in my father. Doctors are notorious for putting things off if they can. When I was a kid, I had terrible tonsils, but my father wouldn't let them come out until it was absolutely necessary. I must have had tonsillitis fifteen times or more. Finally, when I was twelve, they were taken out. They were among the biggest, most scarred tonsils the surgeon had ever seen.

I knew James wouldn't have recommended surgery if it were not absolutely necessary. From my father's work and from having attended medical school, however briefly, I was familiar with some of the procedures and knew that the riskiest part of the operation was the anesthesia.

For the foot surgery, then, I asked for a spinal blockage, a local anesthetic that numbs you from the waist down, rather than the more conventional general anesthetic that puts you out entirely. And even with a mild dosage, I almost nodded out. I didn't want to. I liked the idea of being conscious during the operation. It was a funny feeling, to be paralyzed from the chest down and be cognizant of it.

The surgery was performed in Eugene Hospital, across the street from James' office at the Orthopedic and Fracture Clinic. I was staying with Kenny Moore, and he drove me to the hospital on the morning of April 26. The surgery took about an hour. James was assisted by a visiting physician from Europe, a technician, an anesthesiologist, and a nurse. I was as relaxed as possible under the circumstances and, as is my nature, optimistic. I had faith.

At one point I was struck by what seemed to me the impreciseness of something thought to be as scientifically exact as surgery. Awake, I could hear pieces of conversation. Toward the end, when they were about ready to close, James said something like, "Well, I think we should burr this down a little more just to make sure." It occurred to me that all through the operation he'd been making such judgments based on what he saw inside my foot.

James removed the bone spurs and smoothed out the area. Degeneration of the ligaments that normally connect the two bones in this area was also found and excised. Fortunately, James told me, the major part of the joint appeared to be in very good condition. The injury largely involved the tissues crossing the top of the joint.

I stayed in the hospital overnight. Because I hadn't received a general anesthetic, I didn't have to suffer through the post-operative hangover that usually accompanies it. My foot and leg were placed in a cast, from the knee down. The foot swelled during the night and they had to split the cast to reduce the swelling; then a new cast was made.

I went back to Kenny's. Not surprisingly, word about the surgery had gotten around, and a reporter from the *Eugene Register-Guard* — probably the best "track paper" in the country — wanted to interview me. Sure, why not, I thought. The next day I sat amid the blooming flower garden in Hendricks Park talking to a sportswriter as though I'd just competed at Hayward Field. Only this time I thought not about victory or defeat, but when, and if, I'd be able to run again.

☆

Armed with exercise charts and instructions from James, I returned home to Boulder. The cast was to be on for a month. I was to do no exercise for two weeks, then launch into a program of rehabilitation that would consist of working out on a stationary bicycle and doing isometric exercises. I could not resume running until early July, ten weeks after the surgery, and then only if there were no signs of trouble in the left foot. The running, at first, would be minimal and the rehab work would continue, to be dropped only when total strength was regained and the running became substantial enough to yield a training effect.

All this sounds great, but it was awful. For someone who had run almost every day for ten years — twice a day, at that — not running for weeks on end was very hard on me. It was as though something precious had been taken away, and I didn't know how to react. I became irritable, more introverted, harder to live with. I guess I exhibited the sort of behavioral changes — withdrawal, if you will — that even recreational runners manifest when brought to a halt. The only injury that had ever immobilized me before was a stress fracture in the left arch in 1973, when my father put the foot in a cast to make sure I wouldn't run on it.

Healthy runners take their luck for granted. As soon as that health is taken away, they become angry and then, in my case, contemplative. During my layoff I realized how lucky I had been to be able to run for so long, and so well. I thought a lot on those hard days about what I'd accomplished and what I'd failed to accomplish. I'd considered my second-place finish at Montréal my biggest disappointment. It was a setback not easily put aside. But as I hobbled around in my cast and worked off my frustrations on the exercise bike, my failure to win a second Olympic marathon seemed remote and unimportant.

The rehab worked well, or so it seemed. I rode the bike to maintain cardiovascular fitness and I did the isometrics for muscular fitness. The idea was to be ready to run when the ten weeks were up. To abandon all exercise while on the mend is to invite further injury upon taking on the stresses of running again.

I was on the bike for more than an hour a day. I didn't

enjoy it, but I knew it was right, and it did provide me with an energy release. I rode it vindictively. As I later learned, I put more into it than was necessary; 30 to 45 minutes a day is sufficient to give you the fitness you need.

The exercise bike, or ergometer, has become a popular form of "alternative" conditioning. Runners have been using it, not only as a rehab tool, but also as a supplement to their running even when they are at full strength. One of the ergometer's biggest proponents is Dr. Alex Ratelle of Edina, Minnesota, a fifty-eight-year-old anesthesiologist and national age-group record-holder in the marathon; he regularly runs in the 2:30s. He has said, "If I tried to get all of my calorie burning and cardiovascular conditioning from running, I'd be constantly injured. And there are times when I'm just mentally sick of running. During those times I can ride the bike, and soothe my conscience because I didn't miss my workouts."

Given the choice, I'd pick running anytime, though I have come to rely on the bike more and more in recent years when injury has made running inadvisable. In the fall of 1982, Grete Waitz and I compared notes on the necessary "evils" of the contraption. *The Runner* had asked me to interview the women's winner of the New York Marathon, which Waitz won for the fourth time in five years. She had incurred a stress fracture in midsummer and had had to resort to the bike because she could not run at all for three weeks; she worked on it twice a day, for an hour total. She told me, "I didn't like it. I did it just because I knew it was good for me, and I had to do something." My sentiments exactly.

Isometric exercises are a form of weight training in which the muscles and joints are strengthened merely by flexing the muscles. They are safe and simple, and can be done by tightening the muscles or by pressing them against resistance. You don't need any equipment. Recent research has shown that by exercising the good leg, you'll curb atrophy in the cast leg as well; apparently, there's a transfer effect at work. Now a therapist can cut a hole in the cast and contract the weakened muscles with electrical stimulation, but that technique was not readily available in 1978. When my cast came off, I used equal, light weights on both legs, the theory being that the bad leg would recover at a faster rate and in due time both legs would be of equal strength.

It was a shock to look at myself when the cast was taken off and see the difference. The left one was so much smaller, so lacking in vitality. Regaining full strength would not come easily. And there was still the question of how the left foot, and the rest of me, would respond to running.

During this time I went to Eugene three times: once to have the sutures taken out, another time to have the cast removed, and a third time for a final checkup. On the last visit, in mid-June, James saw no evidence of the bone spurs and told me I could begin jogging in early July while continuing the rehab exercises. I was anxious — anxious to run and get on with it, anxious about the fate of my running.

There were two years to go before the next Olympics. Enough time, I figured; it could be done, and I could do it. It *had* been done. Lasse Viren had done it. In January 1975 Viren had had surgery on his left leg. Months before he'd hurt his ankle, which made him adjust his stride, causing an injury to the upper leg. An operation was required to remove extra ligaments that had attached to the tendon from the injured muscle. Before the surgery, Viren had been unable to run. Viren, of course, recovered from the injury and a year and a half later won two gold medals in the Montréal Olympics. Knowing that reassured me, because in many ways my career has paralleled Viren's.

On July 5, I took my first steps. Louise and I were vacationing that weekend in northern New Mexico. I went out one afternoon, said, "This is it," and "ran" a mile. I jogged for

10 minutes, I guess it was about a mile. I felt out of shape and uncoordinated, as though I didn't quite know how to run. But my foot felt fine. There was no pain. I was relieved and thankful. It didn't hurt the next day either, or the day after that. It seemed to be working!

I continued to run every day, cautiously increasing the distance and improving my pace as James had suggested. By the end of July I was running 5 miles a day in 35 minutes, feeling ready to advance from recuperative jogging into a training program. James agreed. Two weeks later I discontinued the biking (and two weeks after that I stopped the isometrics). I was running an hour a day. I started to feel a slight discomfort now and then in the area of the surgery, but James didn't feel it was cause for concern. I applied ice to the foot and received ultrasound treatments, a form of physical therapy in which sound waves are used to break up scar tissue, increase circulation, and decrease inflammation.

All things considered, I felt pretty good. I was coming back. Maybe I felt *too* good and could not control the impulse to run too hard too soon. Maybe I needed to race. Whatever the reason, by late August, eight weeks after taking my first steps back, I was running 100 miles a week. This was rash, though I probably didn't think so then. Suddenly I was in a hurry again. I had given valuable time to the injury, standing still while the world moved on, and I needed to catch up. It's too bad that I couldn't resist the urge to plunge full speed ahead because, as I later came to believe, it was at this time or shortly thereafter when I did the damage that brought on a second serious injury.

My first major race was the Virginia Ten-Miler in Lynchburg on September 16. It felt secure and promising to be back in the company of the leading runners. Viren was there, and he, too, was marginally fit and recovering from an injury, an ailing knee. He told me a little about his recent injuries, and I told him about mine. Just casual conversation. Viren doesn't say very much, to anyone. That is just his nature, and it has helped him in athletics because no one has ever quite known what he was up to. At Virginia, he finished thirteenth in 52:08. I finished fourteenth in 52:16.

I was encouraged. To have run about 52 minutes for 10 miles eleven weeks after taking my first steps following the surgery was a good sign. Even if I hadn't had the foot injury and the operation, this was where I would have wanted to be with the Moscow Games less than two years away: competitive but not necessarily sharp and certainly not in peak form; training with consistency yet holding back. After the race I told myself, "Well, here I am. I'm back. I'm ready." Ready to make the gradual push that would bring me to full strength by 1980.

The next week I ran 30:45 for 10 kilometers, and the next month my twelfth-place 2:19:32 in the New York Marathon was all the more encouraging. I lowered my 10-kilometer time to 29:29 before the year was over, but soon after — when, exactly, I'm not sure — my back started to hurt. Like the foot pain of '77, the back pain of '79 would come and go . . . and come again. And, like the foot injury, even in its benign state it would affect other parts of my body, producing a cause-and-effect relationship that was insidious. It was responsible for my terrible Boston Marathon (seventy-ninth in 2:21:56) and not so terrible but equally frustrating New York Marathon (seventh in 2:16:15).

The tale of my bad back is thick with implications, assumptions, and guesswork. It is, unfortunately, not the sort of injury that is neatly diagnosed, treated, and cured. That it lingered for two years reflects some of the weaknesses of sportsmedicine — and my own weaknesses. Though I'm proud that I was able to stick with my running through it all, I also regret that I didn't face up to the problem soon enough and give it the attention it deserved. It made me realize, as an athlete, that the troubles that come with running (injuries) sometimes require a devotion to duty (getting better) as single-minded as that which exists when you're in full health. Though by definition your physical state differs once injured, your state of mind cannot be allowed to become impaired because you must remain faithful to the responsibilities of your sport. When well, training comes first; when injured, getting well comes first. It can be a rather selfish and limiting existence, especially if you're a marathon runner. To do it right, you need to be a full-time athlete — something I've not been able to be in recent years, something I'll probably never be again.

At the finish of the 1979 New York Marathon I saw an old college roommate, Ken Davis. Davis is now a professor of psychiatry and pharmacology at the Mount Sinai School of Medicine in Manhattan and chief of psychiatry at the Bronx VA Medical Center, and when I told him about my back problem, he suggested I come up to the hospital and have a specialist examine me. I'd looked down at my legs after the marathon and noted again how the left one looked so much weaker than the right, almost withered; something was preventing it from regaining the strength and muscle it lost to surgery.

Bad back, bad leg. I gave in.

The next day I went to the Bronx, where Ken referred me to Dr. Andrew Fischer, chief of rehabilitative medicine at the VA hospital as well as associate professor of physical medicine and rehabilitation at Mount Sinai. Originally a sportsmedicine practitioner at an institute of physical culture in Prague, Fischer also directed a private pain clinic on Long Island. He's lectured around the world and in 1982 delivered a paper at the World Congress on Sportsmedicine in Vienna, "Objective Evaluation of Soft Tissue Injuries: Tissue Compliance, Thermography, Pressure Threshold."

I was the first top athlete he'd tried it on. First I was

manually examined by Fischer to see if a thermogram was even necessary. When his fingertips applied pressure to certain areas of my back, I jumped in pain. He later called these spots trigger points.

One of the tests was a standard measurement of muscle strength and power. I sat in the chair of a Cybex machine and lifted, with one leg at a time, a weighted electronic device that determines the power (in pounds) of the knee flexors (hamstrings) and extensors (quadriceps). Not surprisingly, my left quadriceps muscle showed 84 pounds while the right showed 96.

I took an electromyogram and nerve conduction study to test the nerves and muscles related to the lower back pain. The findings were normal, ruling out nerve root involvement as a cause of the pain.

I took a test called Pressure Threshold Measurement to quantify the tenderness in my back. For this, a pressure gauge with a tiny rubber disk on it was applied to sensitive areas and I had to indicate when I felt pain. The pressure was increased gradually to determine which areas were most sensitive. Fischer found particularly increased sensitivity in the lower left side of my back and in both sides of my buttocks.

Then I underwent thermography, a "heat picture" that records the distribution of surface temperature over a swatch of the body — in my case, the back, buttocks, and legs. There was no penetration, radiation, or any risk of damage to the patient, according to Fischer. Scanning mirrors were used to reflect the heat shown by an infrared electronic transducer, and from that black-and-white and color pictures were produced that documented the heat pattern, indicating the specific trigger points that were considered to cause my pain. Even small variations in skin temperature are considered clinically significant.

With the thermogram, Fischer confirmed the tender areas

he felt earlier. He also said there was a symmetry of heat emission over the muscles around the spine and over the back of the leg and sensitivity in the gluteus medius, the muscles in the buttocks involved heavily in running. It was all very clear to him. Based on these tests, I was suffering from a condition of myofascial pain — pain in the fascia, or fibrous sheets, that protect muscles — that manifested itself in the many tender spots in the back, buttocks, and legs. It is an "overuse" injury, brought on by the cumulative stresses of running; and it was reasonable to assume in my case, Fischer said, that "uneven loading," due to a weakness in the left leg as a result of the surgery, was another mitigating factor. In short, I was favoring the stronger right leg — the right *side* of my body — and that essentially was causing the trouble.

I then knew what was wrong, according to Fischer and his methods of pain diagnosis, though it was impossible to know how the marathon I'd run the day before might have affected the various test results. Unfortunately, I was unable to follow Fischer's recommendation. He told me the most effective treatment was trigger point injection, a sort of microsurgery in which the damaged tissue is "needled," which breaks up the scar tissue that traps the nerve endings so that the irritating substances can be washed away by the restored blood flow.

Medically sound though it may have been, it seemed a little exotic for my taste at the time, and I wasn't anxious to have it done. And since Fischer wanted me to receive the injections two or three times a week for four to eight weeks, I would've had to remain in New York, which I couldn't do. I had other responsibilities, not the least of which was training for the 1980 Olympic Marathon Trial, which was coming up in May. Even with the obvious physical problems, I still was not prepared to give up on 1980. The Olympics were coming up, which meant my running would take on a certain urgency. If the marathon trial had not been six months away, I might have done the rational thing and taken care of myself. But I had to give it a try. (Of course, two months later, when America kicked off the boycott of the Moscow Games, the point became moot.)

Fischer said he knew of no doctor in the Boulder area who could administer the treatment he advised. He also recommended that I receive physical therapy and do relaxation exercises to relieve tension under the supervision of a physical therapist. I needed, also through exercise, to restore full strength to the weak left leg. But he insisted that without the needling I could not be satisfactorily cured because the condition would flare up when my muscles became stressed.

Ken Davis concurred. Though his work was not in sportsmedicine, he'd been a sprinter at Yale and knew running. He also knew me. He'd seen me tape supporting pads under my feet day after day at Yale. "The same genetics that gave you a great cardiovascular system gave you lousy feet," he said. "To separate yourself from your injuries is to separate a man from his fundamental physiology." Davis agreed that the 1978 surgery had caused me to develop compensatory mechanisms in my running and advised me to remain under Fischer's care.

Instead I went home, and I got worse.

I didn't tell all this to Stan James because he's not a "back man" per se, and I didn't think the needling and the rest of it was something an orthopedic surgeon would take seriously. But a few weeks later, in Milwaukee, I happened to find myself in the company of an orthopedic surgeon, Dr. Gary Guten, who appeared with me on a local "Run for Life" TV program. I told him my story, and he suggested I visit his office later that day for an examination.

Guten, whose primary interest was knee surgery, seemed to know his way around the back. He's a marathon runner himself and in 1981 published a paper on running and back injury in the *American Journal of Sportsmedicine*. At the time he was affiliated with Mount Sinai Hospital in Milwaukee and at present, with a colleague, Dr. Harvey S. Kohn, he works out of the Sports Medicine and Knee Surgery Center, also in Milwaukee.

First he examined my lower body and found "obvious" atrophy of the left thigh and calf. The left thigh measured ¾ inch smaller than the right one and the left calf, ½ inch smaller. He also detected some numbness in my left leg and much the same tenderness in the back found by Fischer.

But Guten also detected something else when he X-rayed my back, something called spondylolistheses Grade I, L_5-S_1. This, he said, was a form of stress fracture in the lower back, a condition not uncommon in female gymnasts, football linemen, pole vaulters, trampolinists, and butterfly swimmers. Stress fractures — slight cracks in the surface of the bone — are common in serious runners, who tend to develop them in the foot and legs rather than the back. My foot injury from 1973, which forced me to drop out of a marathon in Finland, was an example of a common stress fracture in running. The back condition that Guten saw — a weakening of the spine in which the spinal column slipped forward — developed from repeated aggravations of an injured area. I'd clearly been running for some time despite the back discomfort.

Guten's X-rays also showed that I have lumbar lordosis, a muscle imbalance in which the curvature of the lower back is accentuated. It is a congenital condition that serves to pinch the apertures from which the nerves to your legs emanate. To make matters a bit worse, I had, on the left side, a slightly smaller aperture than normal, further predisposing me to the problem.

In addition to the physical manifestations, any emotional stress that I felt seemed to settle in the back, affecting the condition even more. All of life's pressures — my business (still recovering from initial problems), becoming a father (our firstborn, Alex, had arrived that spring), juggling a hectic appearance schedule, and trying to run at the world-class level despite the injuries — found a home in my back. It got to the point where I couldn't sleep comfortably, and I couldn't be sure whether that was due to the actual injury or stress or both.

Guten concluded that my leg symptoms possibly were "related on a neurologic basis" to the spondylolisthesis, and he advised me to see Dr. Douglas Jackson of Long Beach, California, an orthopedist who had a special interest in the condition. Guten spoke with Jackson on my behalf and told me that Jackson had a special computerized X-ray facility that could further diagnose whether or not there was a disk irritating the nerve, causing the negative response in the left leg. Guten also instructed me to continue lumbar flexion exercises (to strengthen the lower back and stomach muscles), to supplement that with isokinetic exercises (moving the muscles against an even pressure) on a "mini-gym" at home, and perhaps to wear a corset while running.

I never contacted Dr. Jackson, nor have I spoken since with Dr. Guten. I was too busy, too preoccupied, too far away, to take care of myself properly. Fischer was in the Bronx, Guten was in Milwaukee, Jackson was in Long Beach, and Stan James was in Eugene. I had to be in Boulder, or somewhere other than the Bronx, Milwaukee, Long Beach, or Eugene, to race, speak, or generally take care of business.

So there I was at the end of 1979: atrophy in the left leg, "hot spots" up and down the body, a possible stress fracture in the back, and more. And not willing to let some very fine physicians help me.

Of course, that didn't stop me from running the Honolulu Marathon four weeks after seeing Guten. I finished second in 2:17:50. Five months later, feeling the full effects of my worsening condition, I bombed out in the Olympic Marathon Trial, finishing eighty-fifth among a hundred and twenty-five finishers in 2:23:24. Afterward I told reporters, "I have to start over and see what happens."

☆

Eventually, I started to heal; it took two years. I cut my running back to one workout a day for an entire year. I used an orthotron machine and other appliances to build up my weak leg. I worked with Nautilus equipment to strengthen my back and did situps and other stomach-strengthening exercises to take some pressure off my back. I went to Eugene to see Stan James. The tension in my everyday life lessened. By late '82, Cybex tests indicated equal strength in both legs. And the pain in my back was gone.

I purchased a little contraption called a Multiaxial Ankle Exerciser, a versatile piece of apparatus that has helped me a great deal in the rehabilitation. Built into the hub of the unit — which is used by strapping your foot into a plate that rests on a tripod — is a unique internal frictional braking system that uses not weights but friction as resistance. It's a streamlined device that gives me greater rotation in the exercises I need to do.

In time, I trained twice a day again. I won a few races, but my performances were still spotty and I couldn't manage to put together a solid marathon. But I felt there was progress, and for the first time I was engaged in a substantial rehabilitative exercise program to supplement my running. I think I have a handle on it now. I'm way past the denial phase, able to face up to the reality that I may never be 100 percent again.

The growth and acceptance of rehabilitative medicine and preventive medicine in athletics are fairly new, outgrowths of another new phenomenon — sportsmedicine. The top

runners coming up today and in the future will be indoctri-
nated with a holistic approach to their sport, a concern for
total body conditioning that is tied to scientific principles
of tissue regeneration, muscle strength, energy levels, joint
flexibility, biomechanics, and the like. I envy them. When
my body started to break down in 1976 — and it was inevitable after many years of all that running — there weren't
the support systems that are available today to injured athletes. Nor was there the environment of approval that might
have encouraged me to take advantage of the latest develop-
ments in rehabilitative sportsmedicine.

I have to try something for myself before I'll believe it.
Until then, I tend to be skeptical. I ran 20 miles a day, and
that worked. I trained at high altitude, and that worked. I
competed in the marathon, and that worked. Running for
so long without serious injury enabled me to perform well,
but it also meant that when I did get hurt, I was vulnerable
to the mistakes of the inexperienced.

Still, I feel lucky — I could have been permanently injured.
I'm still running competitively. On a good day I can run
10,000 meters in 29 minutes or better. Of all the distance
runners competing at the world-class level in the early seventies, I'm one of the few still around and running well.

The feeling that I've used up all my luck is sometimes
in the back of my mind. When will the rubber band snap?
When will I step in a hole and tear up my leg? When the
feeling comes on, it's a feeling that the "percentages" are
catching up with me. But I have to stop and tell myself
how irrational that fear is.

Perhaps this is the American psyche at work. It's our own
brand of compulsion, as athletes in particular, to fret over
the limitations we face. That's why there are people, top
runners among them, who won't take a day off from running.
(I plead guilty.) It's the old story about not running when
the Ethiopians *are*. You fear all of your precious fitness will

dribble out of your big toe. From what I've seen, the Europeans are more apt to rest an injury and take the long view of things. Not Americans; we're in a hurry.

I remember one indoor track meet in New York some years ago when a young miler, Tom Byers, was drawn into a conversation with steeplechaser Barry Brown and me.

"I'm ready. I think I can run fast," Tom said. "But I have this little pain in my right foot here." And he pointed to the painful spot.

"Boy, I wouldn't run on that," Barry told him. "If it really hurts, I wouldn't risk it."

"Really? Maybe I won't run," Tom said.

Byers ran, and with the mile barely under way, he screamed out in pain and left the race. You could almost hear the snap in his foot from across the track. When I was young I might have done the same. But not now. Time hasn't diminished my passion for running, but it's given me the perspective to control it better.

Looking back, I think Ken Davis was on to something when he said that my "fundamental physiology" has been responsible for both my success *and* failure as an athlete. I'd say that the same holds true for my fundamental psychology. The same personality — independent, introverted, single-minded, self-reliant, self-confident, distrusting — that enabled me to excel as an athlete in full health hindered me when I became an athlete in pain.

CHAPTER NINE

Getting Paid

When I was training in 1970, trying to get good, I just had gotten out of college, I was on food stamps, but in between the food stamp line and training I would go out to California, say, from New York for two or three meets, and I would get one plane ticket to get out there and then I would get one or two plane tickets for other meets, and then I would cash these in. Now that is the situation in the United States, plus you get certain per diem payments, and they are allowed to give you twenty-five dollars a day which you say, well, I want to spend three weeks in LA; you know, that can amount to a lot of money which they can legitimately give you.

I don't think it is bad, and it is a heck of a lot less than anybody else gets in other countries. It is substantially greater in other countries.

Well, the way I look at it, if I can get two hundred dollars a month average over the year, that is the ten hours a day that I don't have to work, because it takes me five hours a day to train, and I can't train for five hours in a day and work for ten hours, so to me it is just a means; and with the education that I have — because I was brought up in the old eastern prep school, Ivy League circuit — I have got the education to go out and do something else. And I could make a heck of a lot more money being a professional person, but I want to be an athlete. I went to law school because I started feeling guilty about not doing anything between workouts, and that is just the kind of person I am. If I can get this money, and it makes it easier for me to train,

well, then I have no qualms about it, because I know it is perhaps one-tenth of what everyone that I am competing against is getting overseas.
— My testimony at a congressional hearing of the President's Commission on Olympic Sports, September 9, 1975

I am an amateur athlete. I run and train and compete for the sheer joy of sport. I set goals for myself and structure my life so that I might achieve them. When I am running well, I feel whole and happy, and when I am not running well, I try to figure out why so that I can feel whole and happy again. I run for myself, not for a team, not for a public, not for my country — except when I am competing as a representative of my country, at which time I am delighted to do so. I do not consider myself a performer. When I race and people watch, that's fine; but I do not race for their benefit, only for mine. If no one watches that's just as well: I am seeking an inner satisfaction that only I can determine, not the recognition of applause, headlines, or a lot of money. Running is not my job. Running is not, for me, working, though surely it is, at times, hard work. Running, for me, is a form of self-expression. Though I don't necessarily intend it as such, it is a statement of who I am and a lot of what I hope to be, even if what I someday become takes me away from running. Running is the one absolute in my life, and I admit to its control over me — a control that may not always seem to be in my best interests, but then, who is to say? I think I've reached the point where I am, perhaps perversely so, in control of the controls. This thing is really not so complex, though. Above all else I run for fun, for the expansive feeling I get from running, and while that feeling is enhanced by winning, it is not enhanced by the prospect of being paid for it.

I am a professional athlete. I excel at running and, indirectly, earn a living from it. People pay me for my services much as they would pay a football player or an actor or a commencement speaker. I can get paid just to show up or be somewhere. Or to talk to people about running. Or to endorse a product, company, or organization. Or to compete in a race. There was a time not long ago when such earnings were not allowed by the authorities, but, at some risk, I worked to change the system, and though now I'm one of the leading beneficiaries of the increasingly permissive rules, I'm also somewhat uncomfortable with them. I would have preferred to make a living from something other than running — to have remained an amateur in the strictest sense of the word — but that was impossible, given the demands of the sport and the subsidy system by which the opposition abroad could attain a significant competitive advantage. I was forced to compromise my personal ideals in order to stay in the game. Even so, I do not make a lot of money — not by the standards of professional sports — and I like it that way. All I've ever wanted is the financial security to be able to run.

This conflict between the sporting ideals of amateurism and the practical necessities of athletic life has gnawed at track and field and other Olympic sports for decades. It has been a constant source of friction, polarizing athletes and administrators, and a most prickly issue to resolve. The rules of amateur eligibility, created by the British aristocracy before the turn of the century, were essentially right for their time. But while sport and society advanced, the rules did not; it was as if a Victorian morality were imposed on an enlightened contemporary culture. At their worst, the tight amateur standards inhibited the careers of many athletes, infused a shady underground system of payoffs into the sport, and undermined our efforts to turn out the best teams for major international competition. In the most celebrated case of all, Jim Thorpe was stripped of his decathlon and pentathlon titles from the Stockholm Olympics of 1912 after it was discovered that he had earned a few dollars in professional baseball. It took seventy years for the International Olympic Committee to overturn that decision. And only seven years before it did, I was in danger of being kicked out of running for the very same reason.

In the summer of 1975 I was asked to testify at a congressional hearing of the President's Commission on Olympic Sports. I didn't know much about the commission. I knew that a fellow marathoner, my good friend Kenny Moore, had something to do with it. If Kenny was involved in any way (though, as it turned out, his primary involvement was in the preparation of the Final Report), I felt the commission would be out for the good of the athlete, and I agreed to testify.

I certainly could support its mission, which was "to determine what factors impede or tend to impede the United States from fielding its best teams in international competition," according to Volume I of the Final Report. And I certainly could agree with its premise, again taken from the Final Report:

> The U.S. does not nearly approach achieving its full potential in sports. We have lost international contests that we were capable of winning; we have not even fielded teams in some sports in which we have great talent and resources. Some cry, 'Foul,' or that it is 'our' amateurs against 'their' pros. Others decry their perception of political influence, and still others cling to the purity of the Olympic idea. The fact is that we are competing less well and other nations competing more successfully because other nations have established excellence in international athletics as a national priority.

And I certainly could respect its conclusion regarding amateurism:

> Either amateur rules should be altered or abolished so that our professional athletes can be unleashed on the rest of the world, or the rules should be enforced equally, eliminating the opposition's full-time paid athletes. However, the International Olympic Committee has shown no inclination to suspend Eastern European athletes for violation of amateur rules, or to admit western professionals to the Games.

But despite the PCOS's high-minded intent, when it came actually to supporting the athlete — beyond putting out an encyclopedic position paper — it lacked the courage of its convictions. When I testified that athletes such as myself readily violated the amateur rules, that "we are all professionals," I assumed, naively I suppose, that I would be protected from incrimination in the eyes of the international authorities. That was not so. I feel I was used to draw attention to the work of the commission and that it would have felt most successful had someone like me been "martyred" by exclusion from the amateur ranks.

The commission was created by the Ford administration and came under the purview of the Department of Health, Education and Welfare. It had a staff of twenty-five, led by the executive director, Michael Harrigan, a former athlete who had worked in the personnel office of the Nixon White House. In addition there were twenty-two commissioners, a group composed mostly of former athletes and members of Congress. Among them were Olympic decathlon champions Rafer Johnson and Bill Toomey and two members of the House who had also been distinguished athletes in their day: Jack Kemp (R–New York), a former NFL quarterback, and Ralph Metcalfe (D-Illinois), a three-time Olympic medalist in the sprints. About half the commissioners were present in Washington when I gave my testimony on the afternoon of September 9, 1975.

I was the last of four Olympic athletes to testify that day, the opening day of the hearings. Those who preceded me were Larry Hough, a silver medalist in rowing; Ellie Daniel, a gold medalist in swimming; and Rick Abramson, an Olympian in team handball. I'd never met any of them before.

After some opening remarks by the chairman, Gerald Zornow (who was also the chairman of Eastman Kodak), and procedural instructions from the general counsel, John McCahill, we began. Each of us had been invited to provide, and read, a written opening statement, after which we would be questioned. Hough, Daniel, and Abramson gave their statements, all of which expressed the need for greater financial support for their sports, better administration of their programs, and a more realistic set of rules to enable American amateurs to compete more favorably with their essentially professional counterparts abroad. I was glad to see we were all on the same side.

When it was my turn, I chose to be direct. I'd provided no written statement, but I had a lot to say. I said I'd been training and competing "in spite of the AAU and USOC." I said I was beyond being fed up and "have really run out of axes to grind." I said an Olympic-caliber athlete could not work full-time and be expected "to maintain his form, much less improve." I said that "the U.S. is no longer able to impose its standards of amateurism on the rest of the world," that "most other countries are subsidizing their athletes" and that "we are one of the few pristine nations left." I said, "The purpose of this meeting is to generate winners and I am as much a chauvinist as anyone when it comes to wanting to see America win. . . . If those guys [the AAU bosses] don't like these kinds of situations, then I think we should put the feedbag on them and say thank you and put them out to pasture." I said, "If anyone asks me how it really is overseas with regard to payment of money under the table and federation subsidy, I will tell them. Okay?"

Okay. I told them, and the rule books hit the fan. Perhaps it wasn't only what I said but how I said it that got me into trouble. Essentially I was saying that any experienced track and field athlete could quote chapter and verse on how the federations had been perpetuating a system that favored the Eastern Europeans and how such treatment had put America at a disadvantage in international competition, but since I was there as their spokesman I was going to say what had been going on, and after that it would be obvious what should be done to rectify the situation. The people on the commission were not accustomed to such candor from an athlete, especially an amateur athlete.

The International Amateur Athletic Federation (IAAF) is the world governing body for track and field and road running. Every Olympic sport — swimming, skiing, cycling, and so on — has such a governing body, and all of them are recognized by the International Olympic Committee (IOC) as the organizations that will make the rules for each of their sports and see that they are followed, within the broad guidelines of IOC policy. It is not unlike the relationship between the executive and judicial branches of government, whereby the administration sets forth tone and policy and the courts generally carry out their duties with that in mind. Each world governing body such as the IAAF has, in turn, member federations in virtually every nation — national governing bodies — to enforce its rules in each country. Though these rules, until recently, have been terribly restrictive, they have also been open to interpretation, giving the national governing bodies discretion in determining just what amateur athletes could and could not do.

The Amateur Athletic Union (AAU), at the time of the hearings, was the national governing body in the United States. After passage of the Amateur Sports Act of 1978, which reorganized Olympic sports (based in part on the findings of the President's commission), the AAU gave birth to The Athletics Congress (TAC) as the new national governing body, and the IAAF approved it as well. Though some of the same people who controlled the AAU controlled TAC, the latter group, under great pressure, began to be more responsive to the needs of athletes.

However, through the years, the AAU had been more of an impediment to an athlete's progress, seeking to control his every move, and weeding out transgressors and punishing them. As I stated in my testimony, the AAU made a career out of saying, "No, you can't do that," whenever I'd approach them on something. The AAU routinely prevented us from competing in certain international meets in Europe by denying us travel permits in order to funnel athletes into other competitions more of their choice. Travel permits would also be used to coerce athletes into representing the U.S. in dual meets: If you wanted to compete in Europe (and earn some money), you'd better show up where the AAU wanted you. It had gotten to the point, I said, "where no matter how good they are, they are bad."

While criticizing the AAU, I also explained how amateur athletes in the U.S. and elsewhere made a living. I talked about the system of cashing in unused airline tickets. I talked about the state-supported athletes of Eastern Europe and the payoffs common in Western Europe. "In Italy, you get on the victory stand; instead of a trophy they hand you a white envelope."

I was asked hypothetically what I might have expected to receive from my country had I been a Russian returning with a gold medal from the 1972 Olympic marathon.

Answer: "I would rather have been a Finn. Had I been a Finn, my town would have built me a house. Peugeot would have given me a free car, all of this tax-free, and I could have done endorsements. Every time I would have gone to a shopping center I would have gotten two thousand dollars for cutting a ribbon. I could have demanded two thousand dollars every time I set foot on the track for the rest of the summer and probably all of the rest of the next year. . . ."

Question: "But as an American, what did you get?"

Answer: "You know, I haven't even gotten my Olympic ring from the Olympic Committee yet. That was the one thing I really thought I was going to get. In fact, it wasn't even for me." I wanted the ring for Louise. I still haven't gotten it. Maybe someday I'll call the USOC and see if the ring is sitting around anywhere.

We were not under oath, and my testimony was part of the public record. Reporters covered the hearings, and while the issues were too arcane to impress the general public, word of my assertions got around, attracting the attention of the IAAF. This was hardly the first time anyone had claimed aloud that amateur athletes were earning money and possibly violating the rules, but unless the IAAF is embarrassed into examining its dirty linen, everyone tends to look the other way. But here I was, (a) an Olympic gold medalist (b) from America (c) testifying before a government body (d) and being very open and direct about the whole thing. They had to do something. I gave them no choice.

The obvious hypocrisy in the sport — shamateurism, as it's been called — had been an issue since 1968. *Sports Illustrated* reported in a cover story that Adidas and Puma, then the world's two largest athletic shoe companies, had been falling all over each other that year at the Mexico City Olympics, signing up top track and field athletes to wear their shoes. The issue simmered, and at the end of 1971 *Track & Field News* published a comprehensive two-part article on "track and field's payoffs."

Bob Hersh, a highly regarded authority on the sport, outlined the nature, degree, and scope of "illegal" earnings by amateur athletes, based on questionnaires the magazine had sent to athletes and officials. "By overwhelming evidence," Hersh asserted in the first installment, "violations of the rules are frequent, varied, and widespread." The report included the story that was making the rounds of a leading indoor 600-yard runner "who informed the meet promoter his price was one dollar per yard. The promoter claimed he couldn't afford to pay more than $500, and when (in the race) the athlete reached the 500-yard mark well ahead, he stepped off the track."

On the European summer circuit at that time, when the distance events were even hotter than the mile in terms of spectator appeal, certain top runners could command as much as one dollar per meter, a nice reward for a winner in the 10,000 meters.

Coincidentally, my photograph appeared on the cover of the next issue of *Track & Field News,* which concluded its series by calling for a "redefinition" of amateurism — to include provisions for "open" competition, as there is in tennis and golf — "to make more sense in view of social and economic conditions today." It was the December 1971 issue, but the cover blurbs — "Amateurism Outmoded" and "Focus: Munich Olympics" — were not pegged to me. I had just won the national AAU cross-country title in San Diego and the Fukuoka Marathon in Japan, and so was put on the cover. It's ironic, though, contemplating those cover lines: If there's anything I would be identified with, it's the Munich Olympics and the redefinition of amateurism.

About a month after my testimony in Washington, I got a call from Bob Giegengack at Yale. He was upset. He told me that Ollan Cassell, the executive director of the AAU, had been asked by the IAAF for a "clarification" of my testimony. This was something like reading you your rights before moving in for the kill. Giegengack was one of the few Americans serving on an IAAF committee and knew that if I was not careful — or maybe even if I was — the IAAF could strip me of my amateur standing, making me ineligible for the upcoming Montréal Olympics. It had been done to Paavo Nurmi, the great Finn, forcing him out of the 1932 Olympics, and to Wes Santee, the top American miler, knocking him out of the 1956 Olympics. Both men were charged with earnings violations of the amateur rules. With the 1976 Olympics around the corner, it was not hard to imagine the Eastern European influence in the IAAF taking quite an interest in the outspoken testimony on amateurism by the defending Olympic marathon champion from the United States.

When I called people at the President's commission to see how to get some help, it was apparent I could not count on them. They offered no course of action; they volunteered nothing. "Gee, that's too bad," was the gist of their reaction. They were guilty of nonfeasance: They did nothing wrong. They just did nothing. I realized then that the commissioners wanted a martyr, someone to burn while drawing attention to the "nobility" of their mission. Though they professed to care deeply about the plight of athletes such as myself, they did not seem prepared to come to my defense when — while trying to help them, no less — my career was placed in jeopardy. What could the commission have to gain from any dispute over my amateur standing? Perhaps the people in charge considered it politically advantageous — for them personally or the commission as a whole — for something concrete and punitive to fall out of their work. Maybe they wanted headlines.

Whatever their motives, I was in a tough spot and, as an attorney myself, knew a legal solution might be necessary. The AAU had sent a letter confirming Giegengack's warning, that officially I'd have to "clarify" my testimony to the satisfaction of the AAU, which could then pacify the parent IAAF. Since I was affiliated with the Boulder law firm of French & Stone, I consulted with Joe French. Since my testimony had not been given under oath, we could "clarify" it as much as necessary. I'd been careful at the hearing not to implicate myself but merely to explain what I knew the amateur situation to be.

To resolve the matter, French and I reviewed the testimony, refining my remarks and putting them in the form of a deposition (a sworn statement), and submitted it to the AAU. It was also sent to the President's commission, which duly made it part of their record. And then we waited.

I couldn't sleep; I'd wake up at night in a cold sweat. It was hard to train with such an uncertain fate. Would I be running in the next year's Olympics or fighting it out with the amateur authorities?

I was mad, too. I don't like the idea of other people having such control over me. I like to succeed or fail on my own.

It all worked out. The AAU, the object of scorn in my testimony, supported me. I'm sure Giegengack's influence helped. In effect, he'd told Cassell, "Look, the kid means well." In January 1976, the AAU told me, "We've received your statement and we're satisfied. We'll convey this information to the IAAF." Once the AAU was on my side I felt safe, and in fact I heard nothing further on the matter from the IAAF. Seven months before the Montréal Olympics, I was a reconfirmed amateur.

The ordeal changed me. I learned a lot. I became less naive politically and wiser to the ways things get done when the rules are challenged. I hardened internally from the callousing effect of the friction, becoming more circumspect. And I gained a sense of diplomacy. I realized that the AAU probably had to give up something big to clear me, or perhaps it had to call in a few favors from the IAAF. That's how those things are.

In fact, my contentious relationship with the AAU ended then, for good. I became a friendly adversary and started working with Ollan Cassell on various projects, which served to hasten the reform of the amateur code. I can't say we've become good friends, but we learned to trust one another, and each of us, I think, became more sensitive to the needs of the other side.

Upon reflection, I understood that maybe I should have been less open at the hearing, that I should have realized what the repercussions could be. However, I naively assumed that the commission provided immunity from the "law" and gave a good deal of inside information on that basis. That's what angered me most — that simply by agreeing to testify I was taking some risk, and then when I spoke with candor the presumed protection was not there.

☆

My first summer competition overseas was in 1969. There were rumors about the payments to European athletes by race promoters, and the first evidence I saw of that was at a meet in Malmö, Sweden. An Italian hurdler with whom I'd become acquainted said after the race, "Well, let's go get our money."

I was standing with a group of American athletes. "What money?" we said, almost in unison.

We went running over to our U.S. coaches and managers and repeated, "What money?" We wondered whether the AAU was getting the money that was earmarked for us. The answers were hard to find.

I saw more of the same the next summer. After the U.S.-Soviet dual meet in Leningrad, a number of Americans competed in Stockholm. Ron Clarke, Australia's distance-running world record-holder many times over, was reputedly well paid. So, too, supposedly, was Kip Keino of Kenya, who'd won the Olympic 1,500 in 1968 (and taken second in the 5,000). Everyone in Europe knew what was going on. Though I'd won the 10,000 against the Russians, I was not among the beneficiaries of the Stockholm meet promoter's budget.

Nor had I been earlier that summer in Oslo, where Clarke, nearing retirement, was running his last race in Bislett Stadium. I beat Clarke in Oslo that year, winning the 10,000 in 28:32.6. Clarke was sixth in 29:00.4. I received nothing from the meet promoter while Clarke was thought to have made out rather well. Though I remember thinking about that, it didn't disturb me. I felt Clarke deserved it for all he had accomplished, and besides, the Norwegians paying their hard-earned krone wanted to see Ron Clarke; they'd probably not even heard of me. In fact, the main reason I decided to run was to see Clarke. I wanted to be part of his last race in Bislett Stadium.

Even after my marathon victory at Munich my needs were simple. I needed to train to compete while going to law school in Gainesville. I did some racing in Europe every summer, which helped, and there were increasing opportunities in the U.S., particularly on the indoor track circuit, which was becoming big business.

Following Munich, an attempt was made outside the channels of the ruling bodies to enable track and field athletes to earn money. When it failed I was not surprised. It was called the International Track Association (ITA) tour, or Pro Track, and it was set up in a run-for-money fashion not unlike the carnival events of decades before, when men would race as entertainment for a big purse. The ITA signed up world-class runners from the U.S. and other countries and put together a series of meets, mostly indoors, with prize money, performance bonuses, and some rather unconventional touches designed to spice the package for both TV appeal and the live gate.

It was just too gimmicky. They'd assemble a field of football players to run a Celebrity Challenge sprint; they'd get one top runner to run alone against the clock; they'd flash "pacing lights" on the track to encourage fast times artificially; they'd make huge blowups of checks for pictures at press conferences. I was asked to join but would have no part of it. It had a circus atmosphere that disturbed me. Besides, even if it had had more integrity and had worked, to join meant giving up my amateur status — and the Olympics. Even though such stellar athletes as Jim Ryun, Kip Keino, Gerry Lindgren, Lee Evans, and Bob Seagren signed on, the ITA tour survived only for four years — from 1973 to 1976 — and after that a number of the money-winning pros were banned from all amateur competition. However, in ensuing years The Athletics Congress found a way to approve the reinstatement of several banished runners, including Jim Ryun.

As the novelties of the pro track tour wore thin — if they ever caught on at all — fewer and fewer people turned out to watch. The fields were too often small, the athletes too often out of shape or dispirited. And I don't think the fans were pleased to see the foreign runners beating Americans, which they routinely did in the distance events. The tour folded, an idea whose time, I hope, will never come again.

I like to have people appreciate what I do, but I don't want it to be entertainment. That belief, as much as any other, governs my running. To be an athlete you don't have to be a performer.

There is about running a certain basic integrity that needs to be preserved and protected. I don't hold anything against runners who thrive on "performing." I'm just not one of them. I'm uncomfortable when I see a kind of one-night-stand exhibitionism creeping into the road-racing scene. I'm bothered by that, though I can't say I'm not a part of it. It's funny when you think about it, but many say I had a lot to do with establishing the running boom because people watched me run, and win, in the Olympics on TV. Ironically, I'm most comfortable running alone, without an audience.

☆

After the 1976 Olympics the sport began to change. The enormous growth of running put top runners in a different light, paving the way for them to earn a living. But first the rules had to be reformed; that is, reinterpreted.

A few months after the Games in Montréal, I decided I might be able to support my running with a sporting goods business, a running store bearing my name. This was thought to be outlawed by the amateur rules, but a precedent had been set. In the summer of 1974, when I was competing and studying in Europe, Louise and I passed through Louven, Belgium, the home of Gaston Roelants, the Belgium Olympic champion. He'd won the 3,000-meter steeplechase in Tokyo in 1964.

Gaston invited us to stay with him. I took some interest in Gaston Roelants Sports, a successful shop he ran right there in town. He was still considered an amateur . . . So in October 1976 I called Ollan Cassell and told him I'd like to open a business with my name on it. I told him about Roelants, and how the AAU could use the example to make a point with the IAAF. Cassell reacted positively, took the proposal to the IAAF, and it was approved. The IAAF stipulated that I had to have a "substantial pecuniary and proprietary interest" in the company, meaning that it could not be a deal in which I would simply be lending my name for promotional reasons; it had to be my company. The AAU interpreted that to mean I had to own at least 51 percent of the concern and be active in the business. While the ground rules were being ironed out, I'd made plans to open a store, contingent upon the approval. When it came, we started immediately in Boulder.

I'd also known that Ron Hill, the British Olympic marathoner, had his name on running apparel, and he was still an amateur. I told Cassell about that, too. A few months later, early in 1977, Frank Shorter Running Gear was born, with the same stipulations from the IAAF.

Some months later Ollan and I were talking again. The subject of the amateur rules came up, and he said that as far as road racing was concerned, the underlying philosophy of the rules was that you couldn't get paid for the act of running, but perhaps you could get paid for giving a clinic the night before. So I started doing clinics at races. This was perhaps the single most important step in the reform of amateurism, and in the running movement in general, in the seventies. It gave runners a greater opportunity to train and earn money at the same time, help promote events, and disseminate information about the sport to a growing audience. Soon there were races everywhere, many with clinics, and almost everything of importance going on in running could be connected more or less to road racing.

I was in demand, as other runners soon would be. When I began telling race directors that maybe it was time I re-

ceived more than just expenses for my time and effort, especially if we Americans were to keep up with the East Germans, they agreed. I wouldn't ask for much, and I made
sure that the payment would be for giving a clinic. I just
wanted to make a living, and I wanted the whole thing to
be fair to all concerned.

Even with the clinics, the system of under-the-table payments continued, as it does today. Not every race had a
clinic, and for those that did, some runners began to bargain
for a clinic fee and race fee and bonuses attached to their
performance. So both legitimate and illegitimate forms of
payment were practiced, and I'm not even sure that all the
leading runners realized that the clinic situation could be
fully aboveboard.

Next, in 1979, came the Hilton arrangement. A man named
David Geyer, then with the McCann-Erickson ad agency
in Los Angeles, asked me if I could in some way associate
my name with Hilton hotels, a client of his. This was something new in amateur running, a clear-cut promotional arrangement. David took his idea to Cassell, who saw it as
completely within the existing rules for a corporation to
become a "national sponsor" of the AAU — actually, by
then The Athletics Congress. The three-way, two-year agree-
ment with Hilton International, TAC, and myself called for
Hilton to pay TAC $25,000 a year for the right to use a
TAC athlete (me) in their promotion. I could, in turn, be
paid by Hilton for my services as a consultant, just as a race
director could pay me for a clinic. I helped the Hilton people
develop a training tips booklet, advised them on running
courses around their hotels, and worked with them on a
lighter "athlete's menu" for their increasingly fitness-
minded guests. Technically I was not supposed to be paid
for making a TV commercial; I was paid as a Hilton em-
ployee. TAC went on to acquire many other national spon-
sors, and the precedent was set.

Things were happening fast. TAC's more flexible posture

was perhaps in part in recognition of the millions of new runners who were prospective TAC members, at $6 apiece for a registration fee. This group of nouveau athletes also represented a lot of political influence, and since it was all so new, TAC recognized the need to present a good image and to structure its organization to better support road running.

What still frustrated runners, however, was that they could not be paid prize or appearance money for competing and at the same time retain their amateur status. They could be punished if they openly accepted such a fee, so to survive they took it under the table, as Clarke and Keino most likely had a decade before. They did not like the hypocrisy of it all; many of the runners felt it was undignified to have to earn a living that way when professional athletes seemed to have it so easy.

After a while the under-the-table deals became so commonplace that they were not secret anymore, which added to the hypocrisy, because TAC and the IAAF continued to look the other way, knowing the situation could not possibly be policed. Only when the money was given openly would the ruling bodies act on it.

That did happen, and the result was a trust fund that seemed to finally resolve the dispute.

☆

A number of runners formed a "union" called the Association of Road Racing Athletes (ARRA). It grew out of meetings in 1980, at the Olympic Trials and other events, and in 1981 it formed a circuit of races, with initial funding from Nike, to award prize money openly — a bold challenge to the amateur authorities. These were well-meaning athletes — people like Don Kardong (a marathon teammate of mine at the '76 Olympics, who became ARRA's president), Jon Anderson (winner of the 1973 Boston Marathon), Greg Meyer (who would win the 1983 Boston Marathon) — but there was an element of protest and naiveté that didn't please me. I knew protest was ineffective in this issue, anyway, because protest would have no effect in East Germany. You couldn't stand on a soapbox in the United States and call TAC dirty names and expect that to get an East German in the IAAF to vote your way.

When I was asked to be on ARRA's board of directors I declined. Their approach seemed too harsh, too raw and ill advised. The cause obviously was just — it was my cause, too — but I also didn't like what I saw as the protest view of the leadership.

The inaugural event of the 1981 ARRA circuit was the Cascade Run Off, a 15-kilometer race in Portland, Oregon, on June 28. The previous fall TAC itself had failed to get a Grand Prix series of road races off the ground; its hastily arranged inaugural event in Purchase, New York, outside New York City, so divided the runners that the plans fell apart. At roughly the same time Jordache, the jeans company, got into the act with a marathon offering prize money in Atlantic City, New Jersey. It was the first openly professional road race in the United States in decades and it went off without incident, though some of the prizewinners would be scrutinized by TAC.

Cascade was a mess. The runners were bitter — and foolish, in my opinion — a little like I had been six years before at the PCOS hearings. Cassell was cooperative, but he had the IAAF to answer to, and with some effort he achieved a concession two days before the race. This gesture should not have been spurned by ARRA, but it was. The IAAF told TAC that it would kill the "contamination rule" — a sticky guilt-by-association clause that incriminated amateurs if they were simply in the same race with money-winners — if the race would provide separate finishing chutes, one for those competing for the $50,000 in prize money, another for those competing just for the fun of it, plus the names of the former. This was significant. It meant another senseless rule would be gone. It meant the next concession, in a calmer setting, was bound to be even more significant. TAC obviously was going to get the names anyway; they would be in the next day's papers.

ARRA said no. "It's too late to change the chute," Chuck Galford, the meet promoter, said.

"I don't believe you," I told him.

By giving up the contamination rule, the IAAF was saying, "Let's sit down and talk about this."

I decided not to run, even though I had wanted to run to support ARRA's cause. In fact a week before, in a gesture of good will, I told that to Cassell — that I would run but not take any money, and only if the contamination rule were not enforced. Then he went out and got the concession from the IAAF, expecting that might bring the two sides closer together.

But ARRA apparently wanted all or nothing. You run and take the money and risk suspension, or you run and don't take the money and still risk suspension because you're "contaminated." Everybody in the trenches. That's how I interpreted their position; it was dumb.

Greg Meyer won the race, and $10,000. ("If I have to spend the ten thousand dollars to fight TAC, I will," he said.) Herb Lindsay was second, and won $6,000. Bill Rodgers took fourth and was not competing for money, but he was still considered "guilty" anyway under the contamination rule. Three New Zealand runners — Anne Audain ($10,000), Allison Roe ($4,000), and Lorraine Moller ($2,000) — placed first, second, and third in the women's division. Patti Catalano was the first American woman, in fourth place ($1,500). For not running at all, I was considered a traitor to the cause.

However, I was working behind the scenes on behalf of the runners and their eligibility. When I'd spoken with Cassell about the contamination rule months before, I'd brought up the idea of a trust fund, whereby events could deposit the runners' winnings into an account approved by the national federation, which could then oversee its distribution to the athletes. Something similar was being done in Italy. And if they're doing it in Italy, it must somehow be all right based on the rules. Cassell liked the idea.

When in Portland I told Galford about it, he said, "They'll never go for it."

Philosophically, it seemed a bit absurd; money is money, and what's the difference how you get it into your pocket? The difference was that through the proposed trust system, the national governing body (i.e., TAC) would still control the action by overseeing the funds, which would make the IAAF happy, which, in turn, would make the International Olympic Committee happy.

In Portland, as it turned out, some money-winners, including Herb Lindsay, decided not to accept their prizes. Lindsay never even touched his check. We had a reluctant Galford write "trust account" after Lindsay's name on his $6,000 check. Then we took the check to the French & Stone law offices in Boulder for safekeeping.

"What if we're all suspended?" Kardong had said rhetorically in Portland. "So what. If we stick together and show enough support for an open series, the series will work. Maybe it will be tough at first since we'll have all lost our eligibility . . ."

About three months after the Cascade Run Off, the suspension edict came through. Eight athletes, including Greg Meyer, Benji Durden, and Patti Catalano, were suspended indefinitely. Bill Rodgers was among those cleared because, though the contamination rule was still on the books, TAC and the IAAF were ignoring it.

Lindsay was also in the clear. It was October 5, in Chicago, when TAC's National Athletic Board of Review held a closed-door hearing on the Cascade race. Lindsay had by then split from ARRA; initially he'd been on its board of directors. The suspended runners — indeed, all runners — owe a debt of gratitude to Herb Lindsay because it was his case that resulted in the establishment of the trust. Bob Stone of French & Stone represented Lindsay in Chicago and won his clearance by agreeing to turn over his Cascade winnings to TAC, to be held in escrow pending meetings in Rome in December when the IAAF would decide whether or not to accept TAC's trust fund proposal.

By this time the second ARRA race had taken place, the $100,000 Nike Marathon in Eugene, Oregon (in which the winners, Benji Durden and Lorraine Moller, won $20,000 apiece), thrusting ARRA and TAC farther apart.

TAC liked Bob Stone's trust document. They looked at it as the model for all runners. They liked it so much that they were willing to make it retroactive to the Cascade race, should the IAAF approve it. In that way the suspended runners could be reinstated if they enrolled in the trust program.

We worked hard to complete the trust proposal before the IAAF meetings in Rome. The parties involved were Alvin Chriss, a TAC attorney; Bob Stone; Steve Bosley, the president of the Bank of Boulder; Ric Rojas of ARRA; Herb Lindsay; and me. By the time we were polishing the final draft, almost all of the suspended runners had agreed to go along with the idea.

I continued to work on the trust with Chriss and Cassell, essentially as an intermediary on behalf of the athletes. I had a rapport with Cassell, and I also knew TAC had to get the credit for the idea. But if it had been up to me I would have called it the Herb Lindsay Trust. After Herb had assessed the situation and agreed to try the trust design, Bob Stone could go to Ollan Cassell and say, "Here's one athlete who understands what's going on. Now let's work this out."

It was called the TAC Trust. In early December 1981 it

was formally proposed at TAC's national convention in Reno, and a week later it was ratified by the IAAF in Rome. It was indeed a landmark decision. As Eric Olsen explained in *The Runner:*

> The new trust fund system should go far in stilling the recent controversy over open running and shamateurism, as well as provide a model for similar systems in other Western countries. It's a surprisingly liberal arrangement and there was some doubt at first that the usually conservative IAAF — especially the Eastern Bloc members — would pass the proposal. That it did pass suggests that both the IAAF and TAC are beginning to acknowledge the economic realities that exist in athletics today. The trust fund appears to go as far as possible toward open running while still remaining in accordance with the IAAF rules TAC is required by law to uphold. It will allow an athlete to accept appearance or prize money at a competition while still maintaining his or her eligibility to compete as an amateur as long as those monies are deposited in the trust fund and are withdrawn only for "legitimate training expenses."
>
> The trust fund system, though not philosophically faithful to the ideals expressed by runners seeking to rid the sport of hypocrisy, also appears not to be just another hastily devised political maneuver in the ponderous conflict involving leading "amateur" runners and the methods by which they can earn a living. . . . The system may finally unify many of the different factions in running, create more open prize-money events, enable runners to earn a better living while remaining eligible as amateurs, and put an end once and for all to the divisive dispute between reformists and the national governing body. If all this won't bring about one big happy family, we might still see the closest thing to it in anyone's memory.

At long last it was over.

Now we had to protect what we had — which was quite a bit, since "legitimate training expenses" could include almost anything — and we could not be selfish: We had to think of the sport as well as ourselves.

This was not so easy, either. With endorsements and other

opportunities — for a select few — came the greater need for runners to be represented in financial matters by someone other than themselves, someone who could make a good deal and look out for the long-term benefit of the athlete and the sport. This role might have gone to ARRA had it been better organized.

Enter the agent. It was inevitable. Now that there was real money to be made in running, the agents got involved. To a certain degree this has been good — most runners need agents. Runners tend to be terrible negotiators, and you have to negotiate to get what you deserve, or what you think you deserve. As an independent sort, I've rarely used an agent except to negotiate some TV commercials. Not knowing industry standards, I needed an agent.

In the summer of '81, Sebastian Coe and Steve Ovett, Britain's world-leading milers, were supposed to meet for the first time ever in a mile race. It was to be like Bannister and Landy in '54, "the race of the century." They didn't meet. They never have, at the mile. Perhaps they never will. I was in Brussels with NBC for the race, but before then it was clear Ovett would not be running. From what I gathered, the agents were so busy trying to get the deal to end all deals, the thing fell through and the opportunity passed. Coe ran, setting a world record of 3:47.33. It was terrific, but it could have been even better. The sport lost something by not having Coe and Ovett together.

After setting a women's world record in the 1981 New York Marathon, Allison Roe signed on with an agent. She's not been the same since. I think she was so tied up with fulfilling the commitments made for her, she was unable to care for her post-marathon injuries properly and has never fully regained the fitness she exhibited in New York.

Agents generally are good at what they do, but at times their priorities are mixed up. One agent who refers to his clients as "the product" has been heard to say: "The only reason for a runner to stay amateur now is that he can make more money as an amateur."

That's the sort of thinking that's starting to make an impression on runners. Certain runners nowadays seem to feel it's more important to make money than to run at their best. They overrace and show up everywhere, increasing their earnings a great deal but quite often at the expense of performance.

Sometimes I wonder where runners get their ideas about their worth, about the value of what they do. Running seems to be taking on more of the characteristics of professional sport, and that may not be in its best interest.

CHAPTER TEN

Beyond Running

I had a minor role in *Personal Best,* the 1982 film about women track and field athletes striving for the Olympics and for emotional growth in a sporting world dominated by men. I played myself, but didn't run. I did TV commentary during the climactic scenes of the Olympic Trials, a real-life role for me. My partner and anchorman during the shooting was Charlie Jones, whom I've been working with since 1978 on track meet telecasts for NBC. In keeping with the film's use of athletes instead of actors in many of the roles, the runner and writer Kenny Moore, making his acting debut in the movie, suggested to the director, Robert Towne, that he get Charlie and me for the TV segment. After all, we'd done it at the Olympic Trials in 1980.

There wasn't much to it. One day in the fall of 1981 we were called to Hollywood, to a Warner Brothers studio. They'd erected a commentators scaffolding for us on the set of *The Dukes of Hazzard.* It looked just like the one we'd used at the trials. I'd seen the script and some rough cuts of the film and knew what it was about, but there was no other preparation. When Charlie and I were paired for the shooting, Robert Towne said something like, "Just do it."

No lines were written for us. We were to ad-lib both our

comments on camera about the goings-on and the off-camera play-by-play, which was just like doing voiceovers because we were calling the races while watching the film from the movie on a monitor.

Charlie and I have become a good team, I think, and it took us only a few takes to get it right. In fact, we got so caught up in the decisive race — the one that Chris Cahill (played by Mariel Hemingway) wins to make the Olympic team in the pentathlon — that everyone on the set applauded when we were done.

To tell you the truth, I never saw the movie. I had mixed emotions about the film. The training sequences were marvelous, especially the weightroom scene, in which Cahill and a water polo player, Denny Stites (played by Kenny Moore), who would become her lover, engage in small talk. But if you listened to it, it was not small talk. It had depth and purpose. But what disturbed me was the film's homosexual component. The story line had the two main characters, Cahill and Tory Skinner (played by Patrice Donnelly, a former hurdler), develop a sexual relationship, and it affronted me because it suggested that athletes of the same sex could not become close without the relationship becoming sexual. I don't deny that there is homosexuality in sports, in track and field, but I feel the film exploited that. And did we really need to see so many closeups of Mariel Hemingway's crotch as she went over the high jump bar?

On the other hand, I fully understand that a movie like *Personal Best* would have had little chance of commercial success without its sexual overtones, which some critics hailed for its honesty. How much of a market is there for a film about running, even "the most lyrical instructional film that you'll ever see," as Kenny Moore put it? If you put running in the movies, it can't just be *about* running. *Running* (with Michael Douglas) tried that, and it didn't work, let alone sell. The Academy Award–winning *Chariots of Fire,* a wonderful film, had one sort of angle; *Personal Best* had another.

Television's treatment of running is on the same order. TV has been very selective as far as pure track and field is concerned. Network TV considers running and track minor sports. It seems analogous to the major university seeking minority applicants in order to have a less homogeneous student body. The networks need running and track to satisfy television's concept of variety.

The public doesn't want that much track and field. They want baseball, football, boxing, and *The Battle of the Network Stars.* So that's what they get. A 1983 Miller Lite Report, "American Attitudes Toward Sport," found that 29 percent of TV sports fans participate in running, but it also found that only 1 percent of the respondents said the championship event they would most like to attend in the next year would be a track and field event. Such findings are not lost on network marketing executives, or on the ad agencies that book commercials.

I suppose it could be argued that if TV provided more (and better) coverage of track and field, ratings would be higher. Perhaps. But air time is so precious and competition so keen that TV has to go with the sure thing in terms of viewer appeal.

Even so, more running is on TV these days than ever before, and I'm glad to be a part of it. In 1982, CBS gave same-day coverage to a number of major road races; I was the commentator, working with John Tesh, himself a recreational runner. ABC finally brought live network coverage to the New York Marathon in 1981, in part to get a handle on the tricky logistics of a big-city marathon in preparation for its coverage of the 1984 summer Olympics in Los Angeles. In 1983 I was under contract to work with NBC on a series of events, including the U.S.–East German dual meet that inaugurated the new Olympic track in the Los Angeles Coliseum and the first World Track and Field Championships, held in midsummer in Helsinki. NBC provided, in a week's time, 15 hours from Helsinki, a step forward in non-Olympic track and field coverage. For the Olympics, of course, you can throw away your marketing studies. ABC is planning full-day coverage from Los Angeles — 187½ hours over two weeks, and much of it in track and field, including the marathon.

TV's favorite event — the public's favorite event — is the mile. Everybody knows the mile, and most people even understand it. At the world-class level it has a recognized standard of excellence: the 4-minute "barrier." It's short enough to hold attention, unlike, say, the 5,000 meters, which is twelve and a half laps around the track and a funny metric distance at that. In 1982 David Moorcroft of Great Britain lowered the 5,000-meter world record to 13:00.42, one of the finest track performances ever. Still, that sort of thing won't excite American TV audiences, not unless an American is doing it in the Olympics.

The mile, for better or worse, will. Partly because of the mile's glamour, the event has seen great rivalries: Bannister and Landy, Ryun and Liquori, and, more recently, Coe and Ovett. Marty Liquori admits that throughout his career, he was probably a better 5,000-meter runner than a miler (he held the American record in the 5,000, 13:15.06, for five years), but that "the glory of the mile kept me in the mile."

There's no denying the mile's appeal. I got a firsthand look at it in August 1981, working with NBC at an international track meet in Brussels. We were there for the mile. There was going to be an attempt at a world record, and NBC planned to provide same-day delayed-tape coverage to the States. After the meet, held in the evening, we had to rush to London with the tapes and do the voiceovers there.

Sebastian Coe had the race all to himself. Despite a world-

class field that included Mike Boit (Kenya), Thomas Wessing-
hage (West Germany), Steve Scott (USA), and Ray Flynn
(Ireland), Coe controlled the race just by his presence. Lasse
Viren of Finland is the only other runner I've ever seen
do that. Coe's mastery was extraordinary; it showed how
much mental influence an athlete can have over his competitors, even at that level.

Tom Byers, the rabbit (who has since become an American
Olympic contender), dutifully shot to the lead, with Coe
behind him as planned. You could see the other runners,
all those 3:50 milers, just look at Coe, careful not to get in
his way, in effect conceding him the race. The other men
seemed not to be racing but watching from behind. I tried
to bring that across in the telecast.

Coe won in 3:47.33, a world record by more than a full
second. It was the most exciting event I've covered for TV.
Though no one challenged Coe, the atmosphere was charged
with anticipation, and being down on the track watching
close by was a real treat. World records come and go, but
each one is unique, and this one felt special to me because
of the way Coe went about it.

I interviewed Coe both before and after the race. In a
TV interview situation, I want to hit the critical heart of
the race and at the same time give the athlete "room" to
be both honest and guarded. My role, as I see it, is not to
put the athlete in a corner but, rather, to put him or her
in a positive light while analyzing the essence of the competition.

Before the race Coe told me on camera that he was relaxed
and fit, and though a world record would be nice, the primary objective, of course, was to win. Not very profound,
but I let it go at that. He couldn't very well admit the conditions were custom-made for a record because that would
put even more pressure on him. And he's so careful you
could lead him all you wanted and you wouldn't get any-

where. He's sharp enough to control the race, not the type who'll be led in an interview. Coe impressed me as being bright and fully confident in his ability to train properly for key races (which still doesn't mean he'll always win; Coe's lost his share of big ones).

Coe's confidence shaped my line of questioning after the race. Since he'd expected to break the record, there was no point in dwelling on the wonder of it all. He came, he saw, he ran . . . and he did it. We spoke a little about the conditions being ideal — the weather, the crowd, the rabbit — but I wanted to find out more. In doing so, I'd be careful to avoid the uninspired questions thrown at me over the years: "How does it feel to have run well?" "Are you satisfied with your performance?"

Coe's ¾-mile split was a little slow at 2:52, but I wouldn't say, "Gee, you were slow at three-quarters, then you picked it up, didn't you?" I'd ask him how the 2:52 compared with his hoped-for split, and how that one came to be and what it signified, to try to get him to deliver an analysis. Coe had tripped on the infield curbing at one point on the first or second lap, but I wouldn't say, "Tell us about where you tripped. Did it bother you?" It had to bother him, but I wanted to ask him if it affected his rhythm because I suspected he was so poised that it hadn't, and then he could bring out on TV that his mental framework was such that nothing, not falling or almost falling, was going to prevent him from doing what he'd set out to. It reminded me of the 10,000 at the Munich Olympics: Viren fell, got up, recovered the lost ground, and won in world record time. That's the instinct of a great champion.

☆

My first network telecast was at the 1978 Millrose Games in New York, for NBC. Peter Diamond, a track enthusiast and NBC sports producer at the time (he's now with ABC, working on the '84 Olympics), asked me to team up with Charlie Jones and Fred Thompson, the coach of the Atoms Track Club of Brooklyn and an authority on women's track. That night Thompson handled the field events. We went over the schedule and the lineups a few hours before the meet, but otherwise there was no coaching. They just said, "Okay, do it." I did it, and they called me again.

I did a handful of meets for NBC that year and next, being groomed for the 1980 Olympics. That, of course, was not to be, but I've continued working with NBC except in 1982, when I turned down their invitation to do the Millrose Games because I had to attend a sporting goods show in Chicago that same weekend. I guess they thought I was no longer interested because they stopped calling me for a while. Asked by CBS to do some road racing telecasts that spring and summer, I agreed, returning to NBC the next year.

I find the TV work suits me. There's a deadline aspect to it that makes you alert in doing the job. It's an enforced efficiency; you don't waste time. Yet the pressure to make the whole thing work isn't on me because I'm just a supporting player, unlike my situation in business, where I have to be the one most responsible for its ultimate success. All I have to do on TV is be myself.

They don't seem to mind my eccentricities, either. When I showed up after the first couple of shows wearing a big fat red bow tie, they thought it was great. At one summer meet, where the temperature was nudging up to 100 degrees, I took my suit off and worked in my running shorts — no shirt, no socks, no shoes. Charlie Jones was in full dress uniform and there I was, my 2.2 percent body fat exposed for all to see. They didn't mind. A little personality has to come through, especially in the commentators, and the bow tie and the running shorts were just me. The TV people realize that and they're good about it; they know when to leave you alone.

The only suggestions they've made are that I look more into the camera, which I tend not to do, and that I get more excited in my commentary, show more energy, because when I'm calling a race and analyzing the nuances I don't *think* about it excitedly and therefore come across too subdued. For the sake of television, I've learned to sound more excited than I'm thinking. "Be up! Be up!" they say.

As "up" as I may have to be, I find I'm always a bit melancholy, too, at not being on the track myself. I'm one of the few active athletes doing TV commentary. Marty Liquori no longer competes. Nor does Bruce Jenner, the 1976 Olympic decathlon champion who works with Charlie Jones and me for NBC. Most of the time during the last few years I've not been at my best and would have had no business being in those races. I'm glad to be feeling the competitive urges nonetheless and, given the choice, would trade in my TV position for a world-class performance in the 10,000 meters.

Since I haven't been fit enough lately to compete in the major meets, TV gives me a reason to attend an event, other than just as a spectator. TV provides me with a role, something to *do*. This enables me to keep up with the sport because to do the best job I can, I have to stay current. I have to know the latest performances, the athletes, and to some extent the technical nature of some of the more specialized events. As a "track nut," I enjoy it.

At a meet, I make a point of checking with some of the leading athletes before their events get under way so I'll be prepared to comment during the competition and in the interviews afterward. With the running events that's easy — I'm a runner. With the field events . . . well, I have a working knowledge of most of them, but I couldn't possibly know as much as the competitors. So I'll hang around the pole vault or high jump to get a better feel for the event. My approach is *not:* "Teach me about your event so I can sound smart on the air." Rather it's: "Tell me what you'd like the people to look for so they can appreciate what you do." Field athletes are always trying to perfect a particular aspect of their events — the plant in the pole vault, the takeoff in the high jump, leg extension in the long jump. When I started in TV I'd go up to the pole vaulters and ask them, "How come you can vault eighteen feet eight inches and so-and-so sitting over there can only do seventeen feet six inches? What aspect of your technique allows you to do it?" In the mile, such distinctions are more obvious.

The field athletes appreciate the attention because it's rare for anyone outside their event to try to understand what they do. They can tell when a reporter just wants a quick quote and when someone really wants an explanation of their performance. One of the most interesting is the high jumper Dwight Stones, an Olympic bronze medalist in 1976 and a former world record-holder. It's a pleasure to interview him. He's bright, friendly, a student of track and field, and he knows as much about the high jump as anyone.

The requirements of a TV broadcast are not always compatible with the needs of athletes. Moments after a hard race, the last thing a runner needs is a microphone in the face. I can't change the fact that we might have to do an interview before an athlete has had much of a chance to recuperate, but because I've been on the other side of the mike and the athletes know me, the intrusion becomes less objectionable. I'm not so much TV as a peer congratulating an athlete on a fine effort. And if you have run quite well there is an impulse to talk about it, to share it with people who have empathy for you.

Sometimes it takes an athlete a while to feel at ease with the role of television. A few years ago Edwin Moses, the unbeatable intermediate hurdler, would be difficult to pin down for an interview. He'd come up with objections: It was too soon before his event; he had to find his sweats after his event; he had to jog . . . And yet he's one athlete who's complained about the lack of attention given to track in America. You can't have it both ways. And in time Moses realized that. You have to give a little if you want the exposure. Now Moses is much more cooperative and, like Dwight Stones, he's an expert on the technical complexities of his event.

I'm an example of an introverted athlete who's had to come to terms with being in the public eye. I think I've been cooperative with the media and that they've appreciated it. It's not always easy. I had to be analytical after I failed to win the 1976 Olympic marathon, a time when silly questions tend to carry a particular sting. Of course I was asked, "Are you disappointed?" Even then I tried to be polite. I've had to practice responding so as to cooperate while maintaining a certain degree of privacy. Like Coe does. Or Viren. It's a fine art. After all, you can't tell your opponents exactly what you think or what your plans are.

I don't think it's possible for a journalist to really capture the essence of running unless he's done some running himself. If he's good, he can pick up the vibrations and give a fairly accurate account of the sport and its people. But unless you know the feeling of running, you're at a disadvantage.

Kenny Moore of *Sports Illustrated* is noted for his sensitively drawn portraits of leading runners. When *SI* decided to do a profile of me before the '76 Olympics, they gave the assignment to Frank Deford because they felt Kenny's relationship with me could jeopardize his objectivity. That was a hard call.

I was leery of Deford because I'd read some of his work and he seemed cynical. I was extremely guarded when he interviewed me, but I had no complaints when the piece appeared. It was actually flattering. The worst thing he said was that I'd become so wrapped up in my running that I may have lost control of it. He was right.

As hard as it is for TV to cover track and field effectively, it's harder still to handle road racing, which, not being confined to a stadium, makes the logistics complex, untidy, and subject to severe mechanical failure.

The shorter distance events are less difficult because the course is more compact, but that also means you have less time to communicate your story and get it right. One time I'm sure we got it right was in 1982 at the Falmouth Road Race on Cape Cod. The race got a lot of same-day air time, and we were successful in keying on the pivotal points on the course, such as the spot 2½ miles out where the leaders came out of the woods and onto the path along the shore and Alberto Salazar, the eventual winner, made his breakaway.

☆

My clothing company was formed early in 1977 and named Frank Shorter Running Gear (now Frank Shorter Sportswear). I formed a partnership with three men — Jim Lillstrom, John Kubiac, and Rob Yahn. Though Lillstrom lived in Boulder, I hadn't known him, and it was in a chance meeting with him on a plane to New York in the fall of '76 that the idea for a small manufacturing company came up. Lillstrom was doing some promotional work with the pro ski tour and took Kubiac, a skiing buddy of his from Seattle, the plans. Kubiac already was in the business of making ski clothing. I brought in Yahn, a teammate from Yale and a Harvard Business School graduate who was working as an accountant in Massachusetts. We were so rushed those first few months that at the National Sporting Goods Association Show in Chicago in February 1977, we were sewing the labels on samples at 6:00 A.M. for a nine o'clock opening. I didn't know at the time that this would become a standard way of doing business; Kubiac, experienced in manufacturing, was the person in charge of production (working out of Seattle), and as things turned out he was regularly late with the goods.

In a year, we reached the point where we had about a million dollars' worth of orders on the books, waiting to be filled. And Kubiac had about a half-million dollars' worth of finished product in his Seattle warehouse.

In February 1978 we all met to discuss the business. Kubiac and Lillstrom had just returned from a skiing trip in Canada, and apparently they'd used their time together to formulate a course of action. At the meeting Kubiac announced that he wanted me to sell him my controlling interest in the company, and if I didn't, he said he wouldn't deliver the goods in his warehouse so the orders could be filled because the company was a bad credit risk. Though we had a million dollars in orders waiting, Kubiac couched his threat in a "business judgment," claiming I wouldn't be able to afford to pay him for the goods he held. (Kubiac was essentially the firm's manufacturer, receiving a percentage markup for the goods he sent us.)

Lillstrom was allied with Kubiac, and the two of them tried to convince me to agree to their demands. I said no. Yahn said nothing.

Other meetings ensued. Finally, I told Kubiac that if he persisted I'd take the matter to court. Kubiac's last words to me were: "I take no prisoners."

However, pressured by my attorney, Kubiac turned over some of his goods to avoid possible legal action. I would guess we got about a third of the stock. We should have gotten all of it, but I didn't want to spend the time and money fighting it out in the courts.

Kubiac took the rest of the inventory and started a competing company, called G.U.T.S. He switched labels and quickly had quite a bit of clothing to sell. Lillstrom went with him. (Eventually, G.U.T.S. was bought by the Brooks shoe company, which had had problems of its own. Brooks went through a shakeup and was acquired by Wolverine in 1982.)

One battle was over, but another was just beginning. With such a low inventory on hand, we could hardly fill our orders. In addition, it meant we would not get reorders. This came at a critical point, when we needed to generate the cash flow to help keep the business afloat. Instead, we developed a reputation for nondelivery, which was deserved because we simply did not have the product to deliver.

Yahn, too, left, believing that we would go bankrupt. Though stung by Yahn's departure, I agreed to let him out of his contract, which had a "noncompete" clause that prevented him from working for another company in the industry for a period of time. I was not going to prevent him from going on with his professional life. I suspected Rob would go off and start a clothing company like mine with Bill Rodgers, and he did.

This was in mid-'78, probably the low point of my adult life. My business was in the throes of collapse, a friend had left me for a likely competitor, and I was going through surgery to repair a damaged foot that had made running all but impossible. All this placed a strain on my marriage as well.

I went searching for fresh financing for the company and found it; but that, too, was fraught with bad luck, and we went through a series of investors before settling into a stable financial arrangement. Recovery took five years. It was not until 1983 that we were on the verge of going into the black. Though we'd quickly acquired a following among runners for producing high-quality clothing that is both functional and stylish — indeed, we've been an innovator in the field — the financial wounds were too deep and complex to overcome easily.

Basically Rob is a decent person who I believe simply did not want to go down with the ship. He thought our company would go under and figured he'd try and set up shop with someone else. That Bill Rodgers took him up on it was not surprising since Bill seems to have been following my every move over the years. I think he somehow wants to better me, to be very much like me but "better." I take it personally because that's different from wanting to beat me in a race. Let him beat me in a race. He's certainly beaten me more times than I've beaten him. Bill's a terrific runner, one of the greatest marathoners we've ever seen. Despite that, he seems to feel he's been in my shadow, so he's imitated me as a way of competing. But that's the problem: By imitating me he's *created* the shadow because I've done everything first. Bill hasn't shown individuality; he hasn't struck out in a direction of his own, and it's made me feel almost as though I have to protect myself in some way.

☆

The days of the old gray sweatsuit are, of course, long gone. The running and fitness boom revolutionized the athletic and sportswear industry, creating a demand that, in turn, led to sophisticated, "high tech" attire. Our market includes both the casual jogger and serious runner — and those who want to look like one or the other. Recreational athletes today have discriminating needs, and to meet those needs we review our line all the time for fit, fabric, comfort, style, color, design, and durability. Materials are becoming lighter and more breathable. Styling is becoming sleeker and more utilitarian. Colors are becoming more fashionable. Accent features are becoming more functional. All this enables the runner to look better and feel better.

I like the feeling of looking good when I run, and I've always believed others do too. I'd even go so far as to say it could be psychologically advantageous in competition to feel that you look right. It serves to reinforce the effort. When I organized a racing team of top runners a few years ago, I didn't care which brand of clothing anyone wore in a race as long as the colors matched.

I was concerned about my running attire even back in the days before anyone would *want* to look like a runner. In 1970, competing for the U.S. team in Europe, I switched the heavy USA shirt we'd been issued with a Yale jersey I'd brought. The Yale top was one of the first mesh singlets and therefore far more breathable than the American issue. I had to peel off the USA lettering and sew it onto the Yale shirt turned inside out. If you look at the issue of *Sports Illustrated* that covered my victory in the 10,000 meters against the Russians, you can see the "Yale" outline coming through the inside of the uniform.

By the 1972 Olympics, not much progress had been made. For competition in Munich I wore old training shorts and a makeshift singlet ordered by the Olympic coach, Bill Bowerman, with some advice from Kenny Moore and myself. Kenny wore his green Oregon shorts dyed blue. The regular issue uniform was so shoddy that Bowerman went looking for new stuff once the team was assembled in Europe. I'm not even sure which company finally made the uniforms, but they were shipped over from the States, and in the process some athletes ended up competing in uniforms that weren't exactly their size.

Things were only marginally better at the 1976 Olympics. The shirt had a lot of extraneous piping on it, unnecessary trim under the arms. I just cut it all off. I don't like to feel the weight of my uniform during a race, especially in a marathon. I'll frequently cut off most of my racing number, leaving just the numeral, to scale down its weight and size. At the Olympics, that's discouraged.

I wanted to help improve the uniform quality for the 1980 Olympics and asked to have our clothing considered for the U.S. team. I personally presented our line to the Olympic officials, and before the boycott hit, our company had been selected to provide the competition uniforms.

There's something special about wearing a USA uniform. You have to earn it, and once you do it invests you with a certain responsibility to carry yourself with dignity on and off the track. I'm not involved with the uniforms for the 1984 Olympics. For the sake of all those competing, I do hope the uniforms look sharp and feel good.

CHAPTER ELEVEN

Los Angeles: 1984

One year before the 1984 U.S. Olympic Trials in track and field, I was in Middletown, New York, for the annual Orange Classic, a 10-kilometer road race that snakes through the streets I first ran on as a boy. It was good to be back home. Of all places, it was Middletown that came to represent the ability I felt I still possessed as a runner. Though weakened by recurrent injuries since the 1976 Olympics and counted out by followers of the sport, I won the Middletown race in 1981 and 1982, beating Bill Rodgers the first year and Rod Dixon the next.

But in 1983 it wasn't the same. I was injured again. I'd picked up a little tendinitis in my left foot, near the ankle, and this time I wasn't taking any chances. It was early in June and I planned to rest the foot completely. I would do some light jogging or not run at all the rest of the month, and maintain cardiovascular fitness and muscular strength with swimming, weight work on the Nautilus system, and daily sessions on the stationary bicycle. I wanted to be fresh and mended by July, when I would begin a year-long training program — free of interference, I swore to myself — for the 1984 Olympic Games.

In Middletown I stayed with my grandmother, Ethel Shorter, who still lives in the house where my father grew

up. My father also was in town for the race. He now lives
in semiretirement in Lake Wanasink, New York, an emergency room physician at a nearby hospital. My parents are
divorced, and my mother lives in Taos. Two of the ten
Shorter children remain in Taos today: Michael, who is
mildly retarded, lives with my mother and attends a special
school, and Amy, the fifth girl. She was also in Middletown
for the 1983 race.

I'd notified the race officials that I'd come down with an
injury, in case they no longer wanted me, but they insisted
I come. The race is conducted by the *Middletown Times
Herald Record,* and it's been built into quite a regionally
popular sports event. When it comes to sports I'm Middletown's favorite son, and I'm proud of that because I have
fond memories of the place and its people. I told the officials
that I couldn't try to win this year but would run at a pace
that wouldn't put too much pressure on my bad foot. They
were happy to have me on that basis and, sniffing out every
angle, a photographer from the *Record* took some pictures
of me on an exercise bike at a workout center in town.

In the days before the race I sat on my grandmother's
front porch and thought about my running. It was quiet
on Jackson Avenue, and warm; a good time to stretch out
and contemplate what the next year might bring. When I
thought about the Los Angeles Olympics, I grew a bit tense
with anticipation, but I was careful to catch myself and con-
tain my emotion. I was also frustrated by this most recent
injury, which had developed just when it appeared that,
after six and a half years, I might soon be able to train consistently at full strength again.

My training had been going well, and I'd won a 5-mile
road race in Denver in April. My time was a modest 24:39,
but I beat Herb Lindsay (though Herb was not as fit as he'd
been in 1980 and '81, when he was the top road racer in
the country). Indeed, everything was going well. My back

and leg ailments had cleared up. My clothing business was doing fine. I'd signed a contract with NBC for my track commentary. The amateur rules were significantly changed for the better, and my work to reform the old system was largely over. Life was more tidy than it had been for some time, a welcome environment in which to train.

But speedwork brought me down again. I do much of my interval training at the University of Colorado indoor track, and I guess I'd become increasingly vulnerable to its tight turns. (Running center that Boulder is, it doesn't have a really good *outdoor* track.) In May my foot started to hurt, and I couldn't run hard on Memorial Day in the Bolder Boulder 10-kilometer run, which is to Boulder what the Orange Classic is to Middletown. I had won the Bolder Boulder from a good field in 1981, six weeks before defeating Rodgers in Middletown. That had been my finest period of running in years.

The summer of '83 was a pivotal time for me. When the Olympics roll around, it always is. I had to get in a position that might enable me to come back all the way.

Once I resumed running in July, I would try to train consistently but not race much. The summer would be broken up by an important TV assignment in Helsinki, the inaugural World Track and Field Championships, and I needed to develop a steady routine in which I would become, by the fall, as much of a full-time runner as I once was.

I didn't want to be thinking too much about the Olympics, not until the beginning of 1984. That's how I'd always done it. I was committed to getting into good shape, knowing it could lead to the Olympics but not dwelling on that. I wanted to feel fit but not mentally tired before launching into a peaking timetable that would have me focused on that one goal. And an auspicious goal it was, considering my recent running history.

When January arrived, had my training fallen into place,

I would compete a little on the indoor track circuit for the first time since 1977. If I ran well and survived that, I might run the Olympic Marathon Trial, assuming I'd made the qualifying standard in the months before. It was not with the marathon in mind, however, that I'd been pondering the Olympics. I no longer felt the marathon was my best event. It's never been my favorite event. My favorite event is the 10,000 meters, and that's what I hoped to run in Los Angeles.

☆

After the 1980 Olympic Marathon Trial, in which I'd run miserably because of injuries, I told reporters I'd have to cut back on my training, from two workouts a day to one. The second half of the year I didn't run that badly, getting some seconds, thirds, and fourths, but after another disappointing Honolulu Marathon (fourth in 2:20:11) I did pare down my training. That, coupled with my continued rehab work on the orthotron, seemed to help. The muscle imbalance in my left leg that stemmed from my 1978 surgery and hurt my back needed to be corrected, and with the orthotron I could help it by putting my leg into a hydraulic bar and moving it up (to strengthen the quadriceps) and back (to strengthen the hamstrings).

I wouldn't say I was a new man by 1981, but by the time I was invited to compete in the Middletown race that year, my injuries had gone into remission. I hadn't been home since the Munich celebration of September 1972, and I knew I'd be under a lot of pressure to run well. What I didn't know was that the good people of Middletown had also invited Bill Rodgers — and they hadn't bothered to tell Bill I was running, either.

Bill was having a fine season. Coming into Middletown, he'd won fifteen of nineteen races, had set a lifetime best for 15 and 20 kilometers, and had run one of the fastest marathons of the year, 2:10:34, while placing third at Boston. I was pretty fit myself, and I'd decided even before I knew Bill was running to peak for two races that year — Bolder Boulder and Middletown.

The memories of those two races give me encouragement. With my injuries subsided, I was able once again to do the kind of speedwork that puts me on equal terms with almost anybody. With the challenge so inviting, I could harness the kind of mental toughness that was necessary in top-flight competition. I was free to try as hard as I could, and when trying hard is the deciding factor, I'm set.

I was, in a sense, something of my old self again. I started my speedwork a month before Boulder: ¾-mile, ½-mile, and ¼-mile repetitions. At my sharpest I could manage twelve quarters in 63 seconds with a 220 jog in between at the university's indoor track. When Bolder Boulder came around I was ready, and I won it in 29:28, an excellent time for 10,000 meters at altitude. Living in Boulder and being so identified with its much-talked-about running scene made that victory so wonderful, even just. Because of the altitude factor I considered it my best performance of the year.

Middletown was six weeks later, on July 12. It was hot and humid, my kind of weather. I'd won my eighth race of the year, a 10,000, the week before in St. Louis. Bill had also won the previous week, the Pepsi national 10,000-meter championship, run over the George Washington Bridge from New Jersey to New York.

It was the perfect matchup: Bill and me, both of us fit, both of us ready. And the added impetus of *Middletown*. It was more pressure than I've felt for any race since the '76 Olympics.

It felt strange, almost eerie, to be running through Middletown again. To run from the Orange County Fairgrounds near Middletown High down Main Street, past the Thrall Library, where I'd spent many afternoons, up over Highland

Avenue two blocks from our big old house, around the periphery of Fancher Davidge Park, where I used to ride my bike and fish, and back through the other side of town to the fairgrounds finish — more memories were stored there than I could possibly handle in one morning.

My strategy in the race was to stay close to Rodgers because I knew I could outkick him. I'm faster, and on that day no one was going to push any harder.

We ran together, literally side by side. Bill's one of the few runners I can do that with. In the pictures of the race you see an uncanny resemblance; it's as though our duel had been choreographed. We appear to be running in unison; the angle of our bodies, the beat of our arms, even the squint in our eyes is set the same. The only difference (other than his Bill Rodgers uniform and my Frank Shorter uniform) was that I wasn't wearing a watch. (Remember my superstition.)

We never spoke. At one point Bill offered me some of his water but I refused. I wasn't being antisocial. I just love the heat.

With a mile or so to go I surged, felt an advantage, and pulled away. What a boost that was! It encouraged me to run harder still up the long ascent of Carpenter Avenue near the finish, and I won by 19 seconds in 29:33. It was one of those races in which two guys go at it until one guy breaks. To me, those are the most fun — especially if I'm not the guy who breaks. I had to win in Middletown — even my grandmother was out there watching.

I could not have been more satisfied. I was training only once a day and had won the two races for which I'd peaked. I told myself, "This is going to be all right."

But it wasn't. I didn't recover well from Middletown, which told me I hadn't been extraordinarily fit to begin with. I'd run over my head. When I'm really peaked I recover easily; four days after the 10,000 final I'd won the mara-

thon in Munich. This feeling was far different. I'd beaten
Rodgers more on emotional tenacity than anything else. In
a way, that made me feel better. It showed how psychologically strong I could still be and affirmed my belief that if I
could ever endure optimal training again, I'd be tough to
beat.

But the main reason I'm still running hard is not so much
to win a particular race or even to go to the Olympics again.
I just want to get back into the shape I was in before I
got hurt. I want to have that totally controlled and masterful
feeling of being in the best condition possible. It's been several years since I've experienced the rapture of being physically tuned to a perfect pitch, and one day I may not long
for it anymore. But I do now. And I'm glad that I still do.

The only other race of 1981 I focused on was the Honolulu
Marathon. But I failed again; I couldn't hold up. I couldn't
take the good form I'd shown over distances of up to a half-
marathon and extend it to 26.2 miles. I was never in contention and finished eighth in 2:24:07, my slowest marathon.
It was the third time in a row I'd run Honolulu — Louise
and the kids would come with me and we'd make a vacation
out of it — and each time I've come up short. It happened
again in 1982 when, after leading for 9½ miles, I faltered
and finished fifth in 2:22:57, almost 7 minutes behind the
winner, Dave Gordon. My best performance at Honolulu
came in 1979, when I finished second to Dean Matthews
in 2:17:51. The only marathon other than Honolulu that I've
run seriously since the 1980 Olympic Trial is the America's
Marathon in Chicago, and there too I've been disappointed,
running a 2:23:58 for ninth in 1980 and 2:17:27 for third place
in '81.

It would have been foolish to expect to run a good marathon again soon. That's why I set my sights on the 10,000
for Los Angeles. I believe my problem with the marathon
is that my left leg, even with the rehab work, has not re-

gained full strength since the surgery, and no matter how my training goes, the leg seems not to have the capacity to develop the stamina for the longer distance. At a certain point it slips to a lower gear, throwing my form off.

Dr. Stan James, who performed the surgery, warned me at the time that even with full recovery, one is sometimes no longer quite the same afterward. Invading the body changes it, and it may be that after the operation, my left leg was destined never to be the same, never to have the "memory" it once had. I think I've come to terms with that, though I'll continue to try to achieve equal strength in both legs, at least as indicated theoretically by the equipment.

By 1982 I was starting to feel almost "normal" again, which I attribute to my use of the Multiaxial Ankle Exerciser. This machine, unlike the orthotron, allows me to work on the motions at which I've found my leg to be weakest — eversion (turning outward) and inversion (turning inward). A greater range of motion is possible in the ankle and rear of the foot with the exerciser; on the orthotron I'm restricted to dorsiflexion (upward) and plantarflexion (downward). Still there's a Catch-22: I was probably working too hard on the exerciser at first, and that may have been responsible for the tendinitis near my ankle at the time of the 1983 Middletown race.

Frankly, I would've had to have been at my very best to have won in 1983 because the race officials — who never let me off easy — also invited Michael Musyoki of Kenya. Musyoki, a graduate of the University of Texas at El Paso, was the top road racer in the U.S. in 1982. He won handily in Middletown, breaking my course record by 27 seconds; just how fit he was at the time was evident three weeks later, when he ran 42:28 to set a world record for 15 kilometers in the Cascade Run Off in Portland.

Similarly, when I faced Rod Dixon of New Zealand in Middletown in 1982, Dixon was running as well as anyone.

The circumstances were much like those the previous year against Bill Rodgers: The home folks expected me to win, and because it was Middletown I felt the pressure. I was in better shape against Dixon. I'd run 29:26 at the Bolder Boulder (placing sixth) despite a midrace hamstring cramp, and two weeks later, when the hamstring was better, I won a hilly half-marathon in Kansas City. The speedwork was paying off, and I was ready for Dixon — so ready that to top off my training, I did twelve fast 220s two days before the race. When I'm fit, I'll do that.

Dixon may have been the better runner at the time, but I was emotionally. I'd watched Dixon compete two weeks before in Portland, Oregon, and saw that he didn't run especially well on the downhills. My plan was to run the downhills hard and try to get a bit of a lead to work with, and that's what happened. I drew ahead with 2 miles to go, and ran 29:18 to win by 21 seconds. Dixon was gracious in defeat, saying he'd underestimated me. I'm sure he was bothered by the heat; it was even a little hot for me. Both the temperature and humidity were in the 90s, and there was little shade to protect the runners. I ran shirtless and took a little water.

It's too bad the Olympic Trials won't be in Middletown.

☆

By leaving the marathon for the 10,000 meters, I'm going against a trend. Track runners, as they get older, sometimes gravitate to the marathon, finding their lessening speed and increasing endurance better suited to the longer road races. They also find that training for the marathon is not much different from training for the 10,000 — though training for the road, for some athletes, may be different from training for the track. The rhythms, the style of competition — the entire environment differs. The transition from the 10,000 to the marathon can be a mistake, though, because being a successful marathoner at the high levels takes something more than you can attain through training and experience. There's something about the marathoner that makes it hard to "become" one. By your very nature either you are suited to it or you aren't. It is perhaps some intangible quality that leads to such compatibility. I don't know. Maybe it has to do with temperament, a willingness to wait for success. Kenny Moore, for example, was right for the marathon. Steve Prefontaine would not have been. He was in too much of a hurry.

I'm going about this thing backward. I'm returning to the track. I never enjoyed the marathon as much as the track. I was obviously suited to it, so I ran it, and I'm glad I did. But I feel I run best when I'm running on the track, competing in the shorter events. All along I've found it's a better way for me to train anyway. I didn't get in good shape for road races by running road races but by running on the track.

So I won't miss the marathon. I have no emotional attachment to the distance, and if I ever had, it was in the context of an allegiance to performance. I had to work toward the event I could consistently win internationally, and that turned out to be the marathon.

It may seem peculiar to claim that I've felt cool toward the marathon and at the same time say that I was the sort of person naturally suited to it; one would think that being right for an event means, among other things, that you have a passion for it. Of course I've had a passion for running, if that needs to be said at this point. But maybe, deep down, I've found the track races more alluring and compelling because I could never achieve the success in them that I could in the marathon. They were harder. There was frequently something unfinished about a tough 10,000, something concrete I could take away from the race and work at for the next time.

At thirty-six, I'll be one of the oldest Olympic aspirants

running the 10,000 in '84. I don't worry about age. Runners
in their mid-thirties have done well at the world-class level.
Miruts Yifter, the great Ethiopian, won the 5,000 and 10,000
at the Moscow Olympics, and he was believed to be about
forty — no one knows for sure — at the time. Carlos Lopes
of Portugal, at thirty-six, ran one of the best races of his
life in April 1982, when he finished right behind Robert de
Castella of Australia in the Rotterdam Marathon. His time
was 2:08:39. When I heard that it made my day.

When I compare my running at twenty-five versus thirty-
five, the only noticeable differences concern injury. First,
I get injured more often. Second, the healing process takes
longer. Third, during training I think more about how I
run, my form — what happens precisely as I'm doing it —
because of the injuries. Years ago I never gave it a second
thought; I just did it. It was more fun that way. Now I tend
to monitor my running and worry too much about detecting
signs of dysfunction. It's a habit I must break. It tends to
hold me back, and I can't let that happen.

When I was younger, I could run "through" a lot of routine
minor injuries simply by cutting back on my training. That
no longer works, and I've learned to take more of an all-
or-nothing approach when pain strikes. If I can't make a
total effort, I won't run at all. Many of the Europeans use
this approach successfully. Eamonn Coghlan of Ireland sat
out most of 1982 with injuries, then set a world indoor mile
record (3:49.78) in the winter of '83. David Moorcroft of
Great Britain, who broke the world 5,000 record in 1982,
got hurt and took sick and missed all of '83, but he used
the layoff as a period of renewal before building up for the
'84 Olympics.

I haven't noticed any differences through the years in
my basic training capacity, recovery time, or competitive
instincts. In fact, I now tend to feel less stiff or achy in the
mornings, but I guess that's because I haven't been running
terribly hard day in and day out due to scattered injuries.

As I pondered the 1984 season in the summer of '83, I knew that if I couldn't train hard I could forget about the Olympics. I needed to be able to tolerate intense training, and for that I had to be free of injury. And I needed an atmosphere conducive to highly focused running, so I had to cut way back on my business commitments and travel. I needed to approximate once again the sort of both free and controlled running lifestyle that worked so well a decade ago. It wouldn't be easy, but then, making the Olympic team never is.

The only "easy" thing about it was that there would be little pressure on me. Nobody would expect too much of a thirty-six-year-old runner beyond his peak with a troublesome left leg. I'll be lucky to make the fine print in the pre-race coverage. That could change if I do make the team.

The way I look at it, the three berths in the 10,000 are wide open. America's only world-class 10,000-meter runner is Alberto Salazar, the U.S. record-holder (27:25.61), but he's expected to concentrate only on the marathon; and if he does run the trials and make the team he'd likely give up his spot in that event, as Bill Rodgers and I did in 1976. Not that I feel Salazar has a 10,000 spot assured if he wants it. Off an easy pace, he'd be in trouble. I don't know any major 10,000-meter runner who's slower than he is when the race comes down to an all-out kick.

After Salazar, the leading Americans have not shown themselves to be medal contenders. Greg Meyer ran a fine 27:53.1 two weeks before his 1983 Boston Marathon triumph, but after that he was injured and missed the World Championships in Helsinki. He's more of a marathon prospect anyway. Another frustrated candidate is Craig Virgin, one of the world's most versatile runners before he was riddled with illness and injury in 1982. Since then he's not been near the form that produced an American record (27:29.16) in 1980 and won the U.S. Olympic Trials race so convincingly that year. Bill McChesney, like Salazar an Oregon graduate, has some fast times to his credit but never seems to put together one solid season. Jimmy Hill, Oregon's latest young talent, broke 28 minutes as a sophomore and with 3:56-mile speed he had a lot going for him. But both McChesney and Hill may have a better shot at the 5,000. Another developing runner is Pat Porter, the 1982 and 1983 national cross-country champion who's benefited from training at the high altitude of Alamosa, Colorado. By mid-'83 he'd improved his track times but still lacked experience.

I'd guess that on June 19 in the Los Angeles Coliseum two men will break away in the trials 10,000 final and run under 28 minutes, but not that much under — say, 27:45 or 27:50. The third berth will be won in over 28 minutes, and that's not too much for me to hope for.

While the track and field trials for men and women (June 16–24) will be held at the Olympic facility in Los Angeles, the marathon trials won't, and that's a mistake. The women's trial (May 12) is in Olympia, Washington; the men's trial (May 26) is in Buffalo, New York, where it was held in 1980. I have nothing against either city, but I would have liked the marathon trials to have been awarded to Los Angeles. The marathoners who make the U.S. team would have acquired a terrific psychological advantage by having run the Olympic course before the Games. They'd have an intimate knowledge of the route and would come away from the trials with the memory of having run well there despite the infamous LA weather. Why put the marathoners in a different environment for the trials? It also bothers me that the American men's trial will be run mostly in Canada. Buffalo has a handsome course as such, but after just a few miles the route enters Canada and stays there for the remainder of the race, finishing near Niagara Falls. That seems wrong.

It's too bad that with all the improvements in the amateur system, the location of the marathon trial can turn out *not* to be in the best interests of the athletes. According to The Athletics Congress, the sites are chosen on the basis of the bids submitted by local TAC associations. At a certain point, however, you have to take a Thomas Paine point of view and say, "Look, we're going to hold this thing here. Somebody come up with the right bid." The Olympics is too important to have cronyism get in the way.

The American women, fortunately, as well as women from other countries, did get a chance to run on the 1984 Olympic course, in the Avon International Women's Marathon in June 1983. Julie Brown, should she make the team (and I think she will), received quite a boost by winning that race, and in 2:26:24, the fastest run in a women's race to date. America's other leading woman marathoner, Joan Benoit, the world record-holder (2:22:43), did not run Avon and in fact was a proponent of Olympia as a trials site. I hope she doesn't regret it. After Brown and Benoit, the women's field is spread out in the marathon.

The men's field is far less defined. As in the 10,000, I don't give Salazar an automatic berth. Though he's the world record-holder (2:08:13), he set that record in 1981, and though he won Boston and New York in 1982, he started to slip in '83, most notably with a fifth-place performance (2:10:08) at Rotterdam. The Rotterdam Marathon was the sort of significant European race that goes largely unnoticed in the States. Imagine if Salazar had been fifth at New York or Boston.

If Salazar runs up to his potential he'll make the team. But if he overraces, as he did before Rotterdam, I fear it'll be a tragic error. Salazar should understand that to his agent he represents a short-term business interest, a source of income, and as far as the Olympics are concerned, the agent is taking no risk by piling on commitments because he'll sign up whomever the heroes turn out to be.

In the men's marathon it's quite open. After winning Boston in '83 (in 2:09:01), Greg Meyer seemed a good bet; but then he got hurt, as Boston winners seem to do. Of the Boston runners-up: Craig Virgin hasn't been the same since his run behind Toshihiko Seko, a 2:10:27, in '81; nor has Dick Beardsley since his run behind Salazar, a 2:08:54, in '82. Bill Rodgers was third at Boston in '81 (in 2:10:34), but that's the last marathon he's run that's worthy of him. With all the racing he does and with a questionable commitment to the Olympics, I don't see Rodgers on the U.S. team in '84. Tony Sandoval, who as a medical student won our 1980 trial so nicely, is now a physician, and should he put aside his career to train for '84, I think he'll be tough. If I'm high on any American, it's Sandoval. He knows how to peak.

☆

The Los Angeles Coliseum is a great stadium for track and field. It's got a long and glorious history, highlighted by the 1932 Olympic Games, the last summer Olympics held in the U.S. I got a chance to review the spruced-up stadium and its new track in June 1983 while working the U.S.–East German dual track meet for NBC. That was the first meet held on the new track, a Rekortan polyurethane surface, the same kind used at the Munich Olympics. The track had a good, clean feel to it, and though it was a bit too soft, as new tracks will be, the athletes knew it would firm up in time. The runners spoke highly of the track and the entire facility — which, despite its seating capacity of 92,156, has retained a certain personal charm — and I think those who took part in that meet, especially those who did well, gained an advantage by having experienced the Olympic environment ahead of time. Mary Decker, who won a beautifully controlled 1,500 (3:59.93), put it this way: "Down the home-stretch I could envision what next summer will be like."

The use of positive imagery can be an effective training device. I've always imagined myself in the stadium in which

I'd be competing, though I didn't do that at the East German meet; the Olympics seemed too far away at the time. I have never raced in the Coliseum, though I've trained there. In 1969 I was an alternate in the 10,000 in the U.S.–Soviet–British Commonwealth meet held in Los Angeles.

While the facility is terrific for track and field, the LA air, as everyone knows, is not. Training short distances on the track is not bad, but putting in long mileage out on the roads is. LA is the only place I've ever run where I had to stop in the middle of a 20-mile workout because I couldn't breathe anymore. The conditions that make it most severe — heat, humidity, light wind, and atmospheric inversions — are common to midsummer, when the Games are scheduled. The Olympic marathoners, inhaling carbon dioxide, ozone, and other pollutants when they need oxygen, will suffer. It will be a hard race, and I doubt the winning time will be very fast.

The competition should be marvelous: Carl Lewis with a chance to win four gold medals; the Americans versus the British in the middle distances; great duels in the 5,000 and 10,000; the drama of the marathons; Evelyn Ashford against the East Germans in the women's sprints; Mary Decker against the Russians at 3,000 meters; the first women's marathon in Olympic history.

If Lewis does try four events in LA — the 100 meters, 200 meters, long jump, and 400-meter relay — he'll be risking the obvious comparisons to the immortal Jesse Owens, who won gold medals in those events in the 1936 Olympics in Berlin. And what if he falls short? Say he wins two golds — is he a failure? No, but still, he'll be asked why. If he doesn't try to match Owens, he'll be considered a lesser man by the American public, and if he tries and fails he could wind up a "flop." How would you like to be competing in the Olympics against the record of Jesse Owens?

The odds are clearly against Lewis, and people have to

understand that. Though he may be the most exciting and talented trackman of our generation, he can be beaten. I saw him lose a 100 meters to Ron Brown in the spring of 1983. Lewis didn't look smooth and in control; Brown did. In the 200, Lewis has been beaten by Calvin Smith, another American. And even with Lewis on the anchor leg, you can never bank on a sprint relay because of the botched baton passing that has been characteristic of American teams (though a Lewis-anchored team did set a world record in 1983). That leaves the long jump, Lewis' best event. By the time the Olympics get under way, he probably will have gotten his long-awaited 29-footer — or even a 30-footer! — and it's hard to imagine him not winning that event in Los Angeles.

If Sebastian Coe of Great Britain runs the 800, I can't see anybody touching him. But if he runs the 1,500 he may be beaten by Steve Scott, the American record-holder, who impresses me with his steady improvements from one season to the next. Every year he gets a little bit better. But he'll have to run smart to win. If he doesn't kick soon enough, with a good 300 meters to go, he could be run down by Britain's Steve Cram, who outsprinted him off a slow pace in the '83 World Championships. At one time, there was speculation that Coe might forgo the 800 or 1,500 in favor of the 5,000. That's crazy. Coe's run the 800 in 1:41.73. He's got the rest of the world beat by a full second or more.

His own countryman David Moorcroft is in my view the 5,000 favorite. Moorcroft took *six seconds* off the world record with his 13:00.42 in 1982, then lost '83 to illness and injury. But I expect him to return at full strength for the Olympics, and he's just the sort of runner who can win it. He's got 3:49-mile speed, an endurance base built over many years of training, and at age thirty-one the experience to be relatively relaxed despite the pressure of the Games.

In the 10,000 we're likely to see one of the greatest Olympic finals ever. Track aficionados are high on the Africans — the Kenyans, Ethiopians, and Tanzanians — but I'm not. That may seem odd in light of their amazing success over the years and my tendency to favor distance runners from high altitudes, but the African champions of the recent past have slipped behind and those who have taken their place, by and large, currently lack the distance background and racing experience to be considered their equals. Of all the Africans, the best prepared to win a gold medal could be Mohamed Kedir of Ethiopia, the 1982 world cross-country champion, who has perhaps been around long enough by now to know the ropes. Kenya's Henry Rono is a most curious case. Since breaking four world records in 1978, he's never been the same. Henry's a fiercely independent man, frequently defying the orders of Kenyan athletics officials. He was living in Boulder and Eugene for a while in 1983 and, the last I heard, leading a late-night social life that had put an extra 20 pounds on him.

Portugal has a crop of proven 10,000-meter runners, but the Portuguese tend to peak too early and I doubt they can be that influential in '84, especially with their best runner, Carlos Lopes, expected to run the marathon. Another contender is Werner Schildhauer of East Germany, the 1981 World Cup champion who ran 27:24.95 in 1983, 2 seconds off Rono's world record. Schildhauer was second in the '83 World Championships, and the man who won that race would have to be the tentative favorite for Los Angeles — Alberto Cova of Italy.

And the Americans? We'll be lucky to have someone make the finals. If by some chance we do, and it's me, well, all I can say is that I'd hope to improve on my fifth-place in the Munich 10,000 of 1972.

The men's Olympic marathon should be magnificent. So strong is the marathon today that we may see four or five men enter the stadium together for a sprint to the finish.

That's never happened in the Olympics; it's rarely happened anywhere. To avoid a kicker's finish, someone — perhaps Alberto Salazar, who doesn't have basic speed — may try to steal the race with a sharp breakaway or a fast pace drawn out over several miles. In some sections the course is filled with turns, which can help a runner trying to sneak away. But he'd have to hit the halfway point in something like 1:02 for such strategy to have a chance. If he gets there in 1:03, there will be five smiling faces right behind him.

I see Robert de Castella of Australia as the favorite. In 1981 he won the Fukuoka Marathon in 2:08:18, 5 seconds off Salazar's world record. In 1982 he won the Commonwealth Games marathon in 2:09:18 on a brutally tough course. In 1983 he won the Rotterdam Marathon in 2:08:37 over the best field of marathoners assembled in recent years as well as the World Championships (in 2:10:03), looking fresh and spirited all the way. He's built slowly to a peak under the sensible guidance of his coach, Pat Clohessy, and if he tapers off properly after the hard training in '84, he should have everything it takes to win.

After de Castella, I pick Toshihiko Seko of Japan. If a stadium sprint does materialize, Seko would win it. A onetime half-miler, he's got the most basic speed of the contenders. He's won the Fukuoka Marathon four times, most recently with a 2:08:52 in 1983. He's a proud man, an extremely devoted runner, and de Castella will have to run the best race of his life to beat him.

I pick Carlos Lopes of Portugal for third. He was a close second to de Castella at Rotterdam, and that was his first full marathon (after dropping out at New York the previous fall). We view the running scene too provincially in the U.S. Rotterdam was extremely significant, but how many Americans know or care about it? Only the real track buffs do, and that's why the American public, unfortunately, will feel let down if Salazar, a distant fifth at Rotterdam, doesn't win an Olympic medal.

Salazar could win the gold. But I don't think he will. I think he'll be fighting it out in a second group that will include Rodolfo Gomez of Mexico, Juma Ikangaa of Tanzania, and perhaps Waldemar Cierpinski. It'll be a treat if Cierpinski runs, to watch a man try to win a third straight gold medal in the Olympic marathon. If he shows up, we'll know he's fit because the Germans can be merciless when it comes to the Olympic marathon; if they don't think you can win or come close, they won't even let you run. In 1983, however, Cierpinski placed a strong third in the World Championships, running 2:10:37, only 42 seconds slower than he ran to beat me in the Montréal Olympics, seven years before. For Cierpinski, that's right on schedule.

If everyone is healthy and at full strength, it will be fascinating to see how de Castella goes about trying to neutralize the probable wait-and-kick tactics of Seko. De Castella is a grinder and will have to assume the burden of the lead at some point and just run for it. Seko will not lead. He'll sit behind relentlessly and patiently and hope to have the strength to move past late in the race. This could rattle de Castella, who will know he can't outsprint Seko. He'll have to outfox him. It's a chilling race to think about.

Among the women, America's hopes will ride on Evelyn Ashford in the sprints, Mary Decker in the middle distances, and Joan Benoit in the marathon. Ashford's main opponents are the technically sound East Germans, Marlies Göhr (in the 100) and Marita Koch (in the 200). I think she can win both, as she did in the World Cup in 1979 and 1981. I'm just as confident about Mary Decker, who will probably run the 3,000 meters and not the 1,500 because of the tight Olympic schedule. One of the biggest thrills for me as a TV commentator at the Helsinki World Championships was watching the way Decker ran with courage, strength, and poise to win both the 1,500 and 3,000 over the supposedly stronger Russian opposition. It was an unforgettable double victory, and Mary proved she has even more talent than any of us thought. She sent the Soviets back to the drawing board, and you can bet they'll come out in full force in Los Angeles. It will be the challenge of Mary Decker's life.

The women's Olympic marathon is a hard call because it's the first; there's no precedent to draw upon. Joan Benoit, with her 2:22:43, is the world record-holder. Grete Waitz is the reigning world champion, a former record-holder, and most consistent, with six marathon victories at the world-class level. What these two women have in common, aside from their credentials, is that they train like men; that is, essentially with the same intensity. Many women, even top women, don't, and that's a mistake. There should not be any difference between men's and women's training, except that the men will generally be able to run their intervals faster because by their nature they have more muscular strength.

Speaking of Cierpinski and his chances for 1984, I rate him as one of the five toughest runners I've ever faced. The other four, in no particular order, are Lasse Viren (Finland), Steve Prefontaine (U.S.), Brendon Foster (Great Britain), and Emiel Puttemans (Belgium). They were all different types of runners. Viren was the master of peaking, a man of enormous confidence and refinement. Cierpinski is also a cunning peaker but from a different system, that of the scientifically dependent East Germans. Prefontaine was gutsy and relentless, never one to give up, so you knew you had to be just like that to beat him. Foster was smart, always trying to figure out how to beat you, even devising new strategies in the middle of a race. Puttemans was probably the most natural distance running talent to come along before Rono. When he was at his best, he gave the impression he could run fast forever.

☆

As I go about my preparations for 1984, I know I'm coming upon the Olympics for the last time as a prospective competitor. Even if I make the team and do well in the Games, what chance will I have to do it yet again in four years, at age forty? Would I even have the motivation to try? No, this will be my last possible Olympics, the last one the old legs will have a shot at.

When these Games are over, whether I've made the team or not, I think I'll feel a little disoriented. Nothing will be quite the same anymore, and though the time for change may be right, I'll feel awkward, lost. I'll no longer be one whose life is set to the rhythm of a four-year cycle, always with the Olympics in the future. In running, the Olympics have been the only objective arena to determine the best, and they have stood aloft as a pure and compelling challenge to me — a challenge not without its burdens.

I'll always run, and when the time comes for my running to be de-emphasized, I know a part of me will still long for the days when there could be no greater urge than the need to run my best.

Appendix

Frank Shorter's Career Record ☆ Significant Races: 1963–1983

DATE	EVENT	SITE	DISTANCE	PLACE	TIME
1963/64	**(Mount Hermon Prep School, junior year)**				
Nov. 2	New England Prep XC Champs	Mount Hermon	2.5M	5th	13:21
Nov. 19	Bemis-Forslund Pie Race	Mount Hermon	4.55M	2nd	24:35
May 16	New England Track Champs	Andover, Mass.	2-mile	1st	10:13.2
1964/65	**(Mount Hermon Prep School, senior year)**				
Nov. 7	New England Prep XC Champs	Andover, Mass.	2.5M	1st	12:54
Nov. 24	Bemis-Forslund Pie Race	Mount Hermon	4.55M	1st	23:38
May 15	New England Track Champs	Andover, Mass.	2-mile	1st	9:39.6
May 29	Interscholastics	Mount Hermon	2-mile	1st	9:39.3

1965/66 (Yale, freshman year)
Running de-emphasized

1966/67 (Yale, sophomore year)
Running de-emphasized

APPENDIX

DATE	EVENT	SITE	DISTANCE	PLACE	TIME
1967/68	**(Yale, junior year)**				
Nov. 10	Heptagonal XC Champs	The Bronx	5M	2nd	25:18
May 9	Harvard-Yale dual	New Haven	2M	DNF	—
June 1	IC4A Champs	Philadelphia	3M	6th	13:58.0
Aug. 18	Olympic Marathon Trial	Alamosa, Colo.	26.2M	DNF	—
1968/69	**(Yale, senior year)**				
Nov. 8	Heptagonal XC Champs	The Bronx	5M	2nd	24:52
Nov. 18	IC4A XC Champs	The Bronx	5M	5th	25:11
Nov. 25	NCAA XC Champs	The Bronx	6M	19th	30:07
Mar. 1	Harvard-Yale-Princeton Ind.	Princeton, N.J.	Mile	1st	4:06.4
Mar. 14	NCAA Indoor Champs	Detroit	2-mile	2nd	8:45.4
May 10	Heptagonal Champs	Philadelphia	2-mile	1st	8:50.8
May 17	Harvard-Yale dual	New Haven	2-mile	1st	8:58.4
May 31	IC4A Champs	New Brunswick, N.J.	3M	2nd	13:45.2
June 19	NCAA Champs	Knoxville, Tenn.	6M	1st	29:00.2
June 21	NCAA Champs	Knoxville, Tenn.	3M	2nd	13:43.4
June 28	AAU Nationals	Miami	6M	4th	28:52.0
Aug. 6	U.S.–West Germany	Augsburg, West Germany	10,000M	3rd	29:52.6
Aug. 12	U.S.–Great Britain	London	10,000M	4th	29:16.4

DATE	EVENT	SITE	DISTANCE	PLACE	TIME
1970					
Feb. 27	AAU Indoor Nationals	New York City	3-mile	2nd	13:29.8
Apr. 24	Drake Relays	Des Moines	3-mile	2nd	13:15.6
Apr. 25	Drake Relays	Des Moines	6-mile	1st (tie)	28:24.0
May 16	King Games	Philadelphia	5,000M	2nd	13:46.8
May 30	Kennedy Games	Berkeley, Calif.	3-mile	2nd	13:13.8
June 27	AAU Nationals	Bakersfield, Calif.	3-mile	1st	13:24.2
June 27	AAU Nationals	Bakersfield, Calif.	6-mile	1st (tie)	27:24.0
July 8	U.S.-France	Colombes, France	5,000M	2nd	13:42.4
July 23	U.S.-USSR	Leningrad	10,000M	1st	28:22.8
Aug. 5	Oslo Games	Oslo	10,000M	1st	28:32.6
Aug. 11	International Meet	Cologne, West Germany	3,000M	7th	7:57.8
Nov. 25	USTFF XC Champs	University Park, Pa.	6M	1st	29:01.4
Nov. 28	AAU XC Nationals	Chicago	10,000M	1st	30:05.8
1971					
Jan. 1	São Silvestre Midnight Run	São Paulo, Brazil	8,300M	1st	24:27.4
Feb. 19	Indoor Games	San Diego	2-mile	3rd	8:26.2
Feb. 26	AAU Indoor Nationals	New York City	3-mile	1st	13:10.6
Apr. 16	Kansas Relays	Lawrence, Kans.	3-mile	2nd	13:08.6
Apr. 23	Drake Relays	Des Moines	3-mile	1st	13:07.0

APPENDIX

DATE	EVENT	SITE	DISTANCE	PLACE	TIME
Apr. 24	Drake Relays	Des Moines	6-mile	1st	27:24.4
June 6	AAU Marathon Champs	Eugene, Ore.	Marathon	2nd	2:17:45
June 25	AAU Nationals	Eugene, Ore.	3-mile	3rd	13:02.4
June 26	AAU Nationals	Eugene, Ore.	6-mile	1st	27:27.2
July 2	U.S.–USSR–All-Stars	Berkeley, Calif.	10,000M	2nd	28:41.6
July 17	U.S.–Africa	Durham, N.C.	10,000M	2nd	28:54.0
July 31	Pan-Am Games	Cali, Colombia	10,000M	1st	28:50.8
Aug. 5	Pan-Am Games	Cali, Colombia	Marathon	1st	2:22:40
Sept. 26	Springbank Road Races	Ontario, Canada	11.6M	4th	57:00
Nov. 27	AAU XC Nationals	San Diego	10,000M	1st	29:19
Dec. 6	Fukuoka Marathon	Fukuoka, Japan	Marathon	1st	2:12:51
1972					
Feb. 19	Indoor Games	San Diego	2-mile	3rd	8:33.4
Mar. 24	Florida Relays	Gainesville, Fla.	6-mile	1st (tie)	27:22.8
Apr. 28	Drake Relays	Des Moines	3-mile	4th	13:12.6
Apr. 29	Drake Relays	Des Moines	6-mile	1st	27:38.0
June 16	AAU Nationals	Seattle	10,000M	2nd	28:12.0
July 2	Olympic Trials	Eugene, Ore.	10,000M	1st	28:35.6
July 9	Olympic Trials	Eugene, Ore.	Marathon	1st (tie)	2:15:58
Aug. 3	Bislett Games	Oslo	3,000M	6th	7:51.4

DATE	EVENT	SITE	DISTANCE	PLACE	TIME
Aug. 31	Olympic Games	Munich	10,000M(h)	3rd	27:58.2
Sept. 3	Olympic Games	Munich	10,000M	5th	27:51.4
Sept. 10	Olympic Games	Munich	Marathon	1st	2:12:20
Sept. 30	Springbank Road Races	Ontario, Canada	11.6M	1st	55:47
Nov. 25	AAU XC Nationals	Chicago	10,000M	1st	30:42
Dec. 3	Fukuoka Marathon	Fukuoka, Japan	Marathon	1st	2:10:30
1973					
Jan. 20	Sunkist Indoor	Los Angeles	2-mile	5th	8:40.6
Feb. 2	Maple Leaf Games	Toronto	3-mile	4th	13:30.8
Mar. 18	Otsu Marathon	Otsu, Japan	Marathon	1st	2:12.03
Mar. 31	Florida Relays	Gainesville, Fla.	6-mile	1st	27:54.0
May 20	Korso Marathon	Korso, Finland	Marathon	DNF	—
Nov. 24	AAU XC Nationals	Gainesville, Fla.	10,000M	1st	29:52.5
Dec. 2	Fukuoka Marathon	Fukuoka, Japan	Marathon	1st	2:11:45
1974					
Feb. 22	AAU Indoor Nationals	New York City	3-mile	2nd	13:18.0
Mar. 29	Florida Relays	Gainesville, Fla.	6-mile	1st	27:43.6
May 18	Southeast conference (open event)	Gainesville, Fla.	6-mile	1st	27:09.6
June 8	Haywood Field Restoration	Eugene, Ore.	3-mile	2nd	12:52.0

DATE	EVENT	SITE	DISTANCE	PLACE	TIME
June 21	AAU Nationals	Westwood, Calif.	5,000M	2nd	13:34.6
June 22	AAU Nationals	Westwood, Calif.	10,000M	1st	28:16.0
July 1	D. N. Galan Games	Stockholm	10,000M	2nd	28:11.0
Aug. 16	Weltklasse Meet	Zürich	5,000M	2nd	13:36.6
Nov. 30	AAU XC Nationals	Belmont, Calif.	10,000M	11th	30:57
Dec. 8	Fukuoka Marathon	Fukuoka, Japan	Marathon	1st	2:11:32
Dec. 16	Honolulu Marathon	Honolulu	Marathon	4th	2:33:22
1975					
Feb. 19	Intl. XC Trials	Gainesville, Fla.	15,000M	1st	46:32
Mar. 16	Intl. XC Champs	Rabat, Morocco	12,000M	20th	36:24
Apr. 26	Drake Relays	Des Moines	3-mile	3rd	13:19.4
Apr. 26	Drake Relays	Des Moines	6-mile	7th	28:26.6
May 29	Invitational	Eugene, Ore.	5,000M	2nd	13:32.2
June 7	Prefontaine Classic	Eugene, Ore.	3-mile	1st	13:00.8
June 21	AAU Nationals	Eugene, Ore.	10,000M	1st	28:02.2
June 26	World Games	Helsinki	10,000M	4th	28:11.0
June 30	D. Nyheter Games	Stockholm	10,000M	1st	27:51.8
July 2	Intl. Meet	Milan	5,000M	2nd	13:37.8
July 7	Intl. Meet	Nykoping, Sweden	5,000M	2nd	13:29.6
Aug. 17	Falmouth Road Race	Woods Hole, Mass.	7.1M	1st	33:24

DATE	EVENT	SITE	DISTANCE	PLACE	TIME
Aug. 20	Weltklasse Meet	Zürich	5,000M	1st	13:33.0
Aug. 23	Intl. Meet	Edinburgh	5,000M	1st	13:39.0
Aug. 29	Coca-Cola Meet	London	10,000M	2nd	27:46.0
Sept. 20	Virginia Ten-Miler	Lynchburg, Va.	10-mile	1st (tie)	48:17.0
Sept. 28	Springbank Road Races	Ontario, Canada	11.6M	2nd	55:01
Oct. 18	Rice Festival Marathon	Crowley, La.	Marathon	1st	2:16:29
1976					
Feb. 21	Jack in the Box Meet	San Diego	2-mile	1st	8:27.0
Feb. 27	AAU Indoor Nationals	New York City	3-mile	4th	13:16.4
May 22	Olympic Trials	Eugene, Ore.	Marathon	1st	2:11:51
June 22	Olympic Trials	Eugene, Ore.	10,000M	1st	27:55.6
July 31	Olympic Games	Montréal	Marathon	2nd	2:10:46
Aug. 15	Falmouth Road Race	Woods Hole, Mass.	7.1M	1st	33:13
Sept. 18	Virginia Ten-Miler	Lynchburg, Va.	10-mile	2nd	48:53
Oct. 24	New York Marathon	New York City	Marathon	2nd	2:13:12
Nov. 13	AAU Natl. 25-km Champs	Youngstown, Ohio	25,000M	1st	1:17:56
1977					
Jan. 15	Sunkist Indoor	Los Angeles	2-mile	4th	8:36.5
Jan. 21	Philadelphia Classic	Philadelphia	2-mile	1st	8:40.2

DATE	EVENT	SITE	DISTANCE	PLACE	TIME
Feb. 11	Maple Leaf Games	Toronto	3-mile	2nd	13:14.4
Feb. 18	Jack in the Box Meet	San Diego	2-mile	1st	8:27.3
Apr. 9	Pear Blossom Road Race	Medford, Ore.	13M	1st	1:03:42
May 1	Bloomsday Run	Spokane, Wash.	8.25M	1st	38:26
May 28	Indy Half-Marathon	Indianapolis	13.1M	1st	1:03:56
May 29	Wheeling Distance Classic	Wheeling, W.Va.	20,000M	2nd	1:02:32
June 11	AAU Nationals	Westwood, Calif.	10,000M	1st	28:19.8
July 2	Chicago Distance Classic	Chicago	20,000M	1st	1:01:34
July 3	Peachtree Road Race	Atlanta	10,000M	1st	29:21
Aug. 2	Falmouth Road Race	Woods Hole, Mass.	7.1M	5th	33:34
Aug. 24	Weltklasse Meet	Zürich	5,000M	9th	13:26.6
Sept. 2	World Cup	Düsseldorf	10,000M	6th	28:52.5
Oct. 23	New York Marathon	New York City	Marathon	DNF	—
1978					
Mar. 19	Cajun 10-Miler	Crowley, La.	10-mile	1st	48:36
Apr. 17	Boston Marathon	Boston	Marathon	23rd	2:18:15
Sept. 16	Virginia Ten-Miler	Lynchburg, Va.	10-mile	14th	52:16
Oct. 22	New York Marathon	New York City	Marathon	12th	2:19:32

DATE	EVENT	SITE	DISTANCE	PLACE	TIME
1979					
Apr. 16	Boston Marathon	Boston	Marathon	79th	2:21:56
Apr. 28	Trevira Twosome	New York City	10-mile	3rd	48:35
May 28	Bolder Boulder Run	Boulder, Colo.	10,000M	2nd	30:11
June 17	AAU Nationals	Walnut, Calif.	10,000M	3rd	28:28.6
July 7	Pan-Am Games	San Juan, P.R.	10,000M	3rd	29:06.4
July 8	Chicago Distance Classic	Chicago	20,000M	1st	1:00:59
July 21	Diet Pepsi Regional	Denver	10,000M	1st	29:18
July 28	USOC Sports Festival	Colorado Springs	10,000M	1st	29:29.9
Aug. 5	Badgerland 10-Miler	Milwaukee	10-mile	1st	47:23
Aug. 19	Falmouth Road Race	Woods Hole, Mass.	7.1-mile	5th	32:42
Sept. 22	Virginia Ten-Miler	Lynchburg, Va.	10-mile	5th	48:23
Oct. 21	New York Marathon	New York City	Marathon	7th	2:16:15
Nov. 18	Viren Invitational	Malibu, Calif.	20,000M	4th	1:01:11
Dec. 9	Honolulu Marathon	Honolulu	Marathon	2nd	2:17:51
1980					
Mar. 21	King Games	Stanford, Calif.	10,000M	2nd	28:52.4
Apr. 27	Trevira Twosome	New York City	10-mile	7th	48:34
May 24	Olympic Marathon Trial	Buffalo, N.Y.	Marathon	85th	2:23:24
Sept. 28	America's Marathon	Chicago	Marathon	9th	2:23:58

DATE	EVENT	SITE	DISTANCE	PLACE	TIME
Dec. 7	Honolulu Marathon	Honolulu	Marathon	4th	2:20:11
1981					
May 25	Bolder Boulder Run	Boulder, Colo.	10,000M	1st	29:28
June 21	Chicago Distance Classic	Chicago	20,000M	1st	1:01:25
July 12	Orange Classic	Middletown, N.Y.	10,000M	1st	29:33
July 25	Bix Road Race	Davenport, Iowa	7-mile	2nd	33:59
Sept. 27	America's Marathon	Chicago	Marathon	3rd	2:17:27
Dec. 13	Honolulu Marathon	Honolulu	Marathon	8th	2:24:07
1982					
May 2	Trevira Twosome	New York City	10-mile	4th	47:37
May 31	Bolder Boulder Run	Boulder, Colo.	10,000M	6th	29:26
July 11	Chicago Distance Classic	Chicago	20,000M	1st	1:01:21
July 18	Orange Classic	Middletown, N.Y.	10,000M	1st	29:18
July 24	Bix Road Race	Davenport, Iowa	7-mile	3rd	33:24
Dec. 12	Honolulu Marathon	Honolulu	Marathon	5th	2:22:17
1983					
Apr. 24	Cherry Creek Run	Denver	5-mile	1st	24:39
Oct. 9	Governor's Cup	Denver	10,000M	4th	30:32
Nov. 5	Run for the Roses	Boulder, Colo.	15,000M	1st	47:00
Dec. 11	Honolulu Marathon	Honolulu	Marathon	DNF	—